THE LUNATIC AND THE LORDS

The Lunatic and the Lords

Richard D. Schneider

IRWIN
LAW

The Lunatic and the Lords
© Irwin Law Inc., 2009

Published in 2009 by

Irwin Law Inc.
14 Duncan Street
Suite 206
Toronto, ON
M5H 3G8

www.irwinlaw.com

ISBN: 978-1-55221-132-8

Cover image: M'Naughten's trial at the Old Bailey, *Illustrated London News*, 1843
Cover photo: © Picsfive, 2009, used under licence from Shutterstock.com
Author photo: © Phil Brown
Design: Heather Raven

Cataloguing in Publication available from Library and Archives Canada

The publisher acknowledges the financial support of the Government of Canada through the Book Publishing Industry Development Program (BPIDP) for its publishing activities.

We acknowledge the assistance of the OMDC Book Fund, an initiative of Ontario Media Development Corporation.

Printed and bound in Canada.

1 2 3 4 5   13 12 11 10 09

Contents

Foreword

A BRAZEN AND shocking crime committed by a strange loner. An acquittal because of the accused's mental disorder. Public outcry at the verdict. Suspicion about the role of medical experts who testified for the accused. Demands on judges and legislators to restrict the insanity defence so that more people do not "get away with murder."

Such a story could be from more recent headlines including those arising from the 2009 verdict for Kenneth Li who was found not criminally responsible for killing and beheading Tim McLean on a Greyhound bus in Manitoba because of mental disorder and John Hinckley's 1982 acquittal on grounds of insanity for his attempted assassination of President Reagan.

This compelling book, however, does not speak directly to those modern cases. Justice Richard Schneider, a former clinical psychologist who now presides at Toronto's widely acclaimed mental health court as a judge, has chosen a less direct but more fruitful and enriching path. In this book, Justice Schneider accounts the 1843 case of Daniel M'Naughten in full and colourful detail. In doing so, Justice Schneider draws on his wealth of experience with the law and mental disorder.

As most students of the law and psychiatry know, M'Naughten was acquitted on grounds of insanity for the shooting of Edward Drummond, the private secretary of the Conservative Prime Minister Robert Peel. Fewer know the controversy caused by the acquittal. The public reaction to the verdict was captured by a statement attributed to Queen Victoria: "How could he have been found not guilty? He *did* it, didn't he?" As will be seen, Queen Victoria had already had some unhappy encounters with the insanity defence that may have left her somewhat jaded.

The controversy caused by the acquittal forced the House of Lords to demand that the judges explain themselves by answering a series of questions closely tied to the facts of the M'Naughten case. The judges' answers became widely known as the "M'Naughten Rules." They form the foundation for the insanity defence in most common law jurisdictions. They articulate a fairly restrictive approach to the insanity defence, one which requires the mental disorder to be so extreme that it deprives the accused of the capacity to understand the nature and quality of the act or know that it was wrong.

The M'Naughten Rules are studiously ambiguous about the particular issue that led to the M'Naughten acquittal: namely, the effects of delusion produced by a mental disorder. They provide that delusions will only support an insanity defence if they cause the accused to believe in a state of affairs that would have legally justified or excused his actions. This rule attempts to combine the worlds of mental disorder and the law, perhaps without success. It raises the question of whether M'Naughten's delusions of persecution by the Tories caused him to have a valid self-defence claim for shooting Drummond in the back. This question would not have been of much interest to the doctors who examined M'Naughten and were convinced that he had shot Drummond because of paranoid delusions, or in the parlance of the time, monomania. In any event, this specific part of the M'Naughten rules was repealed in the 1992 reforms to the Canadian mental disorder defence so that today in Canada, M'Naughten's defence would depend on whether his mental disorder rendered him incapable of appreciating the nature and quality of his act or knowing that it was legally or morally wrong.

M'Naughten's case was controversial at the time in part because it was a case of so-called partial insanity. There was ample evidence that M'Naughten had long-standing delusions of conspiracies against him and that these delusions had taken a toll on him. At the same time, however, M'Naughten could function in society and his activities in the days leading up to the shooting suggest a good deal of planning and premeditation. The medical experts who testified in his defence were unanimous that these delusions were a sign of mental illness and explained the killing. At the same time, the law has jealously guarded its ability to shape the ambit of the insanity defence in its own image.

Although the M'Naughten Rules are well known, the trial that produced the demand for them is much less so. Justice Schneider details the context and characters behind the most influential insanity defence trial in history.

The trial was held in the Old Bailey of Dickens' London. It was the London of Karl Marx and Friedrich Engels, and, as such, it was one seething with class tensions. In 1840, a man named Oxford had been acquitted on the basis of insanity for firing shots at Queen Victoria and Prince Albert while they were out riding. In the wake of two insanity acquittals for political crimes in a space of three years, the editors of the medical journal *The Lancet* expressed concerns that an expansive insanity defence might sacrifice public safety.

The public, including Queen Victoria and the editors of *The Lancet*, need not have worried. Daniel M'Naughten did not "get off." As a result of an 1800 decision that had found a man who had fired a pistol at King George III, the grandfather of Queen Victoria, not guilty by reason of insanity, Parliament had quickly enacted a law requiring insane acquittees to be kept in strict custody until His Majesty's pleasure was known. (A similar law existed in Canada until 1991 when it was struck down by the Supreme Court as arbitrary detention.) M'Naughten spent twenty years confined in Bethlehem Hospital, or Bedlam, as it was better known. He died at the age of fifty-two years in the equally infamous Broadmoor asylum.

This book provides a riveting account of the trial drawn from a variety of primary sources, including the extensive news reports ,as well as case reports. The reader learns how M'Naughten was ably defended by the leading and colourful barrister Alexander Cockburn who would later serve as attorney general and Lord Chief Justice of London. Cockburn successfully urged the judges and jury to defer to the opinion of various medical experts, including some who had not even examined M'Naughten, all of whom stated that the accused was insane. The reader also sees how Sir William Follett, the solicitor general and prosecuting barrister, was unable to present one medical witness who would testify to M'Naughten's sanity even though he called twenty-six witnesses.

This story would be very different if it occurred today. M'Naughten would likely not have faced a murder charge if only because the infection that killed Drummond would be treated by antibiotics, not leeches. Although medicine has improved greatly, our use of the English language has not. One of the many pleasures of this book is that its extensive use of primary sources allows the reader to be immersed in the subtle intricacies of the language of Victorian England. One of my favourite examples is *The Times*' report that when arrested, M'Naughten was neither "disheveled, unkempt, or notably malodorous."

Today, the trial would not have begun let alone be completed within three months of the shooting and in two days (including a Saturday!) of court sitting. If, as Justice Schneider predicts, M'Naughten was also found not guilty because of mental disorder today, he would enjoy the legal right to have the necessity of his continued confinement regularly tested and to be released unconditionally if he was not a significant threat to public safety. M'Naughten would likely be treated with drugs and released back into the community rather than detained in asylums for the insane that constituted prisons.

At the same time, readers familiar with modern law and psychiatry will also find much in this marvellous book that is familiar. Public suspicion and even fear of those who suffer from mental disorder remain a regrettable constant. Today, as then, defence lawyers and other advocates for those with mental disorders argue that the law should be more readily accepting of the proof behind science and medicine. The law, however, remains cautious and often resistant to change. It is more rooted in concerns about moral responsibility than in the lessons of psychiatry or modern science. Today, as in 1843, the public is still addicted to tales of murder and madness.

I learned much from this book and enjoyed reading it, and I hope that you do as well.

Kent Roach

PROFESSOR OF LAW AND PRICHARD-WILSON CHAIR IN
LAW AND PUBLIC POLICY, UNIVERSITY OF TORONTO

This book is dedicated to Twins,
Eggy, and Nooner

Introduction

THE MOST PROMINENT story on the front page of *The Times* for
4 March 1843, under the headline "Assassination of Mr. Drummond,"
was an account of the previous day's proceedings at the Old Bailey,
London's Central Criminal Court:

> This day having been appointed for the trial of the assassin Daniel
> M'Naughten,* every avenue leading to the court was at an early hour
> thronged to excess by numbers of well-dressed persons of both sexes,
> anxious to hear a case, the excitement of which has not been surpassed
> by any of the extraordinary events of a similar character which have
> taken place during the last quarter of a century.

Of compelling interest to readers were details about the atmosphere in the courtroom, where the sheriffs had arranged for every door
leading to the court to be kept locked until a few minutes before nine
o'clock, the usual time for commencing business. A number of police
officers were stationed at each of the court entrances to prevent any
rush from taking place.

Several of the desks were removed from the bench, and their places
were occupied by chairs for the accommodation of those who had obtained tickets of admission. One of the entrances to the court was also
blocked, with benches and chairs placed in front of it in order to accommodate the public.

On the bench and in other parts of the court were a number of
ladies, though fewer by far than the court was evidently in the habit of
seeing when such trials took place. The main section of the courtroom

---

* Please note the spelling of M'Naughten. While modern-day writers refer to Daniel
as "McNaughten," this text maintains the original spelling. See p. 29 for a more
detailed explanation.

was almost entirely occupied by young barristers, the majority of whom had never before been observed in the court. Present on the bench, amongst other persons of distinction, were the distinguished Count D'Aumale of France along with ministers and government officials from Belgium, the United States, and the German principality of Saxony; the Earl of Surrey; Lord A. Lennox, Lord Paget, and Mr. C. Russell, MP; and Mr. W. Ellice, Jr., MP.

At precisely ten o'clock, Lord Tindal, the Chief Justice of England, Mr. Justice Williams, and Mr. Justice Coleridge took their seats upon the bench. Gold chains of office resting on the front of their ermine-collared, scarlet robes, they peered impassively from under their great silver-braided wigs as the prisoner, Daniel M'Naughten, was led into court and immediately placed at the bar. He walked to the front of the dock with a firm step, though it was evident to all in the room that he was very excited; he was dressed, apparently, in the same clothes as he had been wearing when examined several weeks earlier at his preliminary hearing in the lower court at Bow Street. He seemed to have altered very little, if at all, both his physical appearance and general demeanour.

The solicitor general, Mr. Waddington, and Mr. Russell Gurney appeared on behalf of the prosecution; the eminent attorney Mr. Cockburn, Queen's Counsel, with Mr. Clarkson, Mr. Bodkin, and Mr. Monteith, were retained to defend the prisoner.

Mr. Clark, the clerk of the court, then read out the indictment as follows:

> That Daniel M'Naughten (the prisoner) on the 20th of January, at the parish of St. Martin-in-the-Fields, did feloniously assault Edward Drummond, private secretary to the Prime Minister, with a certain loaded pistol, which he then and there held in his right hand, loaded with gunpowder and a leaden bullet, and which he of his malice aforethought discharged at, and against, the said Edward Drummond, thereby giving him a mortal wound in and upon the left side of the back a little below the blade-bone of his left shoulder, of the breadth of half an inch, and of the depth of 12 inches, and of which wound the said Edward Drummond did languish until the 25th of January, on which day, of the said mortal wound so given in manner aforesaid, died, and that Daniel M'Naughten did willfully kill and murder the said Edward Drummond.

Upon the clerk of the court inquiring of the prisoner how he wished to plead, Daniel M'Naughten replied with a firm "not guilty." He was then charged upon the coroner's inquisition with the same offence, to which he also pleaded "not guilty." A chair was then placed in the dock for M'Naughten, upon which he immediately sat down and, closing his eyes and throwing his head back, appeared to be asleep. He remained in this same position for the duration of the solicitor general's opening address, though later, when witnesses were under examination, he appeared suddenly to awaken, listening attentively to all that was said.

And so the trial began ...

∿∿∿∿

DANIEL M'NAUGHTEN'S CASE is arguably not only the most celebrated insanity trial in modern legal history, but also the most important. I decided to write this book because the actual story of M'Naughten's trial is one that is not widely remembered today, although its significance remains enormous.[1] Sitting, as I do, for the most part as a judge of the Ontario Court of Justice and frequently in the Mental Health Court where determinations of criminal responsibility are routinely made, this fascinating case maintains its importance in the decisions made by my court on a daily basis.

The story of M'Naughten's trial is an interesting one that I am convinced is very worthy of re-telling. In offering this account I should make it clear that I am not an historian, and in writing of M'Naughten's case I am in no way holding myself out to be one. It is therefore inevitable that the rigorous attention to detail and sophisticated analysis expected of the historian will be given over to a more general – though no less factual – presentation of circumstances and events surrounding this most compelling of trials. I have attempted to review the relevant material as I have found it and interpret it as I am able. I should point out at the outset that the accounts of M'Naughten's assassination of Edward Drummond and his subsequent trial, as related by the court reporters and the press, have been edited and abbreviated as little as possible, since I hoped to make my rendering of the story as clear, correct, and complete as possible.

In the last century there have been a number of notorious insanity trials. The names Jeffrey Dahmer, David Berkowitz, John Hinckley, Jr.,

Jack Ruby, and David Chapman all come to mind; their infamy was derived from their horrific deeds as well as from the suggestion that their acts were precipitated by insanity. The public is always intrigued and often outraged with the successful insanity defence, largely due to the misapprehension that the accused "got off." As witnessed in the almost-universal outcry over the verdict in the O.J. Simpson case, no one wants to see anyone else "get away with murder." In reality, except where the "acquittal" of an accused leads to avoiding the death penalty, there is often little practical difference in the outcome of a conviction versus a successful insanity defence. Often, as we shall see later, the difference in verdicts is only relevant in terms of where an accused will be housed upon conviction.

Mention should be made here of what constitutes "insanity." It is not simply a "mental disorder" or, borrowing the terminology of the nineteenth century, "lunacy." When we speak of insanity we must remember that we are dealing with a legal rather than a medical concept. The term "insanity" is not synonymous with "mental disorder." Mental disorder is primarily a medical concept whereas insanity is a legal concept. However, mental disorder also has a legal meaning that may differ from the meaning of the term as it is used in a medical context. Originally, the terms were imprecisely defined in both arenas and meant virtually the same thing – a break with reality, or the mind misperceiving what others would call reality. Other bizarre behaviours were typically expected from someone to whom the label "insane" was applied.

It is helpful to consider the difference between a mental disorder from a health practitioner's view, and the view which is held in criminal law. First of all, the *Diagnostic and Statistical Manual of Mental Disorders* (fourth edition),[2] the international standard for the classification of mental disorders, concedes that "no definition adequately specifies precise boundaries for the concept of 'mental disorder.' The concept of mental disorder, like many other concepts in medicine and science, lacks a consistent operational definition that covers all situations."

Mental disorder then, for the purpose of civil legislation,[3] means "any disease or disability of the mind." Thus we can see that from the perspective of the mental health practitioner and mental health legislation, mental disorder is not something with precise boundaries or rules of exclusion or inclusion. In order to speak of mental disorder, we do not need certainty as to whether the condition is schizophrenia, mania, drug-induced psychosis, or "psychotic disorder not otherwise specified." Precise diagnoses are sometimes not possible. What is important is that a mental disorder is present and that the symptomatology causes such a departure from "normalcy" that the individual is significantly compromised.

In contrast, the view of mental disorder maintained in the field of criminal law, as one might expect, is defined differently in different jurisdictions. For the purposes of England's *Mental Health Act* (which deals with mentally disordered individuals in both a civil and a criminal context) mental disorder means "mental illness, arrested or incomplete development of mind, psychopathic disorder and any other disorder or disability of mind and 'mentally disordered' shall be construed accordingly."[4] In Australia and the United States, criminal law differs from state to state, and considerable variability exists, for example, as to whether or not intellectual disabilities or personality disorders are included as mental disorder.

In Canada the *Criminal Code of Canada* defines mental disorder as "disease of the mind." The Supreme Court of Canada, in a criminal law context,[5] has previously defined disease of the mind as embracing "any illness, disorder, or abnormal condition which impairs the human mind or its functioning, excluding, however, self-induced states caused by alcohol or drugs, as well as transitory states such as hysteria or concussion." Thus, personality disorders may constitute disease of the mind. In *R. v. Rouse*[6] the court found that "mental retardation" is a mental disorder within the meaning of section 2 of the *Criminal Code of Canada*. Similarly, *delirium tremens* has been found to fall within the ambit of "disease of the mind."[7] From the criminal law's perspective, the term "mental disorder" is quite broad. What is of critical importance here is the impact of the mental disorder upon an accused person's functioning at the relevant time – the time of the otherwise criminal act, not whether or not a condition can be precisely defined diagnostically.

"Insanity," on the other hand, is a strictly legal term – it is caused by mental disorder of a certain quality and intensity. If proven,[8] it constitutes a "defence" to a criminal allegation. It refers to a state in the accused caused by mental disorder that so compromises his or her functioning at the time of the otherwise criminal act that the individual will not be held criminally responsible. So, mental disorder is not synonymous with insanity; rather, it is a necessary but insufficient condition for a finding of insanity. Therefore, not all mentally disordered accused will be found insane, but all accused found by a criminal court to be insane will have been mentally disordered at the time of the criminal act. A very small number of those found to be suffering from mental disorder will be acquitted by reason of insanity.

These terms are often confused and it is very important that the distinctions be quite clear at the outset of this story. M'Naughten's case marks the beginning of modern insanity pleas. By employing the term "insanity," it is critical to remember we are referring to a legal concept rather than a medical one. As we have seen, there is a wide gulf between the expansive range of symptomatology referred to by the medical community as constituting mental disorder and what, for the purpose of criminal law, will be recognized as mental disorder.

The present story is a timely refresher in light of the fact that the Western world has never before seen such an enormous number of mentally disordered individuals flocking through the criminal courthouse doors. In Canada the annual increases over the last decade or so have been as high as 10 percent or more.[9] This trend has no doubt been caused, at least in part, by cutbacks in mental health care spending by governments. Individuals who were previously treated in the traditional civil mental health care system are more often than not left untreated and find their way into the criminal justice system charged with, for the most part, rather minor nuisance offences. Often, they leave the criminal justice system once they are "fit to stand trial" and have been "diverted" back to the civil system. Others avail themselves of the insanity defence. Insanity, the legal concept, has never before been so prominent in the criminal justice system.

This sentiment returns us to the story of Daniel M'Naughten's trial and why it was not only one of the most spectacular ever, but also why it is considered to be the most important insanity trial in the history of criminal law, with the most enduring influence. Indeed, it could be said that M'Naughten's trial gave birth to the modern definition of insanity.

While the other cases referred to above were all spectacular and received tremendous media attention, none has had a comparable impact on the evolution of our criminal law. The trial took place at London's Old Bailey in 1843.[10] Daniel M'Naughten killed Edward Drummond, secretary to Sir Robert Peel, Prime Minister of England, presumably believing him to be Peel. He held the delusional belief that he was being persecuted by the Tories, the governing political party of the day. M'Naughten was assessed and the consistent medical evidence adduced at trial revealed that he was a "lunatic" and, as a result, he was found to be not guilty by reason of insanity. While the botched attempt upon the life of the prime minister makes the offence spectacular in and of itself, Edward Drummond, as we shall see, came from a very prominent family, one which traced its lineage to the thirteenth century. Drummond's ancestors included two queen consorts of Scotland. Queen Anabella (née Drummond), consort of Robert III of Scotland, was the ancestor of all succeeding monarchs in the United Kingdom after James I came to the English throne in 1601.[11]

In 1843, "lunacy" was the medical term applied to aberrations we now refer to as mental disorder. And lunatics were kept in lunatic asylums. Originally, the disordered thinking of the lunatic was thought to be brought about by the phases of the moon (from the Latin noun *luna*) – hence, the term. At the outset it should be emphasized that use of these historically accurate terms is in no way intended to cast the mentally ill in a negative or pejorative light. Lunatic was a medical term of art used well into the twentieth century. Now the term, like "idiot," "moron," and "imbecile," which were also medical terms of art, has a negative connotation and is used more commonly as an insult. It is a term no longer used in medicine or psychiatry. However, use of the term is appropriate for our purposes because this is also the story of insanity.

Finally, M'Naughten's case is not just fascinating but extremely important for several additional reasons. First, it was a sensational event covered closely by a burgeoning press whose rapidly growing readership had an equally fast-growing appetite for "news" of the day. M'Naughten's trial didn't disappoint. It was a sensational event with a sensational outcome, about which Queen Victoria was so wildly outraged that after the trial she referred the case to a committee of the House of Lords. Their examination led to the articulation of a set of "insanity rules" as it were – the so-called M'Naughten Rules that thereafter formed the basis of the insanity defence in England, most of the Commonwealth, and in most American and English-speaking jurisdictions around the world. They continue to be the most widely used rules in insanity trials; not surprisingly perhaps, they also remain extremely controversial.

In telling this story, I have relied fairly extensively on articles published in *The Times* of London. *The Times* covered M'Naughten's trial closely and carefully. I have found no better account on which to base my narrative, with the exception of the *State Trials Reports* from which I have quoted extensively and also abstracted numerous details of what was, by any measure, a most unusual and most unusually interesting legal drama that has implications that are still being felt more than 150 years later. I have left much of the story telling in the words of *The Times*. By present-day standards, the accounting of M'Naughten's story in *The Times* and the *State Trials Reports* is particularly rich, given that today much of what was reported during M'Naughten's trial would have been kept from the public by way of court-ordered publication bans. Where I have added personal explanations and comments, as well as occasional background material, I have done so to give readers a more insightful look at M'Naughten's crime, his trial and its aftermath. Periodic comparisons to and with current law and current psychiatric concepts are offered for this reason as well.

PART I

The Assassination of Edward Drummond

Chapter One

THE PROSECUTION OF Daniel M'Naughten for "a most determined attempt to assassinate the private secretary of Sir Robert Peel in the open street, and in the broad face of day," as *The Times* put it, might have seemed straightforward enough. At about 3:30 on the afternoon of January 20, 1843, Edward Drummond had left the prime minister's Downing Street office in the company of the Earl of Haddington, the First Lord of the Admiralty, a staunch member of Peel's cabinet and a close personal friend of Drummond's since the 1820s when both men had served under Prime Minister George Canning. They proceeded together up Whitehall to Haddington's residence at the Admiralty, Drummond bidding his colleague farewell and continuing up Whitehall to Drummond's Bank on Charing Cross Road. One of England's leading financial institutions (many of the royal family's accounts had been kept there since the time of George III), the bank had been founded by Edward Drummond's grandfather.

After a short visit with his older brother, Charles, who was a partner at the bank, Drummond headed back to his apartment on Downing Street at about four o'clock. He was partway between the Horse Guards and the Admiralty when a man approached him from behind, drew a pistol from inside his jacket, and "putting the muzzle into the back of the unsuspecting gentleman," then fired.

Immediately after the pistol was discharged, a policeman, who had witnessed the act, rushed up to the criminal. In the meantime, the gunman returned the recently-fired pistol to his jacket, then drew another loaded pistol and was in the act of pointing it at Drummond when the policeman seized him and pinioned his arms from behind. The pistol was discharged, but "the aim of the assassin being thus diverted, the contents did not touch Mr. Drummond, nor was any other person injured by them."

The assassin, on being secured by the police constable, was conveyed to the police station in nearby Gardiner's Lane. He gave his name as M'Naughten but refused to give his place of residence, it being supposed that he was either a Scot or a native of the north of Ireland who had perhaps been living in Glasgow. He was then searched, and found upon him were two £5 notes, £4 in gold, and a deposit receipt from the Glasgow Bank for £750, made out in the name of "Daniel M'Naughten," thus confirming the statement made by the prisoner as to his name.

Yet from the moment of his arrest there appeared to be little that was straightforward about the case of Daniel M'Naughten. In its first reports (21 January 1843) *The Times* declared his motives to be shrouded in mystery, with "not the slightest clue being yet obtained to the cause that could have impelled him to the commission of so aggravated a crime." Indeed, during initial questioning and police investigation of the crime, "nothing transpired that could with certainty lead to knowledge of the motives which induced the prisoner to commit this dreadful act." All that the policeman who apprehended him could report was that on his being arrested, M'Naughten was heard to say "He . . ." or "She . . ." (the policeman was uncertain which) "shall not disturb my mind any longer."

It did not appear that M'Naughten had any grievance with, or complaint against, Edward Drummond, nor that he had ever corresponded with Drummond or was ever known to him. Indeed, throughout preliminary questioning we are told that M'Naughten's demeanour was cool and collected, *The Times* assuring its readers, almost with a sense of relief, that although the attempted assassination of Edward Drummond was carried out "with the most cold-blooded determination," there did not appear to be any evidence of "insanity."

୭ଡ଼ଡ଼ଡ଼

IN ORDER TO better understand the significance of M'Naughten's case, and to appreciate that behaviours that we, with our present understanding, observe and recognize as mental disorders – but which were not in the past consistently recognized as such – it is important to retrace the evolution of the interface between mental disorder and the law in some detail.

It is not my intention to provide a history of mental disorder within the criminal justice system, nor do I intend to delve in any great depth into the evolution of psychiatry or mental illness. However, any discussion of mental disorder and the law, and specifically the history of mental disorder in the criminal justice system, must start with the recognition that the behaviours, deficits, or symptomatology we currently interpret and label as mental disorders were not always viewed as such. That is, while it is probably true that the range of departure from "normalcy," both qualitatively and quantitatively, has remained relatively static over time, these aberrant behaviours were periodically viewed as signs of demonic possession, humoral imbalances, punishment for offending an oracle, indicia of being blessed by a god, or disorders of the soul, rather than psychopathology. And different characterizations of the same syndromes would periodically co-exist depending upon who was doing the interpretation and in what forum – the church, the court, or the physician.[1]

Several hundred years ago the world was dichotomized into good/ evil, orderly/disorderly, the work of God/the work of the Devil, rational/irrational, healthy/sick. Thus, we see "witches" (who were almost certainly mentally disordered from today's "enlightened" perspective) being burned and tortured in a benevolent ritual designed to make their bodies no longer habitable hosts for the devil, at the same time, similar manifestations were being treated as illnesses.[2]

In 1484 two Dominican monks, Heinrich Kramer and James Sprenger, produced a document entitled *The Malleus Malificarum*[3] (The Witches' Hammer) under a Papal Bull of Pope Innocent VIII. This document served as a professional manual for witch hunters that remained in use and was present on every magistrate's bench, especially in Catholic jurisdictions,[4] for nearly three hundred years. The text is divided into three main sections: (1) treating of the three necessary concomitants of witchcraft which are the devil, a witch, and the permission of Almighty God; (2) treating of the methods by which the works of witchcraft are wrought and directed, and how they may be successfully annulled and dissolved; (3) relating to the judicial proceedings in both the ecclesiastical and civil courts against witches and indeed all heretics.

It was the objective of Kramer and Sprenger to expose the heresy of those who did not believe in witches and to set forth the proper order of a world with devils, witches, and the will of God. Contemporary cases were presented that illustrated methods by which witches might attempt to control and subvert the world: for example, how and why women roast their first-born male child; the confession of how to raise a tempest by a washwoman suspended "hardly clear of the ground" by her thumbs; methods of making a formal pact with the devil; how witches deprive men of their vital member; and many others. Methods of destroying and curing witchcraft, such as remedies against incubus and succubus devils, were exemplified and weighed by the two Dominican authors, writing in ecclesiastical support of their pontiff.

Against this background we can perhaps approach the evolution of mental disorder and the law more clearly, since in spite of the dominance of these different views, they were never universally held. In fact, it would appear that society recognized the presentation we currently label mental disorder in a rather sympathetic light, no matter how it was construed, notwithstanding the circumstances and context of a particular case. The point to be stressed is that the phenomena captured by use of the term "mental disorder" have not changed significantly over time – what has evolved is our interpretation of the phenomena and the resulting label. The early examples cited later in this chapter are obviously instances where the courts viewed the accused as suffering from a mental disorder rather than as operating in league with the devil. Regardless of how the symptomatology was interpreted, we must also realize that the so-called remedies of the day – even burning at the stake, drowning, and torture – were not seen as punishment but were performed to rid the host of the devil. In other words, for the most part these procedures were carried out by well-meaning "practitioners."

Today, while the likely reaction of most people would be to attribute bizarre behaviour to the presence of mental disorder, we periodically hear of exceptions, as a recently reported[5] case from Bucharest exemplifies. In 2006, Daniel Petru Corugeanu, a Romanian monk, left a nun tied up for days without food or water and chained to a cross, believing that he was exorcising the devil from her. This was done with the support of the nuns at the secluded Holy Trinity convent in the northeast of the country. The "patient," one Maricia Irnia Cornici, who was twenty-three, had been treated for schizophrenia in the past but apparently relapsed, causing her to believe the devil was talking to her. Corugeanu and the nuns then took it upon themselves to perform the exorcism, which ended with the death of the afflicted nun because of dehydration, exhaustion, and suffocation. Cornici's death prompted Romania's dominant Orthodox Church to promise reforms that would include psychological testing for those wishing to join the monastery.

Although most agree that the modern history of the criminal law's consideration of mental disorder and its impact upon determinations of responsibility commences in 1800, with James Hadfield's attempted assassination of George III at the Theatre Royal in Drury Lane,[6] it is nevertheless useful to look at developments prior to the nineteenth century in order to put Hadfield's case and subsequent decisions, including those arising from the trial of Daniel M'Naughten, into historical perspective.

According to historian Nigel Walker, it would appear that in pre-Roman England, as a result of an adherence to strict liability due to a lack of differentiation between "criminal" and "tort" law, there were rules or conventions, uneven in substance and application, that an insane killer was not to be killed in a retributive fashion but rather that the family of the victim was to be compensated for its loss.[7] There was "simply a straightforward rule for ensuring that compensation was paid for an insane killer's victim, and that the insane man did not become in turn the victim of the spear," or as it has alternatively been described, "buy off the spear or bear it." By secular law, compensation was determined not by the extent to which the accused was to blame, but rather by the status of the victim and the extent of the injury.[8] On the other hand, the Church was not concerned with compensation or restitution, but with culpability for sin. The accused therefore had to satisfy both the secular legal system as well as the dicta of Church law whereby penance was prescribed to match the gravity of the offence according to Church strictures.

By the eleventh century, certain of the most serious crimes were identified as "botless," that is, ones that could not be resolved by compensation but were punishable by death and the forfeiture of property without a pardon from the king. From this emerged a certain group of wrongs that were identified as "criminal," leaving the rest (the compensatible) to develop civilly as "torts." This crude emergence of a criminal law was as well based upon strict liability. Royal pardons, therefore,

became the accepted method of dealing with an obviously insane offender.[9] Presumably, the offender's family was to then take charge of
the offender or else he would be kept in jail.[10] So far as forfeiture and
the non-insane offender were concerned, "his goods and lands were
also to be seized; but he was to be allowed sustenance from them, and
the persons charged with their management were not to commit any
waste."[11] It should be noted that this scheme of forfeiture was not the
same as the present criminal forfeiture where the offender loses all
rights to the property or its use.

The insane offender, on the other hand, was apparently excused
from the penalty of forfeiture, although his property was governed
initially by his parents, then his feudal lord, then ultimately by the
Crown. This became a very profitable procedure where the king would,
out of the profits of the lands, provide the mentally ill with "necessaries" and then, upon the death or recovery of the accused, return
the land to him or his estate. Nigel Walker indicates that there was a
distinction made between "madness" and "idiocy"; in the former case
the profits were returned to the accused upon his recovery, while in the
latter case (a permanent condition) the king took profits from the land
for the life of the idiot – a procedure that lasted up until the end of the
eighteenth century.[12]

Even by the late-thirteenth century, when the system of trial by
jury was well established, insane offenders were occasionally dealt
with outside of the courts and the trial process. An exceptionally well-
documented example of such a "diversion" is set out in the case of
Richard (Blofot) of Cheddestan, in the year 1270.[13] In this early case,
King Edward I instructed the sheriff of Norfolk to conduct an inquiry
to determine how it was that Blofot had come to kill his wife and two
children.

In volume 1 of *Crime and Insanity in England* we are told that the
king wished to know whether or not it was true that Blofot had killed
his wife and children in a frenzied seizure, or, if otherwise, how and in
what fashion he had done so. He also wished to find out if Blofot, who
at the time had been imprisoned in the jail at Norwich for six years,
was restored to his former soundness of mind and whether it would be
dangerous to release him from prison on the grounds that he was ill.

Appearing before the inquiry, Blofot declared he was not guilty
of the crime of which he was accused, claiming that he was returning

from the market at Reepham with his wife, when passing "a certain marl-pit full of water" he was seized with a "frenzy" and cast himself into the pit, wishing to drown himself. His wife, with much difficulty, dragged him from the marl-pit before he drowned and took him peacefully back home to Cheddestan. Soon after, while his wife was out "in search of necessaries," Richard claimed that he was again seized with a fit of frenzy which so took control of him that he killed his two children. When his wife returned home she cried out in grief and tried desperately to calm him down but was killed by her husband who was still in the grip of the frenzy. Alerted by the noise and commotion, when neighbours reached the house they found Richard trying to hang himself from a roof beam. Though he continued in the throes of his frenzy, they were able to get control of him and prevented him from doing himself harm, later swearing on oath that it was in the grip of a "frenzied sickness" that Richard had killed his family and that even afterward the frenzy showed no signs of abating. The sheriff of Norfolk concluded at the time of his inquiry that while the evidence showed Blofot was, for the most part, restored to good health, there was still a danger in setting him free.

It can be seen from this case that the king was prepared to release the accused, notwithstanding the criminal act, if he did not present as dangerous. "Diversions" of the sort described above were within the exclusive jurisdiction of the king and no one other than the king could interfere with what would otherwise be an automatic sentence.

Although by the middle of the thirteenth century acquittals on the basis of insanity were apparently not the norm, the writings of Bracton at that time cited by Nigel Walker[14] suggest that, so far as Bracton was concerned, that is what should have been the case:

> For a crime is not committed unless the will to harm be present. Misdeeds are distinguished both by the will and by intention [and theft is not committed without the thought of thieving]. And then there is what can be said about the child and the madman, for the one is protected by his innocence of design, the other by the misfortune of his deed. In misdeeds we look to the will and not the outcome.

Walker notes that the "[t]he period during which it became the regular practice to acquit the insane instead of leaving him to be pardoned by the king cannot be identified with certainty."[15]

Nevertheless, Walker does find an early example of such a judicial outcome in the case of an accused referred to briefly in the *Year Books of Henry VII* in 1505, which read: "A man was accused of the murder on an infant. It was found that at the time of the murder the felon was of unsound mind (*de non saine memoire*). Wherefore it was decided that he should go free (*qu'il ira quite*). To be noted."[16] Walker's investigation of the era led him to conclude that the insanity defence was actually used much more commonly prior to 1800 than previously thought, perhaps due to the fact that there was no discernable standard test; "if the jury were trying an ordinary theft or case of violence – not a Jacobite or a terrorist – the important question for them was whether the defendant was really insane." If the jury found that the accused was insane he may have been discharged; however, the practice did not appear to be uniform or consistent. "Much depended on whether the relatives were willing to take care of the prisoner and guarantee his future behaviour. If no such person could be found, the court could send the discharged lunatic back to jail" until he was fit to be discharged although, again, no fixed practice was apparent.[17] It is not clear that any distinction was made between insanity at the time of the trial (now referred to as fitness or competency to stand trial) and insanity at the time of the offence.

By the early-seventeenth century, Sir Edward Coke was observed discussing the criminal liability of persons *non compos mentis* in *Beverly's Case*[18] (of *Non Compos Mentis*) where he relied upon the writing of Bracton:

> But as to his (a) life, the law of England is that he shall not lose his life for felony or murder, because the punishment of a felon is so grievous, *sc.* 1. To lose his life. 2. To lose his life in such odious manner, *sc.* by hanging, for he shall be hanged between heaven and earth as unworthy of both. 3. He shall lose his blood as to his ancestry (for he is as a son of the earth without any ancestor) and as to his posterity also, for his blood is corrupt (b), and he has neither heir nor posterity. 4. His lands. 5. His goods; and in such case the King shall have *annum, diem, et vastum*, to the intent that his wife and children shall be ejected, his houses pulled down, his trees eradicated and subverted, his meadows (c) ploughed, and all that he has for his comfort, delight, or sustenance, wasted and destroyed, because he has in such felonious manner offended against the law; and all this was, *ut* (d) *poena ad paucos, metus*

as omnes perveniat: but the punishment of a man who is deprived of his reason and understanding, cannot be an example to others. 2. **No felony or murder can be committed without (e) a felonious intent and purpose;** *et ideo dict' est felonia, quia fieri debet felleo animo*: but *furiosus non intelligit quid agit, et animo et ratione caret, er non multum distat a brutis*, **as Bracton saith, and therefore he cannot have felonious intent.** [emphases added]

Although this excerpt from *Beverley's Case* is a clear recognition of the fact that the insane offender should be spared, there is no indication of the degree or type of insanity that would qualify for the defence or exemption.

Sir Matthew Hale, in his book *The History of the Pleas of the Crown*[19] does distinguish between cases of insanity that will excuse the accused from criminal liability, and those that will not:[20]

Man is naturally endowed with these two great faculties, understanding and liberty of will, and therefore is a subject properly capable of a law properly so called, and consequently obnoxious to guilt and punishment for the violation of that law, which in respect of these two great faculties he hath a capacity to obey: The consent of the will is that, which renders human actions either commendable or culpable; as where there is no law, there is no transgression, so regularly, where there is no will to commit an offense, there can be no transgression, or just reason to incur the penalty or sanction of that law instituted for the punishment of crimes or offenses. And because the liberty or choice of the will presupposeth an act of the understanding to know the thing or action chosen by the will, it follows that, where there is a defect of the understanding, there is no free act of the will in the choice of things or actions. But general notions or rules are too extravagant and undeterminate, and cannot be safely in their latitude applied to all civil actions; and therefore it hath been always the wisdom of states and law-givers to prescribe limits and bounds to these general notions, and to define what persons and actions are exempt from the severity of the general punishments of penal laws in respect of their incapacity of will.

Hale goes on to describe various conditions or types of mental illnesses recognized at the time of his writing. He describes disorders resulting from natural or accidental causes and "civil incapacities or defects." Natural defects are those of infancy, accidental defects are "dementia, casualty or chance, and ignorance," whereas civil defects include "civil subjection, compulsion, necessity, and fear." The law "in some cases, and under certain temperaments takes notice of these defects, and in respect of them relaxeth or abateth the severity of their punishments."[21] Hale devotes Chapter III to *Touching the defect of infancy and nonage* (under the age of twelve) and Chapter IV to *Concerning the defect of ideocy, madness and lunacy, in criminal offences and punishments.*[22]

Hale's very early writing reveals a conceptualization of the problems of mental disorder and the determination of culpability which is consistent with contemporary views. First of all, as noted earlier, the presence of mental disorder is not, by itself, sufficient for a defence, and secondly, that the matter of determining culpability is a matter for the trier of fact. So far as a test for responsibility is concerned, he goes on to say: "the best measure I can think of is this; such a person as labouring under melancholy distempers hath yet ordinarily as great understanding, as a child of fourteen years hath, is such a person as may be guilty of treason or felony."[23]

We have, above, in Hale's 1736 *History of the Pleas of the Crown*, a rudimentary test for lack of criminal responsibility based upon mental disorder that was widely adopted and came to be known as the "child of fourteen years test."[24] Williams Hawkins, in his 1724 edition of *A Treatise of the Pleas of the Crown*[25] also sets out a test for determining criminal responsibility based upon an ability to differentiate between good from evil.[26]

This "good and evil" test, described by William Hawkins in 1724, very much resembles the "right and wrong" test that was eventually adopted by the House of Lords in *Daniel M'Naughten's Case*[27] in 1843. In contemporary variations, it became known as the "M'Naughten Rules" seen, for example, in section 16 of the *Criminal Code of Canada* and in many other Western jurisdictions. The primary difference between the "right and wrong" test as set out above, and the later version seen in *M'Naughten's Case*, is that the ability to determine or know right from wrong was in the latter case directed specifically to the otherwise criminal act or omission, rather than the absence or presence of the ability in the abstract.

At about the same time as the publication of Hawkins' treatise came the decision in *Arnold's Case*[28] in 1724. Here, the court employed what subsequently came to be widely known as the "wild beast test."[29] Edward Arnold was tried for felony, "in maliciously and wilfully shooting at, and wounding, the Right Hon. the Lord Onslow." The wild beast test, emanating from *Arnold's Case*, came to be known as such as a result of the following notable excerpt from the judge's direction to the jury (at 764):

> It is not every frantic and idle humour of a man that will exempt him from justice, and the punishment of the law. When a man is guilty of a great offence, it must be very plain and clear, before a man is allowed such an exemption; therefore it is not every kind of frantic humour or something unaccountable in a man's actions, that points him out to be such a madman as is to be exempted from punishment; it must be a man that is totally deprived of his understanding and memory, and *doth not know what he is doing, no more than an infant, than a brute, or a wild beast,* such a one is never the object of punishment [emphasis added].

Although the wild beast test is referred to by some writers as if it represented a different substantive test, a further reading of the charge to the jury, not usually cited, suggests otherwise, putting an entirely different gloss on the "wild beast" reference. It reads as follows:

> [T]herefore I must leave it to your consideration, whether the condition this man was in, as it is represented to you on one side, or the other, doth shew a man, who knew what he was doing, and was able to distinguish whether he was doing good or evil, and understood what he did . . .

It is fairly clear that The Hon. Robert Tracy was using the "wild beast" as an example of the sort of condition the jury might look for in the accused rather than suggesting a qualitatively different test than the good and evil test enunciated by William Hawkins. Indeed, earlier on the same page the direction is as follows:

> If he was under the visitation of God, *and could not distinguish between good and evil, and did not know what he did, though he committed the greatest offence, yet he could not be guilty of any offence against any law*

whatsoever; for guilt arises from the mind, and the wicked will and intention of man. If a man be deprived of his reason, and consequently of his intention, he cannot be guilty; and if that is the case, though he had actually killed Lord Onslow, he is exempted from punishment.[30] [emphasis added]

The charge ended with "and if you believe he was sensible, and had the use of his reason, and understood what he did, he is not within the exemptions of the law." Perhaps too much has been made of the so-called wild beast test because of the rather dramatic imagery conjured up by its name alone.

Later in the eighteenth century came the trial before the House of Lords of Lawrence Earl Ferrers[31] for the murder of one John Johnson. Lord Ferrers was tried by the House of Lords because of his title. There was, therefore, no charge to the jury and no reasons given by the members of the Court for their individual verdicts. In his argument, the solicitor general for the Crown relies upon Sir Matthew Hale's *The History of the Pleas of the Crown* as being the law of England with respect to the defence of insanity, as follows (at 947):

My lords, the result of the whole reasoning of this wise judge and great lawyer (so far as it is immediately relative to the present purpose) stands thus. If there be a total permanent want of reason it will acquit the prisoner. If there be a total temporary want of it, when the offence was committed, it will acquit the prisoner: but if there be only a partial degree of insanity, mixed with a partial degree of reason; not a full and complete use of reason, but (as Lord Hale carefully and emphatically expresses himself) a competent use of it, sufficient to have restrained those passions, which produced the crime; if there be thought and design; a faculty to distinguish the nature of actions; to discern the difference between moral good and evil; then, upon the fact of the offence proved, the judgement of the law must take place.

Although the House of Lords gave no reasons for their verdict (Lord Ferrer was convicted and hanged), one might assume that the Court agreed with the submissions of the Crown and if that were the case that, so far as the House of Lords was concerned, the law regarding the defence of insanity was as suggested by the Crown relying on the writings of Hale.

Chapter Two

WOUNDED BUT STILL conscious, Edward Drummond requested of the crowd which had quickly gathered that he be conveyed to his brother's bank a short distance away in Charing Cross Road. Drummond's brother Harvey sent immediately for an apothecary by the name of Richard Jackson who was known to Drummond's family and whose shop was located nearby. Upon examining the wound, Jackson found that the bullet had penetrated the skin of Drummond's back, through the coat and undergarments, but, not having the necessary instruments, he could not trace it further. As Drummond did not seem too debilitated by loss of blood, Jackson advised Harvey that his brother should immediately be moved to his own residence in Grosvenor Street.

By five o'clock, less than an hour after the shooting, Drummond was being tended to by George Guthrie and Bransby Blake Cooper, two of England's most eminent surgeons.[1] Though unable to find the bullet at first, they turned Drummond on his back and discovered it about a half inch below the skin in the lower portion of his chest. Having no operating instruments at hand, Guthrie (a former war surgeon whose specialty was gunshot wounds) used a lancet to make an incision; Bransby Cooper extracted the bullet which, although it had ripped through Drummond's diaphragm, was thought by both doctors not to be life-threatening. Indeed, they notified the press soon after that the bullet had been removed, that none of Drummond's vital parts had been injured, and that they had every reason to believe their patient was "doing very well."

✿✿✿✿

NEWS OF THE attempted assassination sent shock waves throughout England, many believing that M'Naughten's intended target was the prime minister, Sir Robert Peel, the leading Tory politician of his day. The Tory government was struggling to cope with various movements for political and social reform among the newly emerging industrial or "labouring" class, most notably the Chartists, who felt that although it gave the vote to the middle class, the *Reform Act of 1832* had betrayed the interests of working people. Not only was political opposition to Peel's government mounting, but in the previous two years, strikes and protests, fuelled by a severe depression, had turned violent, with many protestors advocating the widespread use of force as the only means of attaining their goals.

In this particular respect, M'Naughten's shooting of Drummond – possibly mistaking him for Peel – as an act of Chartist resistance, was not too unreal for either the government or the public to accept. After all, it was only three years earlier, in June of 1840, that a man named Edward Oxford shot at Queen Victoria and Prince Albert while they were out riding in Constitution Park. Although Oxford's bullets missed the queen and her husband, the police search of his rooms turned up evidence that suggested ties to the Chartists and other politically radical groups that were threatening the government. Oxford, who was eighteen at the time of the shooting and who had a family history of mental illness, was tried for high treason. At trial it came to light that he worked as a "potboy" in a tavern and indeed suffered from a delusional belief that he belonged to a non-existent society, a world of fantasy and imagination far removed from the grim reality of his life in the poorest, most dismal part of London – a world "with guns and swords and means of escape and concealment, and so on."

The jury in *Oxford's Case*[2] was instructed by the judge Lord Denman that the law was as follows:

> Then as to whether the prisoner, owing to the state of his mind at the time, was exempt from criminal punishment, every man is *prima facie* taken to be responsible for his acts until the contrary is proved, but a man's state of mind may make him irresponsible for an act in its nature the most criminal. If he was in that state of mind that you cannot say he was a free agent, but that some controlling disease was the acting power which he could not resist, he would not be guilty, and would be entitled to be acquitted. In some cases where insanity is pleaded, it is

difficult to decide upon the mark between occasional eccentricity and the delusion which leads to the commission of the offence.

. . .

The ancient law on this subject is laid down in Latin words which have become very familiar to us. That man charged as a criminal is not responsible for the act who, in the language of our law, is *non compos mentis*, or not able to distinguish between right and wrong. The meaning of it is that he, from a diseased state of mind, is wholly unconscious that it is wrong in him to do the act charged upon him. That is the law . . .

The question is whether the prisoner was labouring under that species of inanity which satisfies you that he was quite unaware of the nature, character, and consequences of the act he was committing, whether he was under the influence of a diseased mind, and was really conscious at the time he committed the act that it was a crime.

Hence, the jury returned a verdict that the prisoner was "[n]ot guilty, he being at the time insane." Oxford was then ordered detained during Her Majesty's pleasure pursuant to the *Act for the safe Custody of Insane Persons charged with Offences* of 1800, commonly known as the *Criminal Lunatics Act*.[3] He was sent to Bethlehem Royal Hospital (Bedlam) where he remained until 1864 when the criminal patients of the institution were transferred to the new hospital for the criminally insane at Broadmoor.

While the preceding case was significant in the evolution of the insanity defence, there is really very little doubt the most celebrated and important case ever is that of our subject, Daniel M'Naughten. His case resulted in a formal articulation of the insanity defence by the House of Lords that remains the most pre-eminent in all of the Western world. As a result, he has acquired a permanent place in medico-legal history.

NOTORIOUS AS *Oxford's Case* had been from a political point of view, it was significant from a legal standpoint because the *Criminal Lunatics Act* of 1800, a statute which was precipitated by the case of James Hadfield, was often viewed as marking the beginning of modern jurisprudence. This was not so much due to the court's articulation of the test for insanity, but more importantly, for the formal process of dealing with the post-verdict *acquittee* that was legislated as a result of this case.

On the evening of 15 May 1800, at the Theatre Royal in Drury Lane, twenty-eight-year-old James Hadfield fired a pistol at King George III who stood in the royal box for the playing of the national anthem. The bullet missed, Hadfield calling out, "God bless your royal highness – I like you very well, you are a good fellow." Apprehended at the scene, with no doubt among any as to what he had done, Hadfield was charged with high treason for "compassing and imagining the death of the King [George III]" by discharging a pistol at the monarch at close range while in his box at the Theatre Royal in Drury Lane.

The most significant part of the case, which included the evidence of two surgeons and a physician who testified that Hadfield's delusions were a direct result of earlier head injuries, was the speech of counsel for the accused, The Hon. Thomas Erskine, the leading barrister of his day (later to become Lord Chancellor of England). The attorney general, Sir John Mitford, essentially conceded the case. Lord Kenyon, speaking for the Court, virtually directed the jury to return a verdict of "not guilty" by reason of insanity.

While Erskine conceded the law to date, as expressed by both Coke and Hale, he questioned the requirement that the accused be totally deprived of his memory of the otherwise criminal act and introduced the concept of delusional thinking at the relevant time as a basis for the defence (at 1312–14):

> The attorney-general, standing undoubtedly upon the most revered authorities of the law, has it laid down, that to protect a man from *criminal responsibility*, there must be TOTAL *deprivation of memory and understanding*. I admit, that this is the very expression used by both lord Coke and Lord Hale; but the true interpretation of it deserves the utmost attention and consideration of the Court. If a TOTAL *deprivation of memory* was intended by these great lawyers to be taken in the *literal* sense of the words: – if it was meant, that, to protect a man from punishment, he must be in such a state of prostrated intellect, as not to know his name, nor his condition, nor his relation to others – that if a husband, he should not know he was married; or, if a father, could not remember that he had children; nor know the road to his house, nor his property in it – then no such madness ever

existed in the world. It is IDIOCY alone which places a man in this helpless condition; where, from an original mal-organization, there is the human frame alone, without the human capacity; and which, indeed, meets the very definition of lord Hale himself, when referring to Fitzherbert, he says – "Idiocy or fatuity *a nativatate, vel dementia naturalis*, is such a one as described by Fitzherbert, who knows not to tell twenty shillings, nor knows his own age, or who was his father." But in all cases which have filled the Westminster hall with the most complicated considerations – the lunatics and other insane persons who have been the subjects of them, have not only had memory, *in my sense of the expression* – they have not only had the most perfect knowledge and recollection of all the relations they stood in towards others, and of the acts and circumstances of their lives, but have, in general, been remarkable for subtlety and acuteness. Defects in their reasonings have seldom been traceable – the disease consisting in the delusive sources of thought; all their deductions within the scope of the malady, being founded upon the *immoveable* assumption of matters as *realities*, either without any foundation whatsoever, or so distorted and disfigured by fancy, as to be almost nearly the same thing as their creation.

. . .

Such persons, *and such persons alone (except idiots), are wholly deprived of their* UNDERSTANDINGS, in the attorney-general's seeming sense of that expression.

. . .

Delusion, therefore, where there is no frenzy or raving madness, is the true character of insanity . . .[4]

Erskine's interpretation of the law accords very closely with the manner in which insanity is treated today. Clearly, most individuals suffering from mental disorder of a sort that would afford them a defence have some, if not a complete, recollection of the events in question. As well, most insanity defences are indeed founded upon delusional thinking that caused the accused to believe events and people to be related in a manner that does not accord with reality.[5]

The evidence adduced at trial further revealed that Hadfield had been a soldier serving under the Duke of York and that in battle six years previously was, amongst other injuries, almost completely decapitated by a sword. The evidence was that the accused was from that point on "bereft of his senses forever."[6] Indeed he was discharged from the army because of his insanity. At the time of the offence (at 1321):

> He imagined that he had constant intercourse with the Almighty Author of all things; that the world was coming to a conclusion; and that, like our blessed Saviour, he was to sacrifice himself for its salvation; and so obstinately did this morbid image continue, that you will be convinced he went to the theatre to perform, as he imagined, that blessed sacrifice; and, because he would not be guilty of suicide, though called upon by the imperious voice of Heaven, he wished that by the appearance of crime his life might be taken away from him by others.

As indicated, the case was cut short by Lord Kenyon because of the overwhelming state of the evidence and Hadfield was found to be not guilty by reason of insanity – the characteristics of which have been, in part, described earlier in this chapter. Although it is not entirely clear precisely what test was applied by the court, it is apparent that the court accepted that delusional thinking can be a basis for a finding of insanity.[7] This was seen as "partial insanity" in that it pertained to circumscribed delusional (insane) thinking in an individual who in every other respect was rational and apparently sane. Earlier, more primitive constructions had required that the individual be completely and fully affected by mental disorder – devoid of all rationality.

Hadfield's acquittal prompted a public furor. He had carried out a premeditated attack on the king and yet he had somehow "got off." The court was confronted with the issue of what to do with him, not only because of the angry public reaction that would ensue if he were released, but also given Hadfield's remaining dangerous mental condition, it appeared that neither setting him free, nor sending him to prison, was appropriate. In response to the predicament caused by the case, Parliament speedily passed the *Criminal Lunatics Act* (*Act for the safe Custody of Insane Persons charged with Offences*). The Act provided *inter alia* that a person found to be insane, for his own sake and the sake of society at large, shall be ordered by the Court "to be kept in strict custody, in such place and in such manner as to such Court shall seem fit, until His Majesty's Pleasure shall be known."[8]

In the case of M'Naughten, *The Times* had noted that the day after the shooting that he showed no obvious signs of mental disorder when he was arrested, other than what might be inferred from his statement that "He" (or "She") . . ."shall not disturb my mind any longer." True, he had been seen loitering about the public offices in and around Downing Street for some days previously; on one occasion the keeper of the Privy Council Office observed him standing on the office doorstep. But his response, when asked what he was doing, whether he might be in the service of the police (many of whom were not in uniform at that time) was a harmless if equivocal reply in the affirmative. And he assured the man he need not be afraid for his property. This may be interpreted to have meant that while his plan was in place, he was accurately indicating that no one's property was at risk, although at the same time, one might argue, he was avoiding any guarantees with respect to personal injury. All in all, however, there was nothing about M'Naughten that was conspicuous. "He was neither," as *The Times* reported, "disheveled, unkempt, or notably malodorous," as good an indication as any to readers in Victorian England that there was "no evidence of insanity."

And while it was known that he was a native of Glasgow, and that the family name was likely McNaughton, a certain curiosity was aroused about Daniel M'Naughten in the way he spelled his name. *The Times* used M'Naughton, but accounts in other newspapers, in court transcripts and in other documents pertaining to the case contained variant spellings, such as: Macnaughton, Macnaughten, Macnaghten, M'Naughten, M'Naughton, McNaughton, and McNaughten. Though an actual signature of *M'Naghten* has been found, it is insufficiently clear to put the matter to rest. So far as the House of Lords and legal reference were concerned, the name continued to be spelled M'Naghten. The best explanation has been offered by J. Thomas Dalby in *The Case of Daniel McNaughton*,[9] who, referring to the authors of a book on the M'Naughten trial, points out that at the time a printing convention existed that used a reverse apostrophe to create the small *c*, which was above the printer's range of type. It may have been from errors in this execution that variations occurred.

What would become increasingly interesting about M'Naughten was the fact that his demeanour throughout his time in prison was always precisely the same. He always appeared to be calm and composed. He had a hearty appetite and ate well. He appeared very attentive to conversations between other people in the jail: other prisoners, attorneys, police guards, and is said to have frequently laughed at any jocular observations that were made. At no time did he ever allude to the crime with which he had been charged, nor to why he might have committed it. He entered into conversation with the jailer and other persons connected with the court, but he never spoke about himself or his life. Most assumed that, like many other Scots of his day, M'Naughten, a wood-turner by trade, had recently come to London in hopes of finding work.

Chapter Three

WITH THOUSANDS POURING into London each month hoping to find work, and with its metropolitan population having ballooned as a result to well over 2 million people, the city to which Daniel M'Naughten first came in the summer of 1841 was a study in contrasts. London was at once an ancient city, built by the Romans in AD 45, and a modern one, with a dozen railway lines running trains in and out of London daily while hundreds of steamships plied the waters of the Thames, bound for or returning from Britain's imperial colonies around the world. People of staggering wealth lived and worked alongside the poor and poverty-stricken. Royalty and aristocracy, as emblemized by the monarchy and the House of Lords, continued to rule "Brittania," the young Queen Victoria and her husband Prince Albert were beloved by all. At the same time mass working-class labour movements agitated for social and political reforms with an ever-growing willingness to use violence to achieve their ends.

Indeed, London in 1843 (the time of the murder) was a city like no other. Frederick Engels, arriving the year before to work with Karl Marx on the seminal works of dialectical materialism (Communism), marvelled at the city's vibrancy and dynamism:[1]

> I know of nothing more imposing than the view the Thames offers during the ascent from the sea to London Bridge. The masses of buildings, the wharves on both sides, especially from Woolwich upwards, the countless ships along both shores, crowding ever closer together, until, at last, only a narrow passage through which hundreds of steamers shoot by one another.

We can almost visualize the frenetic harbour and hear the blaring horns of the "countless ships" docking and departing from the bustling port with columns of smoke from the coal-fired engines clouding the skies over the city. We can almost see the marketplaces in the busy public squares, sidewalks along the narrow streets crowded with pedestrians from all walks of life, the roads thick with horse-drawn Hansom cabs, with coaches, carriages, carts, and wagons. We can almost hear the whistles of great black steam locomotives constantly chugging into and out of London, the clatter of thousands of horses' hooves on the cobblestones, the din of curbside vendors hawking their wares, the cheers and jeers of Londoners reacting to soapbox speakers spouting religion, politics, and populist philosophy, the barked orders of British soldiers in their red coats, and busbies changing guard in front of Buckingham Palace.[2]

But we can also see, by the dim light of the gas lamps on Christmas Eve, the Ghost of Christmas Present in Charles Dickens' *A Christmas Carol*, leading the miserly Scrooge through areas of downtown London he had never seen before:

> They left the busy scene, and went into an obscure part of town, where Scrooge had never penetrated before, although he recognized its situation and its bad repute. The ways were foul and narrow; the shops and houses wretched; the people half naked, drunken, slipshod, ugly. Alleys and archways, like so many cesspools, disgorged their offences of smell, and dirt, and life, upon the straggling streets; and the whole quarter reeked with crime, with filth, and misery.[3]

While the spot in Charing Cross Road where Drummond was shot would not have been quite so gritty, we can imagine the pungent and unpleasant smells coming from Grove the fishmonger's, very close by, which, depending upon the prevailing winds, may have caused a "fishy" aroma to mix with the smell of burnt gunpowder from M'Naughten's pistol after it was fired. At the time of the shooting he was said to have been standing by the door of a stationer's store, with Drummond, ironically as it turned out, near a gunsmith's shop no more than 50 yards from his brother's bank.

The day after the shooting, details of M'Naughten's stunningly bold assassination attempt were the talk of London, but they were also the talk of Manchester, Liverpool, Birmingham, and Glasgow, and of cities across Britain, courtesy of what was, after the government, perhaps the country's most powerful and influential institution: *The Times* of

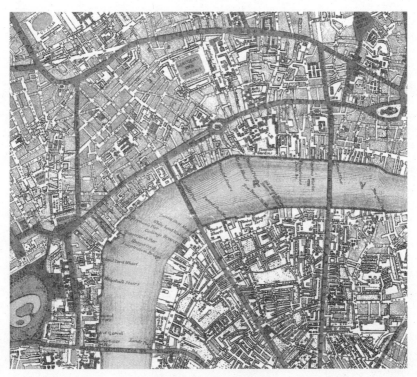

MAP OF LONDON, 1843

London, nicknamed "The Thunderer" because it commanded the largest readership and because, unlike most other papers, it put forward an authoritative brand of informed, objective, and fair reporting.

This policy of keeping to the "middle of the road" allowed *The Times* to increase its sales and advertising revenues so that, by 1840, they so surpassed those of all other newspapers that *The Times* was able to take advantage of new developments in printing: an improved paper-feeding process and a revolving press in place of double cylinders, which quintupled the speed of newspaper production. Along with this, the accelerating pace of developments in train transportation made it possible for *The Times* to have news of the Drummond shooting appear simultaneously in cities throughout Britain the morning following the event.

Newspaper circulation numbers climbed dramatically in London during the early 1840s. The old subscription model gave way to a dynamic new distribution system that saw the rise of "penny papers," sold by newsagents, like the renowned W.H. Smith, who were opening shops in, or near, the crowded railroad stations, and by street vendors who positioned themselves on prominent city corners. Shouting the latest headlines, particularly when they involved the attempted murder of a political figure like Sir Robert Peel, people were only too eager to read about the news.

Though a Metropolitan Police Force had been created by Peel in 1829, its officers (popularly known as "Bobbies") went about unarmed and wore plainclothes rather than uniforms. Because their chief function was keeping the peace, they carried no weapons other than a nightstick, a small wooden club mostly used for subduing drunkards. Naturally, in a city becoming rapidly more populous and more socially complex all the time, crime was on the rise. Robbery and assault rates were climbing at an uncomfortable pace, but the weapon of choice for criminals remained the knife. Indeed, most of those arrested by the police belonged to crews of petty thieves, frauds, and pickpockets operated by dubious characters like the wily Fagan and the bullying thug Bill Sykes in *Oliver Twist*, who used stealth and cunning rather than violence on their favoured prey: the newly affluent middle-class gentry.

The authors of the 1843 *Street Map of London*, produced by the Society for the Diffusion of Useful Knowledge (so that passengers hiring the new Hansom horse-drawn cabs could be assured that they were being taken about the city via the most direct route), described London, and England in general, as "witnessing a new age of youth, enthusiasm and expansion," epitomized by eighteen-year-old Queen Victoria's accession to the throne six years earlier, replacing a long line of indifferent and unpopular Hanoverian (German) kings. In 1840 she married Prince Albert of Saxe-Coburg-Gotha and two years later became the first monarch to travel by one of the greatest transportation inventions of the nineteenth century: the railway train, which had become the chief commercial means of moving all manner of commodities, factory-made goods and products around the country, while steamships, superseding less efficient sailing vessels, shipped ever greater volumes of British manufactured goods to ports throughout the world.

Accompanying this new age of expansion in the early years of Victoria's reign were significant political and social developments. The old, oligarchic, and often corrupt municipal "corporations" who controlled the urban centres were quickly giving way to the rising stature of individual Members of Parliament in the House of Commons, bringing forth new legislation on behalf of an increasingly political, knowledgeable, and reform-minded electorate. The expanding middle-class demanded that government be more responsive and responsible, particularly for such things as commerce, finance, and education. Working-class labour movements like the Chartists pressed for, among other things, all men aged twenty-one and over to have the right to vote, for the secret ballot in elections, for an end to property ownership as a qualification for Parliament, and for members of the House of Commons to be paid.

As a result, government between 1820 and 1840 became a much more complex and fragile business, with power shifting back and forth between the Whigs and the Tories, sometimes as often as every few months, as the two principal parties struggled to either win support for new legislation, or to muster enough opposition in the House of Commons to defeat the government through a vote of non-confidence. With no third party of note, coalition governments were not effectively possible: defeat on a single bill in Parliament meant that a government had to fall, with the result that elections were held and power changed hands sometimes every six months.

A leading figure in British politics and government for over thirty years and M'Naughten's presumed target, Sir Robert Peel, had entered the House of Commons in 1809 at the age of twenty-one. The son of a wealthy cotton manufacturer, Peel was trained from childhood to become a politician, as his father (himself a Member of Parliament) required him to repeat from memory both the morning and evening sermons delivered in church each Sunday.

Ambitious, determined, and politically astute, at the start of only his second year in the House of Commons he was made undersecretary of war and the colonies, helping direct military operations against Napoleon. In 1812, at all of twenty-four years old, he was made chief secretary for Ireland where the Protestant-Catholic conflict was dangerously heating up under the leadership of Daniel O'Connell, a revered figure in the Irish nationalist movement. Such was the enmity between Peel and O'Connell that in 1815, Peel challenged the Irishman to a duel, but O'Connell was arrested on his way to Ostend, a coastal

SIR ROBERT PEEL, 1843
SOURCE: ILLUSTRATED LONDON NEWS, 4 FEBRUARY 1843

town in Belgium where the duel was to have taken place. Ironically, it was Peel who, several years later and in spite of violent opposition from King George III, would introduce the *Catholic Emancipation Act* in Parliament, an act that proposed the end of preferment for Protestants over Catholics in government service.

At the age of thirty-four, Peel served as home secretary in the short-lived Tory governments of Lord Liverpool and the Duke of Wellington; from 1830 to 1833, he was a member of the opposition when a Whig government passed the *Reform Bill*, an Act that introduced some of the most significant social and political changes in British history. But in 1834, King William IV (Victoria's father) dismissed the Whig government and, because of the regard with which he was held in the House of Commons, appointed Peel prime minister. He immediately called an election and, though outnumbered by Whigs in the House of Commons, he did manage to work with them in a coalition government for more than a year.

Power continued to pass back and forth between Whigs and Tories for the next several years; however, in the election of August 1841, two years before Drummond's murder, Peel won a majority in the House of Commons, the first in several decades, due largely to his having changed public perception of the Tories as a hidebound, repressive party, to a new and more enlightened "conservative" party. Solidly in control of Parliament, with what all regarded as one of the best cabinets in a long while, over the next five years he and his Conservatives (as the party was coming to be called) enacted legislation that effectively created the model for modern government administration. Peel introduced an income tax and revised outmoded tariff structures to promote "free trade," a policy that led to the reduction of Britain's deficit and allowed the government to earn more than it spent; he instituted policies that brought about much-needed reforms in business, labour relations, banking, trade, agriculture, and transportation, gaining the confidence of the working- and middle-classes in the process, while at the same time his respect for history and tradition allowed him to retain the support of ancient institutions like the monarchy and the Church; among his large-scale reforms of the British legal system, he took the first steps towards giving women and children permanent protection in labour law and, although unsuccessful, he advocated a national system of schools for the poor.

By 1843, Robert Peel was the most powerful and popular political figure in the country, solidly at the head of the House of Commons and widely regarded as an outstanding prime minister, even by many of his harshest critics and ardent political foes. That someone would attempt to kill him, considering the esteem in which he was held by the British public (Londoners in particular), was shocking; but that the attempt should end up being made against Edward Drummond, Peel's personal secretary, was nothing short of bewildering.

The shooting having occurred late in the day on the 20th of January, a Friday, Drummond's condition remained a top news story in all the London papers throughout the weekend. Reporters and writers stationed outside the Drummond home crowded around the attending doctors at their every arrival and departure, plying them with questions as to the state of their patient's health – questions that the physicians obligingly answered. Prime Minister Peel and his wife Lady Peel were among Drummond's most frequent visitors, but many of the nobility and gentry who were "in town" at the time either called at the house in Grosvenor Street or made regular inquiries, as did numerous high-ranking government officials and relatives and friends of Queen Victoria herself.

Indeed, not only had Edward Drummond been a fixture in British politics for nearly twenty-five years, serving as private secretary and trusted adviser to three other Tory prime ministers besides Robert Peel – George Canning, Lord Goderich, and Arthur Wellesley, the first Duke of Wellington – but the Drummonds were also leading members of the Scottish peerage. Edward's uncle James was the current Viscount Strathallan; his great-grandfather the fourth Viscount William Drummond who had died at the Battle of Culloden in the second Stuart uprising of 1745, and for whom the Scottish bard Robert Burns had written the moving *Strathallan's Lament*:

Ruin's wheel has driven o'er us
Not a hope that dare attend,
The wide world is all before us –
But a world without a friend.[4]

The Drummonds had also been a prominent English banking family for over a hundred years – their eponymous Drummonds Bank being one of London's most eminent financial institutions, with well

DRUMMONDS BANKERS

over five thousand accounts in 1843, customer deposits in excess of £3,000,000, and an elite clientele that included many of the city's leading businessmen, as well as members of the royal family. Edward's older brother Charles, whose offices he was taken to after M'Naughten's assassination attempt, was a partner in Drummonds Bank. The youngest of the four brothers, Arthur, an Anglican rector at Charlton in Kent, set out for London immediately upon being informed that his brother had been shot, while brother Berkeley, a colonel in the Scots Fusilier Guards, who had recently been appointed one of the grooms-in-waiting to Queen Victoria, was on duty dining with the queen when a special messenger arrived "with the lamentable and alarming intelligence of the diabolical attempt which had been made on his brother's life." Stricken by the news, Berkeley left Windsor Castle soon after and proceeded to town, "both Her Majesty and His Royal Highness Prince Albert," reported *The Times*, "having manifested the most intense anxiety for the fate of the unfortunate sufferer."

Chapter Four

WHILE BERKELEY DRUMMOND made his way to London to be with his brother, the man being held for shooting him was making his first appearance before the court. *The Times* reported that "[i]t having become known that the person charged with attempting the life of Mr. Edward Drummond would be examined at Bow Street on Saturday morning, the court, as soon as the doors were thrown open, was densely thronged by persons anxious to hear the proceedings."

After disposing of other business before the court, a Magistrate Hall, who was hearing the case, had Daniel M'Naughten brought in and placed before the bar. "He was a young man," according to *The Times* (M'Naughten was then thirty), "rather above middle height, having the appearances of a mechanic, and was respectably dressed in a black coat and waistcoat and drab trousers. He was rather thin, had good colour and his countenance betokened nothing ferocious or determined."

It is remarkable by today's standards that M'Naughten was brought before a court and arraigned (his case given a preliminary inquiry) within two days of his alleged offence. Nowadays a preliminary inquiry, or a grand jury if such is the case (mainly in American jurisdictions), upon hearing the evidence of the Crown, would conclude that there was *prima facie* evidence to support the charge and then issue a "true bill" (had the evidence not supported the charge, the jury would have declared "no bill"). As well, a preliminary inquiry is usually not held for a number of months after arrest, so that a determination can be made as to whether or not there is enough evidence to put an accused on trial. The defence is first supplied with the Crown "disclosure," which consists of a synopsis of allegations, statements of witnesses, police notes, and any other evidence to be relied upon at trial.

As well, pretrial hearings are typically held where the Crown and defence discuss possible resolution or agree on certain matters if the case is to go to trial. Today, these procedures take many weeks and, more typically, months to sort out. Of course, at this point, Drummond was still alive, so M'Naughten was accused in the police sheet read out by the clerk of the court, only of "discharging two loaded pistols at Mr. Edward Drummond, at Charing Cross, and wounding him."

When the clerk asked him his name, M'Naughten replied in a broad Scottish accent, "Daniel M'Naughten."

The first witness examined was James Silver, a police constable.

"On Friday afternoon about ten minutes or a quarter before 4 o'clock, I was on duty at Charing-Cross when I heard the report of a pistol on the opposite side of the street – the same side as the Horse Guards. I immediately directed my attention to the spot, and then saw the prisoner with a pistol in his hand."

"Did you see him do anything with it?" asked Mr. Hall.

"Yes," answered Constable Silver, "he immediately put it into his left breast pocket, and at the time drew another pistol, which he cocked and was about taking a deliberate aim with when I ran up and seized him."

"Did you observe whether the prisoner was pointing the pistol at any person?"

"Yes, he was pointing it at a gentleman."

"Had you previously observed the gentleman?"

"Yes. I saw him reeling near the spot."

"That was after the first shot was fired?"

"After the first shot," Constable Silver nodded, "and before he drew the second pistol. I then noticed that the gentleman's coat-tail was on fire, in a small place, but not in a flame, and I also saw something which looked like a small piece of paper burning at his feet. The gentleman appeared to be wounded, and placed his hand to his side."

"Did you see where the prisoner took the second pistol from?"

"He took it from his breast. When the prisoner presented the second pistol, I seized him by the arms, and it was discharged in my struggle to secure him. I have since searched for the ball, but could not find it."

"Did the prisoner use any violence when you seized him by the arms?"

"He struggled with me till I overpowered him."

"Was the second pistol aimed at the same gentleman?"

"It was. As soon as the pistol was discharged, I took it from the prisoner's hand, and also took the other from his breast. I then conveyed him to the station-house, and on our way there he said – 'He,' or 'She,' I cannot say which, 'shall not destroy my peace of mind any longer.' He said nothing more."

"Did you say anything to him to induce him to make that observation?"

"I did not. He said it voluntarily. When I got the prisoner to the station-house, I searched him and found in his pockets the articles mentioned in the police sheet."

At this point the pistols were produced – pocket-pistols as they were usually known – with percussion locks. They were not of the same pair, but appeared to be quite new.

"Do the percussion-caps fit the pistols?"

"Having tried several, I can say they fitted exactly. After the prisoner was locked up at the station-house, I went and searched his lodgings, where I found, in the pockets of a pair of trousers which his landlady said belonged to him, two more percussion caps, similar to the others."[1]

M'Naughten was then asked by Mr. Hall whether he wished to ask the witness any questions, to which he replied, "I do not ..."

We can see that at this juncture Daniel M'Naughten was unrepresented. There was apparently no inquiry by the court as to whether or not he had counsel, or wished to retain counsel. Today, especially in respect of a serious charge of this sort, and where there is at least the prospect of mental disorder being in issue, the accused would have been represented by counsel. If the fitness of the accused or his competency to stand trial were at issue, the appointment of counsel would be mandatory. A court must, where there are reasonable grounds to believe that an accused may be unfit to stand trial, hold an inquiry to determine the issue. Of course, this issue pertains to the accused person's present condition and his ability to defend himself, rather than to his or her mental condition at the time of the alleged offence. In M'Naughten's case it may be that minds were turned to these issues but no concerns arose; or it may be that the issue arose, but was not reported. Certainly, it would be unthinkable in a court today that an individual in M'Naughten's situation would be subjected to this process without the aid of counsel.

Another curious aspect of the case to this point, by modern legal standards, is that the police officer apparently went to M'Naughten's residence and searched his quarters without a search warrant. Today, a search warrant must be obtained in circumstances such as these. A justice of the peace must receive sworn evidence that an offence has or is about to be committed and that the search of a particular place for particular things is necessary. Police are not permitted to simply enter a premise and snoop around without authorization.

The next witness to be called by Magistrate Hall was Robert Hodge, a carpenter.

> "On Friday afternoon, between 3 and 4 o'clock, I was passing down Whitehall, when I observed the prisoner walking behind a gentleman, who was about three yards from him. I then saw the prisoner draw a pistol and deliberately fire it at the gentleman, and wound him."
>
> "Where was the wound?"
>
> "It was in his side. I saw the gentleman stagger and place his hand to his side. I immediately went up to the prisoner, when I saw him draw another pistol from his breast, upon which I immediately ran away into the carriage road."
>
> "I suppose you were afraid that he would shoot you?"
>
> "I was."
>
> Hall deliberated a moment. "Did you see the second pistol fired?"
>
> "No, I did not, but I almost immediately afterwards heard the report."
>
> "Did you see what became of the wounded gentleman?"
>
> "He was taken into Messrs. Drummond's bank."

Again given the opportunity to question the witness, M'Naughten declined, and so the witness Benjamin Weston was called to the stand.

> "I am a porter at the Ship Tavern, Charing-Cross. On Friday afternoon, about five minutes before 4 o'clock, I was standing near the door of the Salopian Coffee-house, when I heard the report of a pistol very near me. On turning round I saw a gentleman staggering on the pavement, as if he were wounded. He held one hand to his side and with the other pointed to the prisoner, who was behind him."

"Did you see the prisoner near the gentleman you have mentioned?"

"Yes. He was within a few paces of him. The prisoner then turned round and drew another pistol from his breast, which he deliberately cocked, and then pointed it at the gentleman. At that moment, and before the pistol was discharged, the policeman Silver pounced upon him and pinioned his arms."

"At that time you say the pistol was pointed at the gentleman?"

"It was. I immediately ran to the constable's assistance, and laid hold of the prisoner's jacket collar, and during the scuffle which ensued the pistol was discharged."

"Did you see what became of the gentleman?"

"Yes. I went to look after him, and found him in Messrs. Drummond's bank."

"Did you see the constable take the pistol from the prisoner?"

"Yes, after it was discharged, but he struck him on the hand in the first instance, in order to make him drop it."

"Did you not state that I struck the officer?" M'Naughten piped up.

"Certainly not. I said that he struck your arm."

"Did I at all resist the officer?"

"You did, till after the pistol was discharged, and you found yourself overpowered."

"I have nothing else to ask you."

At this point, James Partridge, a police constable who regularly patrolled the streets in the vicinity of Charing Cross, took his place in the dock.

"For some time past I have been doing duty in the neighbourhood of Whitehall, and during the last 17 or 18 days I have frequently seen the prisoner walking up and down near the Privy Council Office and the Treasury, and generally observed that he looked earnestly towards the residence of the Duke of Buccleuch. I have several times seen him standing on the steps leading to the Privy Council Offices. I particularly recollect seeing him there on the morning of the 13th January, I believe it was. I then asked him whether he was waiting for any person, and I believe his reply was that he was waiting to see a gentleman, but he spoke in a hurried manner, and instantly walked away.

"On Friday morning last, about half-past 10 o'clock, I again saw him walking to and fro in front of the Council Office, and after watching him a few minutes I went up to him and asked him whether he had yet seen the gentleman he wanted, to which he hastily replied, 'No,' and walked hurriedly away. I saw nothing more of him for about half an hour, when I next saw him standing near the entrance to Lady Dover's residence: he was then eating a piece of bread. I then left the neighbourhood for an hour or two and on my return, saw the prisoner near the Treasury, and between that time and half-past 3 o'clock I saw him several more times in the neighbourhood."

M'Naughten directed a question at Police Constable Partridge.

"Are you quite sure you ever had any conversation with me?"

"Certainly I am."

"I have no recollection of anything of the sort ..."

Partridge gave Mr. Hall a puzzled look and was soon after allowed to return to his seat in the packed courtroom as attention turned to one of Edward Drummond's doctors, Bransby B. Cooper.

"I am a surgeon, and reside at number 2, New Street, Spring Gardens. On my return home about 4 o'clock on Friday afternoon, I found that I had been sent for to Messrs. Drummond's bank. On going there I was informed that some gentleman had been wounded, and I then immediately went to No. 19, Lower Grosvenor Street, where I understood the gentleman had been taken. I there saw Mr. Drummond, who was undressed, and attended by Mr. Jackson, his apothecary."

"Were you previously acquainted with Mr. Drummond?"

"I was not till I saw him on that occasion."

"Who pointed him out to you as Mr. Drummond?"

"Mr. Jackson."

"Did you address the gentleman as 'Mr. Drummond'?"

"I did. My attention was called by Mr. Jackson to a wound in Mr. Drummond's side, which upon examination I found to correspond with the openings in his shirt and flannel waistcoat. I then searched the course of the wound for the ball, and in order to do so was compelled to enlarge the opening made by the ball in the skin. I could not, however, during this period of the examination, find the ball. In the course of a short time Mr. Guthrie, who had been also sent for, arrived, when the wound was again examined, but still we were unable to find the ball. We then directed Mr. Drummond to be turned upon his back, in order that we might examine the anterior part of his body, when a small projecting lump was observed, which, upon examination, was found to be the ball immediately under the skin, so that a mere incision of the lancet led to its extraction. The opening then made showed that the ball had traversed round the left half of the gentleman's body."

"What has become of the ball?"

"I gave it to Miss Drummond, the patient's daughter."

"I presume it was a pistol ball?"

"It was slightly marked, and had the appearance of having been rifled."

"Do you consider Mr. Drummond to be in any immediate danger?"

"I have not seen him since last night. I then left him in the care of Mr. Guthrie, who is his personal medical attendant, but I am going to attend a consultation as soon as I leave this court. I do not consider that any immediate danger is to be apprehended, although I cannot say there is not danger, as it is very possible inflammation may take place.

"In your opinion, will Mr. Drummond be able soon to get out, or not?"

"In my opinion his confinement will be very protracted, as all the danger has yet to come . . ."

When all the evidence had been presented, the magistrate addressed the prisoner:

"I am about to remand you for a fortnight, and if you wish to say anything in answer to the charge, I am ready to hear you. You are not compelled to say anything unless you think proper. But it is my duty to tell you, that if you do say anything, it will be taken down in writing and made use of, if necessary, hereafter. Now, having given you that caution, do you wish to say anything?"

"I am much obliged to you, sir, but I shall say nothing at present."

"Then you are remanded for a fortnight," the clerk announced, and M'Naughten was immediately taken from the dock and removed to one of the cells attached to the court. He had only been there for a minute or two when he sent a message to the magistrate intimating that he wished to say something. He was accordingly led back into court and placed at the bar.

At this point, although unclear from the way the proceedings were reported, Daniel M'Naughten was committed to stand trial on the charge as originally read – a charge of "wounding." Normally, at the conclusion of the Crown's case, argument would be heard as to whether or not there was sufficient evidence to put the accused to trial. No such argument was reported. This may have been because M'Naughten was unrepresented and the outcome, regarding committal, obvious to the court. Or, alternatively, it may be that there simply was no reporting of the argument on this issue.

Today, at the conclusion of a preliminary inquiry, the court must be satisfied that there is sufficient evidence such that a reasonable jury properly instructed *could* convict the accused. Not that a reasonable jury *would* convict the accused or that it *should*; but that it *could*. Where sufficient evidence is adduced the accused is *committed* for trial; where the evidence is insufficient the accused is *discharged*.

Although at this point it would be today's practice to address the issue of judicial interim release or "bail," in 1843, his alleged offence not being "bailable," M'Naughten would not have had a right to request bail even though he would have been able to post a considerable deposit. While various methods of insuring an accused person's attendance at trial are known to date back to at least Medieval England, the *Statute of Westminster* in 1275 sought to eliminate uneven practice and the sheriff's discretion, and stipulated which offences were bailable and which were not. These provisions were reinforced by the *Petition of Right* of 1628, which relied upon the *Magna Carta* and other laws guaranteeing imprisonment would not occur without due process and "cause being shown." These provisions were, in turn, reinforced by the *Habeus Corpus Act* of 1677 and the English *Bill of Rights* in 1689, which declared that "excessive bail ought not to be required." Still, the *Statute of Westminster* specified which offences were bailable and which were not. It is perhaps therefore significant that the accused, M'Naughten, is referred to throughout as the "prisoner"; the implication being that an accused charged with such an offence will always be in the position of prisoner, so long as the charges remain outstanding.

As noted earlier in this chapter, prisoner M'Naughten had only been in his cell for several minutes when he sent a message to the magistrate intimating that he wished to say something. He was accordingly led back into court and placed at the bar.

Magistrate Hall addressed him.

"I understand that you wish to say something. If so I am ready to hear you."

M'Naughten, after a slight pause, said, "The Tories in my native city have compelled me to do this. They follow and persecute me wherever I go, and have entirely destroyed my peace of mind. They followed me to France, into Scotland, and all over England. In fact they follow me wherever I go. I can get no rest from them night or day. I cannot sleep, in consequence of the course they pursue towards me. I believe they have driven me into a consumption. I am sure I shall never be the man I formally was. I used to have good health and strength, but I have not now. They have accused me of crimes of which I am not guilty. They have everything in their power to harass and persecute me, in fact they wish to murder me. It can be proved by evidence – that's all I wish to say at present."

"Is that all you wish to say?" the Clerk asked.

"I can only say," M'Naughten replied hesitatingly, "that they have completely disordered my mind, and I am not capable of doing anything, compared to what I was. I am a very different man to what I was before they commenced this system of persecution."

"Do you wish to say anything more?" the clerk inquired.

"Oh! Yes, I wish to know whether I am to be kept in that place . . ." Here he pointed towards the cell, "– for a fortnight? If so, I am sure I shall not live."

"Oh, no, you will be taken to a proper place of confinement, where you will be taken care of till you are brought here again."

"Oh, very well, then I have nothing more to say."

"Have you any objection to sign the statement you have made?" the magistrate asked.

"No, I have no objection."

The statement having been read over to the prisoner, it was handed over to him in the dock, whereupon he immediately signed it. He was then removed from the bar.

The prisoner after being cautioned as to his statement says, The Tories in my native City have driven me to this, and have followed me to France, Scotland, and other parts, I can get no sleep from the system they pursue towards me, I believe I am driven into a consumption by them, they crush humbles me that is all I wish to say at present, they have completely disordered me, and I was quite a different man before they commenced this annoyance towards me.

Daniel McNaughten

Taken before me this
28th of January 1843

J Hall

The prisoner upon his examination on the 28th of January instant declined saying anything —

J Hall

M'NAUGHTEN'S STATEMENT
SOURCE: PUBLIC RECORDS OFFICE, CRIM 1/4/270-15

It is clear from these last utterances of Daniel M'Naughten that at trial there would be an issue as to his criminal responsibility, if not his fitness to stand trial. As it turns out, the latter issue – his fitness, or competency to stand trial – was never raised. And, on the basis of his brief utterances thus far, that issue did not appear to be prominent. Nevertheless, his brief statement did have a rather paranoid flavour to it. Competency or "fitness to stand trial" does not require a finding that the accused is not mentally ill. Rather, it requires a finding that the accused is aware of his charges, the pleas available to him, the outcome should he be convicted, and a general familiarity with the trial process. An appreciation of the trial process would today also require a perception on the part of the accused that he is about to undergo an impartial inquiry. Where the accused person's perception of the process is coloured and distorted by delusional thinking of, for example, a persecutory nature, he will likely be found unfit to stand trial.

While M'Naughten's statement set up his ultimate defence and was therefore exculpatory in nature, today great caution would be taken by the court before receiving a statement from an unrepresented accused. What M'Naughten said might just as easily have been a damning inculpatory statement that could have greatly assisted the Crown in its prosecution. The accused is under absolutely no obligation to say anything and would generally, particularly at a preliminary inquiry, be advised by counsel to say nothing.

Chapter Five

A SHORT TIME after the prisoner had been locked up in his cell, he expressed a wish to have some dinner and he was accordingly supplied with a plate of beef, some bread, and potatoes, of which he made a hearty meal. He was moved from the cell to the jailer's room at about three o'clock, and was allowed to remain there (instead of being locked up) until he was taken to Tothill Fields Prison, in the regular prison van.

At about six o'clock, while in the jailer's room, he frequently entered into conversation with Tyrrell, the jailer, and other persons connected with the court; but, of course, the crime for which he had been apprehended was not in the slightest degree alluded to by them, neither did the prisoner ever once mention it. He appeared to be very attentive to any conversation that passed between other persons, and frequently laughed at any jocular observation that happened to be uttered. His demeanour throughout the day was precisely the same, and there was nothing in his appearance or behaviour, with the exception of the statement he made before the magistrate, from which it could be inferred that he was labouring under insanity. Between five and six o'clock he expressed a wish to have his tea, and he was supplied with a pint of coffee and a penny loaf and some butter, the whole of which he ate.

As he did so, Tyrrell read the latest on M'Naughten's case in *The Observer*, two items attracting his interest. A constable searching the prisoner's lodgings found a powder horn filled with gunpowder and a quantity of newly cut balls, which exactly fitted the pistols taken from M'Naughten at the time of the shooting, a piece of evidence, the article pointed out, that had not been mentioned in court that day.

The other item was an interview with "a very respectable widow" by the name of Dutton, residing at Poplar Row, New Kent Road, where

M'Naughten had apparently lived for the past sixteen weeks. He had been well known to that lady for a long time previously, as it was nearly three years since he first came to lodge in her house, and he occupied at that period, on and off, the same apartment which he continued to rent up to the period of his apprehension on Friday, January 20th. He was generally considered by Mrs. Dutton to be of a very quiet turn of mind, and appeared to have no occupation, as he seldom rose before a late hour in the morning when he left the house, and he returned about ten o'clock in the evening.

He remained on this occasion approximately four months with Mrs. Dutton, and her general impression was that he was in search of employment. The rent he paid for his apartment was two shillings sixpence per week, and the payments were always made once a week. On leaving Mrs. Dutton's house he stated that he was going to France, and that lady heard no more of him for many months until he returned and took the same apartment. He stopped for only three weeks in England on this occasion, and then told Mrs. Dutton that he was about to leave for Scotland.

About the first week in October, 1842 he again returned, and on Mrs. Dutton opening the door to him he smiled, and said, "I see you have a bill in your window. Is it for my old room?" Mrs. Dutton answered, "Yes, sir," and M'Naughten replied, "You see I am come back. I said I should do so." Nothing particular was marked in his manner at this time, but the gloomy temperament which marked his general character was considered to be rather increased. He seldom spoke to anyone in the house, though he was always obliging and civil when addressed by any person. He never took meals at home, but on one occasion, about three weeks since, he caught a violent cold, and Mrs. Dutton supplied him during the three days in which he was confined to his bed.

He was never observed to read a newspaper or any other publication, and during the confinement above alluded to, Mrs. Dutton lent him a religious volume, which he appeared to peruse with much interest. It was Mrs. Dutton's impression that M'Naughten always had something on his mind. He was not at all communicative, but on one occasion he did tell Mrs. Dutton that he was in Scotland when Her Majesty Queen Victoria paid her recent visit to that country. He always appeared to be very moderately off, and on his taking up his abode at Mrs. Dutton's on the last occasion, had only one shirt. He purchased a second after the first fortnight, and Mrs. Dutton regularly washed them for him alternately. In other respects, his wardrobe seems to have been miserably provided. He had only two pair of socks and a flannel waistcoat. He had no change of dress and until within a fortnight, when he purchased a new pair, his trousers were patched and darned in every direction, and full of holes.

About a week ago he asked Mrs. Dutton if she could lend him a pair of old boots while his own were mended, and at her instigation he applied to a shoemaker in the neighbourhood who allowed him the use of an old pair for a day or two during the repair of his own. He had no boxes in his room, or property of any description. M'Naughten's habits were remarkably sober and steady. The room he occupied was the apartment on the second floor, and he seldom remained in it, if not labouring under indisposition, after nine o'clock in the morning. It was his habit to get up about that time, clean his shoes in the back kitchen, and then go out for the day. He seldom came home after ten o'clock, and sometimes he was much earlier.

On Friday morning he went out at about nine o'clock as usual, and, after being absent from the house for a short time, returned, and went upstairs for a few minutes. He went out again soon after, and Mrs. Dutton heard no more of him until she was told that he was taken into custody. Mrs. Dutton stated that she never saw much money in his possession, and her belief was that he was a young man in confined circumstances. She also said, distinctly, that she never heard him mention Mr. Drummond's name, or allude in any way to politics. His landlady further offered that it was very difficult to reconcile the apparent poverty of her tenant Daniel M'Naughten, which was borne out by his personal appearance, with the possession of so large a sum of money as £800. There can be very little doubt of the genuineness of the cheque or receipt of the Glasgow Bank for £750, and that fact proves the sum to have been deposited by the prisoner in the bank alluded to.

It should be realized that, while exact conversions are difficult, £800 in 1843 had approximately the same purchasing power as £50,000 or $125,000 CAN today (according to conversion tables which do exist). So, Daniel M'Naughten was, at the time of the incident, in contrast to his living situation, a fairly affluent man. This, again, while only suggestive, is consistent with a more global diagnostic picture that begins to emerge. Extreme frugality is, by itself, certainly not a symptom of mental illness. However, this eccentricity in combination with many others, could eventually paint a rather compelling picture.

The large sum of money to which apparently M'Naughten had access to through his Scottish bank seemed all the more confounding to Mrs. Dutton since in the years during which he had occupied a room at her residence she had never known him to be employed at any type of work. In response to a question as to how M'Naughten might have found the money to pay his weekly rent, she advanced the possibility that he might have been the recipient of some form of relief from a public department, but such, she was informed, had not been the case. It was the opinion of Mrs. Dutton that the sum of money he was possessed of at the time of his arrest must have been acquired during the previous two or three days, although this was in great measure contradicted by the date of the receipt. But some other papers found upon him led a messenger from the Home Office, accompanied by a police-officer, to leave London for Glasgow for the purpose of discovering if he had any family connections there.

Here we have a glimpse of Daniel M'Naughten's daily life and habits. The picture, at a minimum, is suggestive of what we now call a schizoid personality disorder. Personality disorders are not "major mental disorders" and therefore typically do not involve profound breaks with reality. The disorder is defined in the *Diagnostic and Statistical Manual of Mental Disorders* (fourth edition)[1] as "a pattern of detachment from social relationships and a restricted range of expression of emotions in interpersonal settings, beginning by early adulthood and present in a variety of contexts."

Individuals obtaining this diagnosis, while not psychotic (i.e., demonstrating an unequivocal break with reality) are seen as eccentric or weird. They appear to lack a desire for intimacy and derive little, if any, enjoyment from social interaction, even with close family members. And, naturally, they do not miss close family members when apart. "Loner" is a term often used to describe these individuals who are generally indifferent to signs of approval or disapproval from others. As a result, individuals with a schizoid personality disorder are unlikely to be particularly successful with careers unless they are of a kind that permits working in isolation. Aesthetics and enjoyment of more subtle aspects of one's environment (for example, a beautiful sunset) are usually lost upon this group. Consequently, personal grooming and hygiene may also be neglected. An individual with this sort of personality disorder is typically seen as asocial rather than anti-social and will probably be viewed as an "odd ball," which certainly may have been an emerging perception of Daniel M'Naughten: a rather odd or eccentric individual who was a quiet recluse and whose behaviour was not, at that point, suggestive of a major mental disorder.

Chapter Six

THREE DAYS AFTER the "diabolical" attempt on his life, Drummond's medical condition remained headline news for *The Times*, which continued to provide detailed coverage of the story, reporting in its late Saturday edition "with extreme regret," that a very distressing change had taken place in Drummond's symptoms earlier that day. The favourable state in which they had described the unfortunate gentleman's health in previous accounts published on Saturday morning had apparently continued through Friday night, and "the most sanguine hopes were entertained by his eminent medical attendants, that, severe as the wound was, no vital part had been injured."

Shortly before noon on Saturday, however, Drummond showed symptoms of "a considerable uneasiness, and felt so much pain as induced his friends to believe that inflammation had taken place." A consultation between the medical gentlemen was immediately held and another examination of the wound was determined upon. It was then discovered that the lowest of the ribs had been seriously injured by the ball. The doctors decided that the danger which, under the circumstances, was to be feared from the gunshot wound, had indeed made its appearance in the form of an inflammation (not recognized at the time but almost certainly the product of infection); in order to subdue the inflammation, it was arranged that a quantity of blood should be instantly taken from the patient.

Mr. Guthrie accordingly proceeded to open a vein in Drummond's left arm, but the operation proved fruitless. An attempt was then made to obtain blood from the right arm, but still without success. It was then determined that the temporal artery should be opened. This operation was performed immediately and a considerable quantity of blood taken from the patient, which for a time lessened the dangerous symptoms that had appeared.

Towards evening, however, another consultation was held, at which time the inflammation had only but slightly subsided, notwithstanding the application of a great number of leeches to the patient's back in addition to the general bleeding. Consequently it was then determined "that unless a very favourable change took place by 1 o'clock, the bleeding should be repeated." By midday Drummond continued to experience great pain and difficulty in breathing, but both doctors were of the opinion that the unfavourable symptoms that had presented themselves earlier had subsided somewhat. They considered that their patient "was doing as well as can be expected, and his wound is showing a more favourable prospect toward healing." As the bleeding had proved beneficial, they deemed it unnecessary to do more. The business of bloodletting or phlebotomy had, by the middle of the nineteenth century, been practised for hundreds of years. The theory behind the practice was that there were four "humours" in the body – blood, phlegm, yellow bile, and black bile. Most physical and mental diseases were seen as a product of the four humours being out of balance. By letting out between sixteen and thirty ounces of blood it was thought that the body would then rebuild itself in a balanced way with the assistance of various tonics and elixirs.

A variety of instruments were developed to produce the necessary incision, everything from handheld lancets to automatic spring-loaded devices that would produce a cut of consistent shape and depth. Blood was collected, usually in a bowl, until the patient started to lose consciousness. Not surprisingly, the result of the procedure was that the patient was much more "settled" and less flushed. Now, it would be generally accepted that the procedure is of absolutely no utility and would tend to weaken the patient and therefore reduce their prospects of recovery. It must be remembered that in the middle of the nineteenth century the practice of medicine was loosely regulated, if at all, and medical education was, to say the least, poor. Bloodletting instruments were depicted in medical catalogues and available for sale until late into the nineteenth century.

So improved was Drummond's condition by Sunday afternoon that his much relieved brother Berkeley was able to return to Windsor Castle and resume his duties as groom-in-waiting to the queen, conveying "the satisfying intelligence" to a gratified Victoria that Edward had been considered by his medical attendants to be out of danger, and that his ultimate recovery was therefore to be anticipated.

⟋⟋⟋⟍

AT THE SAME time as this news was being reported, *The Times* expressed frustration that "nothing has at present transpired tending in the slightest degree to furnish any clue as to the motives which induced the assassin to make his murderous attack on Mr. Drummond. The mystery which had clouded the affair from the beginning had not been at all cleared up by the previous day's investigation before the magistrate. Hence innumerable rumours were afloat as to the probable cause and intention of M'Naughten's act, however," the reporter conceded, "to allude to them further than the mere mention of the fact would at present not only be premature, but useless."

One troubling piece of information had come to light – one which was deemed to have a bearing on M'Naughten's "condition," his sanity as it were, or lack thereof, was described as follows:

> It is said that Mr. Drummond had, previously to the murderous attack upon him, received threatening letters, which have, it is added, been mislaid, otherwise a comparison of the handwriting with those found on the prisoner, and now in the possession of the police, might have settled the question as to whether they were sent by M'Naughten or not. On Friday morning, Mr. Drummond stated to a friend that he had observed a man lurking about the Treasury, as he thought, somewhat suspiciously, and coupling this fact with threatening letters he had previously received, he remarked he did not take the appearance of the man. His friend replied carelessly, that he did not conceive the matter worth thinking about, and it is supposed it was subsequently dismissed from Mr. Drummond's mind.[1]

To most it seemed improbable, from the general taciturn and reserved demeanour M'Naughten was exhibiting, that he would say anything about the subject. It was understood that since his confinement in Tothill Fields Prison he had not shown the slightest disposition to make any communication beyond the extraordinary and confused statement he had made when under examination at the magistrate's inquiry on Saturday morning. It was felt very probable, on the other hand, that on the return of the officer who had been sent to Scotland for the purpose of gathering information from his family, friends, and associates "that something further might transpire." Vigilant inquiries had also been set afoot throughout the city in order to ascertain, if possible, whether M'Naughten had any connections to people there, or companions who might provide information on the man and how, in the recent past, he had been in the habit of passing his time. For the time being the only source of information on Daniel M'Naughten was his landlady, Mrs. Dutton, though what she had elucidated was felt to be "anything but satisfactory."

Moreover, the general opinion of many people who were present during the Bow Street examination was that making the statement he did – about his having been persecuted by the Tories – was an attempt to have the public believe he was labouring under insanity, even though his previous conduct and behaviour, coupled with his general appearance, entirely negated such a supposition.

On Monday, *The Standard* broke a story that proved more perplexing for those trying to assess the perplexing character of Daniel M'Naughten. Several eminent doctors affiliated with London's various lunatic asylums visited him at Tothill Fields Prison for the purpose of ascertaining whether he suffered from aberration of mind. Although he had made such an extraordinary statement during the inquiry at Bow Street, which at the time was considered indicative of an unsound state of mind, he had not followed up that line of conduct in any way, but on the contrary had maintained a sullen demeanour, and his replies to the various questions put to him were all very sensible.

The result of the interview by these medical experts was in each case the same – namely, the conviction in their minds that M'Naughten was perfectly sane, and that the statement made by him before Mr. Hall at Bow Street was a premeditated one. Mr. Lavies, the prison doctor, had a second interview with Mr. M'Naughten and he was perfectly convinced of the total absence of mental derangement. In Lavies' opinion it was very evident that M'Naughten viewed "with the greatest indifference the atrocious attempts which he made on Mr. Drummond's life, for what meals he partakes of, only his breakfast and dinner, he eats with a keen appetite." These meals were furnished at M'Naughten's own expense, an application having being made to

Mr. Hall for a portion of the money found on him when arrested to be allotted for that purpose. When the meals were taken into him, as well as on all other occasions, M'Naughten was invariably to be found sitting before the fire in his cell.

Although several books had been placed in the cell for his accommodation, he had not yet been found looking at one, nor had he asked for pen, ink, and paper. To none of the turnkeys had he uttered a word further, until, when his dinner was conveyed to him on Monday (which consisted of a rump-steak), he observed "that it was very hard to be prevented the use of a knife and fork." On being informed that it was one of the prison regulations, he maintained his usual silence. Lieutenant Tracy, the governor of the prison, whose opinion was highly valued because of the great practice that he had, decidedly affirmed that M'Naughten was not insane.

ↂↂↂↂ

BY MONDAY NIGHT, an unfavourable change in Mr. Drummond's health was again reported. "The improving state in which we described the unfortunate gentleman last evening continued through the greater part of the night, but towards morning he became very restless."[2] It soon became evident that with the infection worsening, the inflammation was increasing. At ten o'clock a consultation of the medical team took place and it was quickly determined that the patient should again be bled, a task undertaken by surgeon Guthrie.

Drummond's doctors remained in attendance "a considerable time" but the unfavourable symptoms persisted, to the point that a statement was issued that the patient was in "a critical state." It was agreed that Mr. Guthrie would sit up with Drummond through the night.

These regular updates regarding the precarious state of Drummond's health and the somewhat mysterious aspects of Daniel M'Naughten's behaviour and state of mind came amid other news of the day. In particular, *The Times* reported from the Chamber of Peers on the growing and controversial debate regarding Britain's right of search on the high seas. The Baron de Brigode concluded by observing that Great Britain ". . . durst not avow her real motives for insisting on the right of search; inasmuch as they were founded on her ever-increasing desire to arrogate to herself the empire of the seas, and of domineering over all other maritime nations when the apparent pretext for the claim of a right to search was Britain's desire to extinguish the slave trade, which was still very much alive in many parts of the world including the United States."

Also distressing was the disappearance of the Levant steamer, a mail ship, which failed to arrive at Marseilles as expected and for which little hope remained. The cause was apparently a "tempest" that extended from the British Channel to the coast of Egypt. "The Royal Mail steamer *Trent*, Captain Boxer, Commander, with West India, Jamaica, and Havana mails, left St. Thomas on the 26th of December, Bermuda on the 3rd of January, and Fayal on the 16th. She was bringing on freight 50,000 dollars, 173 serons of indigo and cochineal, and 17 passengers." The reports of the activities of various Royal Mail ships included details of another ship, the *Victor*, which was also missing.

Along with the reporting of other criminal activity, including murders and robberies, it was announced that the wedding of Crown Prince of Hanover, Victoria's cousin, was to take place in the third week of February, but that a particular day had not been fixed.

THE LONDON PRESS was still dominated by stories chronicling the state of Drummond's health, together with attempts to piece together M'Naughten's background, mental condition, and motivation in attacking him. *The Times* in its Tuesday edition delivered details of dramatic new developments, first regarding "The Prisoner M'Naughten."

> The few facts which have transpired since our last, in reference to this lamentable event, have rather been of a nature to excite, than to satisfy, the natural desire for information upon the subject. Information has been procured (in the course of the investigations which are being diligently pursued both in the metropolis and in Scotland), the general result of which is, that the prisoner had carried on business in Glasgow under respectable and comfortable circumstances; that about two years ago he had relinquished it in favour of one of his journeymen, assigning as a reason that he was tired of it; that he had been absent for a considerable period, and had stated his having been in the interim to France; that, in answer to interrogatories, he was in the habit of saying he wished to go into the army, but did not like the idea of enlisting as a private soldier; that he had always been most thrifty

and economical in his habits, living on two meals a day, and evidently accumulating as much money as possible.[3]

Among the particulars that had been elicited relating more closely to "the melancholy event itself" it was mentioned that the pistols M'Naughten used to shoot Drummond had a Paisley manufacturer's mark upon them, and that the powder flask had the mark of Dixon's in Sheffield. It appeared that the weapons had been purchased from a pawnbroker who remembered having sold them "to a Scotchman" and their having been paid for by a £10 note.

Meagre as they were, these facts seemed to warrant the conclusion that whatever eccentricity there may have been in M'Naughten's behaviour, there was a considerable amount of "method" behind it – matters of foresight, prudence, deliberation, and design – method that could hardly have been the conduct of a madman. Indeed, it was certainly evident that M'Naughten's condition was very much the reverse of unstable, at least as far as matters of money and "aforethought" or premeditation were concerned.

> But the moment we attempt to divine any imaginable motive for an act so deadly as that which he committed, all appears wrapped in impenetrable darkness. We understand that no inquiries can lead to the discovery of any communication, on his part, with the Cabinet or the Privy Council, so as to have brought him in contact with the unfortunate gentleman under circumstances at all calculated or likely to create any ill feeling toward him. No clue had been discovered of any inducement, no trace found of any instigators, to the dreadful deed. At present, therefore, a mystery conceals the transaction, which will, however, in all probability, be soon in some degree cleared up by the acute and energetic investigations which we find are proceeding, and further results of which we hope to present to-morrow. In the meantime, the prisoner's demeanor, we believe, remained reserved, betokened no disposition to confession, and betrayed also no symptoms of the insanity which one would suppose he at first wished to counterfeit.

A further interesting development was that a letter had been received by Mr. May, the superintendent of police in London's downtown division, from Sergeant Stevens, the officer who had been sent to

Glasgow for the purpose of discovering any connections M'Naughten may have had there. While the contents of the letter had not been made public, there was sufficient reason to believe that the statement made by "the assassin" was strictly correct in all important facts. The letter was placed with the police commissioners, and forwarded by them to the secretary of state for the home department who was supervising the government's investigation of the Drummond shooting.

As well, in its Tuesday edition, *The Standard* published details of "a singular incident" that had occurred to the Duke of Wellington a few minutes after Edward Drummond was wounded, an incident that if nothing else served to indicate the atmosphere of tension and uneasiness about the city. His Grace had left the commander-in-chief's office and was crossing the parade ground in St. James's Park when a stout male youth, about sixteen or seventeen years of age, ran at the duke "with considerable violence," the collision causing his Grace to stagger. A policeman on duty witnessing the occurrence, "and with the fact of the recent attempted assassination being upon his mind," ran up and seized the youth, believing that he had intended some violence upon the duke.

"It is but justice to the lad to state he instantly made an apology, without being aware of the high rank of the person he had so unintentionally assaulted." The Duke of Wellington is said to have replied: "I will take no apology" and instantly carried on. The policeman, believing the duke would bring charges against the boy, took him to the station-house in Gardiner's Lane. It was deemed advisable to detain the lad until it could be ascertained whether or not it was the intention of the Duke of Wellington to charge him with assault, but after three hours the youth was released.

Another article in the same edition informed readers that the prisoner M'Naughten had asked to be supplied with writing materials, which when they were brought to him he wrote a note requesting a person named Gordon, who he said resided in Peter Street, Westminster, to come and see him in prison. The note was duly delivered to Peter Street, but Gordon was found to have left London for Glasgow some days earlier. However, a fellow named Bean who worked as a gas meter maker, his curiosity aroused, came forward and said that he remembered seeing M'Naughten in the company of Gordon about a month before, on Christmas Day. Bean informed Lieutenant

Tracy, who had delivered the letter, that when he saw M'Naughten with Gordon, he understood that Daniel was looking for a job, that if he didn't find one he would be returning to Glasgow. Bean told Tracy he wished to have an interview with M'Naughten, but the lieutenant thought it best to defer the visit for a day or two.

Indeed, the police lieutenant's sense of caution with this acquaintance of M'Naughten's was to prove well-founded, for as of Tuesday afternoon a marked change was noticed in the prisoner's demeanour. Although he had, since the day of the shooting, appeared to manifest "the most perfect indifference" to the awful situation in which he found himself, taking considerable pains with his toilet and showing no degree of excitement about his circumstances, M'Naughten, after eating his lunch Tuesday, began to appear noticeably melancholy and seemed to be brooding over his situation.

A Mr. Spalding, who had called at Tothill Fields Prison for the purpose of speaking with M'Naughten was prevented from doing so, but in a subsequent discussion of the prisoner with police, Spalding provided the first concrete glimpse into the identity of a man whom he claimed to have known upwards of twenty-nine years. M'Naughten's father had apparently carried on a very lucrative business as a wood-turner within a few doors of the house in which Spalding lived in Glasgow. Daniel was apprenticed to his father, and his steady working habits allowed him, during the term of his apprenticeship, to amass a considerable sum of money.

Shortly after M'Naughten completed his apprenticeship, a serious quarrel with his father led him to leave home and nothing was heard of him for eighteen months, until his father, learning his son was in London, sought him out and, having settled their differences amicably, they returned together to Glasgow. According to Spalding, M'Naughten was a Presbyterian, and when in Glasgow attended the kirk (church) regularly. He remained with his father and managed the wood-turning business for him until 1837, when, another quarrel taking place, M'Naughten again left his father, this time setting up in business for himself within a short distance of his father's establishment, but which he gave up in 1839.

Though the information would turn out to be wrong, Spalding claimed M'Naughten's father had died about twelve months previously, in 1842. Daniel being his father's only son, Spalding understood that the several houses owned by M'Naughten, Sr., reverted to Daniel who then sold them, which, doubtless, would account for the receipt for £750 that was found on him when he made his attempt on the life of Mr. Drummond.

Overall then, the press seemed to be of the view that Daniel M'Naughten, although his behaviour may have perhaps been eccentric, was by no means insane. Further, to the extent that his statement days earlier in open court could be seen as a plea of insanity, the press was of the view that it must have been a deliberate manufacturing on M'Naughten's part. Other circumstances, such as the purchase of the pistols and the possible stalking of Drummond, lent further support to the theory that this degree of planning and deliberation was inconsistent with the behaviour of a "madman." This rather simplistic juxtaposition of apparently purposeful behaviour was, as we shall see, not necessarily anything from which sanity can be divined. As well, it is clear that, for the most part, the opinions with respect to M'Naughten's culpability are based upon the few words he had spoken (or not spoken) and the oddness of some of his actions, rather than upon any attempt to determine what his thinking was at the actual time of the event.

Chapter Seven

AFTER THE LAST consultation, which took place between ten and eleven o'clock on Tuesday night, it was announced to Edward Drummond's family and friends "that his dissolution was at hand" – that in fact "mortification" had already set in; all human aid would consequently be of no avail. Although he had gradually been sinking the whole of the day, the final turn occurred about seven o'clock, when his three brothers and sister were summoned and began their vigil at his bedside until the end, comforted by the assurances of his doctors, who were also with him till his last moments, that for some time previous to his death he had been entirely free from pain.

A messenger was dispatched to convey the melancholy tidings to Queen Victoria, whose aunt the queen dowager (widow of William IV) had sent her messenger to Drummond's kin with words "of profound sympathy and condolence." *The Times* closed its headline article "Death of Mr. Drummond" with these words of tribute:

> The unfortunate gentleman, who was in his 51st year, bore a most estimable character, and was beloved by all who had the pleasure of his acquaintance; and it is impossible to describe the gloom which the melancholy event has cast over the circle in which he moved.

As the press would soon report, Daniel M'Naughten, with the death of Edward Drummond, now stood accused of murder.[1]

∾∾∾∾

ONLY THE DAY before, the *Glasgow Chronicle* had run a story, "The Assassin M'Naughten," in which it was revealed that Daniel M'Naughten was the illegitimate son of a Daniel M'Naughten, Sr., formerly a wood-turner in the city of Glasgow, who was still alive, but who, having quarrelled with his son some considerable time ago, had had no communication with him. The father appeared to have bred his son to his own business of wood-turning, and the latter had afterwards embarked "on a separate concern of the same kind on his own account." After doing so for about seven years, he retired as a turner about two years ago. His workshop was first in Turner's Court, and afterwards in Stockwell. On leaving the business he disposed of it to a younger man, who was still carrying on in the Stockwell shop.

M'Naughten appeared to have been very retired in his habits, avoiding society, and occupying much of his time with reading. Acquaintances reported that he usually spent about sixteen hours a day between working and reading. He was known to be very parsimonious, and was understood to have saved a good deal of money. Though he was generally well enough dressed when he went out, his habits when within doors were "of a most filthy kind." Much of the time he was in business he lived in his workshop, cooked his own food, and otherwise attended to his own wants. He was a Radical in his politics and religion; however, his views were regarded by those who knew him as more speculative than practical, that is to say, he was felt to be a dreamer. One of the *Chronicle*'s informants had happened to see him about six months ago, at which time he had the appearance of having been in bad health.

It appeared that M'Naughten, upwards of two years ago, showed symptoms of mental aberration. To the landlady with whom he was living at the time (Mrs. Dutton) he had repeatedly expressed his opinion that there were "devils in human shape" seeking his life. One day he showed her a pair of pistols and declared his determination to use them "against my tormentors." About a year ago it was also reported that he applied to the Glasgow police for protection against Tory persecutors, who he claimed were seeking his life. Further to this a letter was discovered, addressed to the prisoner from Mr. A. Johnston, M.P., in answer to some communication from M'Naughten, in which Johnston expressed his belief that the writer was "not of sane mind." These and a number of concurrent circumstances were thought sufficient testament to M'Naughten's state of mind at the time he made his rash and violent attempt upon the life of Mr. Edward Drummond.

Chapter Eight

The Times – 27 January 1843

THE INQUEST ON THE LATE MR. DRUMMOND

Yesterday an inquest was held at the Lion and Goat Tavern, Grosvenor Street, before Mr. Gall, the coroner for Westminster, assisted by Mr. Higgs, and a jury, to inquire into the cause of the death of the late Mr. Edward Drummond.

THE CORONER'S INQUEST is a process for inquiring into the cause of death in unusual circumstances. From as early as the Middle Ages, violent or suspicious deaths were investigated by a coroner who held a hearing with a jury. The coroner had the ability to bind over witnesses and suspects to appear in court and, in the case of homicide, detain suspects in jail.[1] Although the inquiry may precede a trial where the death has also led to a criminal charge, it may occur after the trial. The jury may conclude that the death was an accident or a homicide, but would avoid attributing responsibility to a particular individual or addressing the perpetrator's state of mind. In addition to usurping the function of the trial court, such a procedure would be highly prejudicial.

The tavern inquest room was crowded by persons anxious to witness the proceedings. The proceedings commenced at a few minutes after four o'clock, the jury comprised of "Messrs. Stanley, Meagoe, Tucker, Mills, Owen, Slack, Christmas, Strachan, Dawes, Evandar, Bailey, Padgett, Davis, Turner, Dunn, Bywater, Clifford, Nobile, Low, and Cooper." Sworn in according to the usual form, they proceeded to go to view the body, which lay at the residence of Mr. Drummond, at No. 19 Grosvenor Street.

On their return to the inquest room, the coroner, seeing Mr. Maule, the solicitor to the Treasury, inquired whether it was the intention of any party to appear on behalf of any person who might be accused? Maule intimated that he attended on behalf of the Crown, and no other person answered. The coroner, in addressing the jury, said it appeared to him that it would in all probability not be necessary for the jury to bestow a vast deal of their time or deliberation "on this melancholy occurrence." He was not aware whether it was the intention of anyone to appear before them "on behalf of any person who might hereafter be accused of the crime by which the deceased had lost his life." But, even if any person were so to appear, he anticipated that under the circumstances with which they all were more or less acquainted, it would not be for the purpose of disproving the fact. Indeed, for what purpose would such a person appear? It would, in all probability, only be for the purpose of proving that the person, whoever he might be, was not of sound mind, with a view of inducing the jury to give a different verdict from that which they might otherwise return.

"If it were intended," the coroner went on, "to make any such attempt," it appeared to him that that would not be the proper place for it. They would return such a verdict and would send the party to another tribunal to be tried, and then a proper opportunity would be afforded for making such an attempt. There the party would have the benefit of an able judge who would explain everything to the jury, both in his favour and against him. It would, therefore, be for the jury to consider whether the evidence that would be brought before them was sufficient to induce them to send the person in question to take his trial.

In reply to a question from a juryman, as to whether the person accused of having caused the death of the deceased ought not to be present, the coroner observed that not a very long time had elapsed since, in a case where the same question arose, the jury had said they would rather adjourn than proceed without the presence of the accused party. He then sent a messenger to Bridewell, to desire the keeper of the jail to send the prisoner before the jury. However the keeper answered that he had no authority to do so; thus the jury adjourned, in order that a communication might be sent to the secretary of state, that the keeper had done quite right in refusing to send the prisoner.

The evidence called at the coroner's inquest was very much the same as that heard before the grand jury on January 22nd. The first witness called was James Silver, the policeman who testified as to the events of January 20th. He described once again and in precisely the same manner how he apprehended M'Naughten, and how the accused had uttered the words "he … or she should not break my peace of mind any longer." After describing a little too modestly his heroics on the day in question, he again described the money and banking documents found on M'Naughten's person, and the powder flask and bullets found in his room at Mrs. Dutton's. Next, the inquest heard from a nineteen-year-old carpenter, Robert Hodge, who had also witnessed the shooting and described the event in much the same manner as James Silver. Finally, there was the testimony of the medical men who attended upon Drummond. They described the care that had been provided, as well as their opinions, upon the completion of an autopsy, as to the cause of Drummond's death which was, not surprisingly, a gunshot wound.

When all witnesses had spoken, the coroner then instructed the jury to consider its verdict, which they gave without the least hesitation: "Willful murder against Daniel M'Naughten." In reply to an inquiry from the coroner, Mr. Maule, who had been present throughout the inquiry, stated that he had not attended for the purpose of then taking any proceedings, but added that he had received directions to prosecute Daniel M'Naughten, against whom the jury had now found a verdict of "willful murder." The policeman Silver, Robert Hodge, and Mr. Guthrie were together bound over to prosecute, and the coroner issued his warrant for the committal of Daniel M'Naughten to the prison at Newgate.

What was extremely unusual in M'Naughten's case is that the jury made findings with respect both to the issue of responsibility in Drummond's death as well as the issue of his state of mind at the time: the act of murder had been a "willful" one. This anomalous outcome (again, because the jury had attributed responsibility to M'Naughten and with "willful" addressed his state of mind at the time) may have been because there was no question as to who the perpetrator was. Inconsistent practice was apparently more commonly found in this era and the functioning of the coroner's inquest appears to have been more intertwined with judicial proceedings than it is today. Today, it would be unusual to have this multiplicity of hearings occur so soon after a death. Today, the coroner's inquest is a hearing that is independent of proceedings before the court, and because of its potential for prejudice is best left till after all criminal proceedings are concluded.

❧❧❧❧

A STORY FROM the *Glasgow Constitutional* appeared in the same day's edition of *The Times*, in which the newspaper regretted to state that the assassin of Edward Drummond was a Scotsman and a native of Glasgow. Inquiries had been made regarding his previous habits, and from what had been discovered, the *Constitutional* had no doubt "that the fellow is insane." The son of a most respectable tradesman in this city, whose name he bears, Daniel M'Naughten was brought up to the trade of wood-turner by his father. Yet his conduct and habits, which were always eccentric, became so disagreeable to his father about ten years ago that their misunderstandings led to a cessation of the correspondence between the parties.

After working for some time as a journeyman, Daniel commenced business on his own at Turner's Court, and latterly had his workshop in Stockwell Street. From the outset he was very abstracted, and "parsimonious to a proverb." To save money he bought and cooked his own food, lodged in his own workshop, and, except when it came to his clothing, in regard to which he was a little vain, his "purse strings were seldom unloosed." He consequently saved a considerable sum of money, at one time his bank account reaching to about £1,000.

Having devoted himself greatly to reading, he became somewhat enthusiastic and romantic in his ideas, wandering about the most remote and unfrequented country roads instead of attending to his business, invariably carrying a book with him, usually political or religious, although he never showed himself a partisan in either respect. His general opinions in politics, it was noted, "were of the most violent and radical description."

About the beginning of January 1841, his "fitful" temperament, as one of his most intimate acquaintances terms it, could no longer submit "to the drudgery and confinement of a workshop," and he disposed of his turning materials and the goodwill he had built up in his business to a young man who had been an apprentice with him for three years. The proceeds of this transaction he evidently devoted "to the replenishment of his wardrobe," and after drawing his funds from the bank, he left Glasgow en route to France, with nearly 1,000 sovereigns

CIRCLE INDICATES THE LOCATION OF M'NAUGHTEN'S LODGINGS AT 90 CLYDE STREET, GLASGOW. SOURCE: WATERCOLOUR BY WILLIAM SAMPSON, R.I., THE MITCHELL LIBRARY, GLASGOW

in gold in his possession. He did go to the continent, where he remained for some time, but according to his own account he had never been more than 58 miles from the coast. On his return to England he came to reside in London.

While in Glasgow he lodged with a Mrs. Pattison, on Clyde Street, Anderston, very close to the spot at which Smith, the cotton-spinner was shot, and some of his letters to Mrs. Pattison and others indicate, at the very least, an aberration of intellect. He came to Scotland, and to his old lodgings, about the time of the queen's visit last year, and called upon a few of his former acquaintances, all of whom observed that his eccentricities had been increased rather than diminished by his travelling.

He again left Glasgow, and went to London, where he seems to have remained. He appears to have been in some degree subject to hypochondria, and on such occasions he would confine himself to bed for days. He was decidedly temperate, and preached temperance to his friends. But on the occasion of these "fits," he availed himself largely of the eau-de-vie medicinally.

M'Naughten was known to be extremely fond of argument, and did not hesitate to let his listeners know whose side he was on, provided he had an opponent. So far as was known, the pistols found on him in London were a pair which he had in his possession in Glasgow, and with which he was in the habit of "fowling" wild game. In his Glasgow lodgings a few scraps of manuscript had been recovered, chiefly notes of medical lectures that it seems he had attended. One paper, however, clearly indicated that his mind had been or became unsettled a considerable time ago. In a reply of 6 May 1842 to some communications from M'Naughten, Mr. Johnston, M.P. for Kilmarnock, wrote: "I received your letter of the 3d of May. I am very sorry I can do nothing for you. I am afraid that you are labouring under a delusion of mind, and that there is no reason for your entertaining such fears." Although attempts had been made to procure M'Naughten's letter to Johnston, it was held to be very probable that it may have been destroyed by Mr. Johnston at the time "as a piece of absurdity."

Once, when urged by Mrs. Pattison to go out and exert himself to get employment of some kind or other, he said he had done every thing he could for that purpose, but that he had been persecuted and tormented "by a parcel of devils." He added, after further questioning on the subject, that if they (the devils) did not give up tormenting him "he would blow their brains out." He had apparently left Mrs. Pattison's for the last time about four months ago, without saying where he was going, or even taking a change of clothes with him. He did carry with him, however, the two pistols and all his money.

In light of the newspaper report's firm contention that M'Naughten was without doubt insane, it is perhaps interesting that it would close by pointing out that at one time he had spent in the neighborhood of three years "with a company of strolling players." One wonders if, during his dramatic sojourn, he might have become familiar with Shakespeare's *Hamlet*, the story of a young man who pretends madness in order to excuse the murder of the uncle he feels is persecuting him.

AS FURTHER PARTICULARS began to emerge in the developing story as to Daniel M'Naughten's state of mind prior to and as motive for the killing of Prime Minister Peel's private secretary, a police official arrived in Glasgow from London for the purpose of gathering information about him. This was principally procured at "the house of the assassin's father," the very respectable Daniel M'Naughten, Sr. Among other things the father recollected that his son had told him, about the beginning of the previous summer, that he was going to call Sir James Campbell, the lord provost of Scotland, which he subsequently did about the end of May or beginning of June 1842, at the provost's Glasgow residence. Sir James apparently had some conversation in the hall with M'Naughten, whom the lord provost described as a jolly-looking man, "who spoke very coolly, although evidently labouring under some hallucination of mind."

M'Naughten told the provost with great earnestness that he had been "increasingly watched and dogged by certain parties" who bore him great ill-will. He said they forced him from his home with their "spiteful machinations," and in fact the night before they had obliged him "to fly to the fields in the suburbs for refuge." Sir James, asking M'Naughten's name, which he gave, as well as the name of his father, tried to reason with M'Naughten as to the folly of his notions. Sir James likewise inquired, pretty broadly, whether he had ever "been treated for suspicion that there was something wrong with his intellects," and receiving a reply in the negative, seriously advised him to consult his family or "some medical man as to the state of his health." During the visit M'Naughten talked neither of religion nor politics, but merely shook his head repeatedly, saying that he "could not get rid of them at all."

Immediately after this the lord provost sent for Daniel's father, who said he "could do nothing with his son at all in his place of business," for although he was generally well behaved, so far as sobriety and hard work were concerned, he was frequently reading books, and keeping others from their work by talking about them. More than anything, he was most anxious about making money and frequently "worked night and day for that purpose."

According to his father, Daniel was a violent Radical, and spoke furiously against the Conservatives of Glasgow, frequently declaring that they and Mr. Lamond, their agent, were constantly after him. The previous November, M'Naughten, Sr., recalled, his son had written from London to draw £10 out of the Glasgow and Ship Bank. It was only on going to the bank to get the money that M'Naughten learned his son had so much money, and to save trouble, he sent him £20, as his son had said in the letter he liked London much better than Glasgow.

So far as any could judge, then, "the assassin M'Naughten" seemed to have been a tolerably sane person, except on the subject of the Tories:

The Times – 27 January 1843

After allowing his mind to ruminate upon the doings of that party for a considerable period, he appears to have come to the conclusion, that extirpation of even one of them would be doing his country a service: and in the absence of all evidence on the subject, we see no reasons for supposing that Sir Robert Peel was his object any more than Mr. Drummond. He had been watching at the door of the Treasury for a considerable number of days, and may have seen Mr. Drummond going out and in frequently, and this fact, settling the unfortunate gentleman as a Tory, and one of his (M'Naughten's) enemies, may have been the sole motive to the commission of the atrocious deed.

Shortly after the death of Mr. Drummond, "the melancholy intelligence" was communicated to M'Naughten, who although he turned very pale and was for a short time slightly agitated, soon regained his usual composed manner. He had previously been informed that Mr. Drummond was in a hopeless state, and was likely prepared for such a communication, but still it was noticed "that the prisoner seemed to treat the matter with perfect indifference." It had been suggested that Dr. Sutherland and Dr. Monroe[2] had visited M'Naughten several times in order to ascertain the state of his mind, but apparently this was not the case. The only medical gentleman who had visited with him was Mr. Davies, the regular prison surgeon: "At all events, no official report has been made to the Government with respect to the prisoner's state of mind."

The accounts put forward by the press supporting the view that M'Naughten was most certainly insane when he shot Drummond are indicative of what we would presently refer to as "delusional thinking of a paranoid nature." A "delusion" is a fixed false belief. So, as the evidence against him accumulates, it is clear, assuming the veracity of the accounts, that M'Naughten's mental condition at the time was not merely of an "eccentric" but indeed a psychotic nature. As such, he would, in today's medical parlance, be seen as suffering from a major mental disorder.

What is worth mentioning apropos of the rather lofty if not esoteric discussion being conducted in the press as to the state of an individual's mind at the moment of committing a murder, is the following account in the same edition of an accused who came within an "inch of transportation" for attempting to steal a "firkin" of butter. A firkin, a term no longer in use,[3] is defined alternatively as either "a small wooden vessel or cask," or "any of various British units of capacity usually equal to ¼ of a barrel." "Transportation" refers to the deportation of criminals to remote areas, most notably for the British to Australia. Punishments, by today's standards, were harsh.

The Times – 27 January 1843

WITHIN AN INCH OF TRANSPORTATION

A well known thief, named William Lancaster, was charged on Wednesday with attempting to steal a firkin of butter on the shop of Jane Fisher. From the evidence, it appeared that the prisoner had raised the firkin on one edge, but had not lifted it from the floor. Mr. Rushton said, that the firkin not having been lifted from the floor, the evidence could not substantiate a charge of felony; and, addressing the prisoner, he said, "You were just within an inch of transportation. One inch more, and you would have been transported." The prisoner was ordered to be indicted for a misdemeanour, in being found on the premises with intent to commit a felony. – *Liverpool Chronicle*.

Chapter Nine

TO COUNTER ACCUSATIONS emanating from some quarters that *The Times*, in its reporting on the Drummond assassination, was giving undue prominence to strong intimations, if not outright opinions, regarding Daniel M'Naughten's sanity or lack thereof – information that was being served up as evidence when in many cases it was no better than hearsay and extremely prejudicial to his receiving a fair and just hearing at trial – the newspaper ran what amounted to a public disclaimer in its edition of 28 January, here reprinted in full:

> We have already stated our determination to say nothing which can in any way prejudge M'Naughten's case, or prejudice his character. The solemn and protecting mantle of justice is thrown over him, and in the courts of justice alone must his innocence or his guilt be proved. We would, indeed, rather be silent on the subject and all its bearings. But silence is rendered impossible by the observations which we have read in contemporary and provincial journals, as well as by the general tone of letters addressed to ourselves. We therefore repeat, once for all, that we shall be truly thankful to see the accused acquitted on the ground of insanity – provided that insanity be proved on testimony positive, irrefragable, and beyond suspicion.
>
> We shall truly rejoice to find that there is not a man in England or Scotland, exercising the faculty of reason, who is wicked and savage enough to commit a cowardly murder on a fellow-creature without the miserable plea of passion or provocation. But the insanity which alone ought to be admitted in defense of the accused is of that forcible and overmastering kind which utterly obliterates all moral sense of right or wrong. It is not sufficient to prove occasional hallucination or erroneous and extravagant hypotheses on particular subjects; the

madness proved must be similar in kind to that which is said to have prompted the horrible deed. Least of all can any laws of reason justify us in inferring an exculpatory insanity from the act itself. The law of England universally and unequivocally forbids a man to take advantage of his own wrong; and if this principle were once admitted as a true one, there is no crime of lust, violence, or malice which might not go unpunished.

But we will say no more. All that we could urge on this point is advanced much more forcibly in the charge of an eminent judge now no more, and which we have reproduced in our columns this day. To this we refer our readers. We have thought it right to resist what we believe to be a fashionable tendency of thought on the subject of criminal penalties. We have no ill-will towards a man whose guilt the law has not yet proved. To that law, severe in its scrutiny, solemn in its punishments, but merciful in its scrupulousness, we leave him, knowing that – whatever may be the result of the awful trial which he is about to undergo – he will be debarred from no benefit which the profound learning and rigid impartiality of his venerable judges or the attentive consideration of a British jury can allow him.

In Scotland, on the other hand, the *Glasgow Chronicle* seemed intent on providing its readers with what today we would call "in-depth" coverage of M'Naughten's past life and behaviour, perhaps in an effort to defend against any present or future imputation that M'Naughten's crime might have had something to do with his being Scottish, as opposed to his having had certain flaws of personal character that led to his being of unsound mind. Or perhaps, from the cynic's standpoint, merely to sell more papers, since the M'Naughten case was attracting ever-widening public interest:

> As any circumstance, however trifling, in connexion with the past history of this 'unfortunate man' (miscreant), and more especially any incidents tending to show a connexion between his previous state of mind and habits of thoughts and the atrocious deed which he has perpetrated, have become of public interest within the last few days, we have exerted ourselves a little among M'Naughten's friends, associates, and relations, to come at a knowledge of his real character, and have to submit the following as the substance of our investigations. We beg to state, at the same time, that from all that we have

collected, we see no reason to alter the opinion expressed in our last, that M'Naughten, at the time he committed the act for which he has made himself amenable to public justice and for years previous was in a state of mental aberration.

However much parties differ as to his sentiments in other matters, all are agreed in this, that he was from his youth upward an exceedingly provident, careful, and saving man – not a whisky drinker – not a jovial companion – not an attender of public entertainments. It is also generally known that he was a close and earnest book reader – not of any particular sect or party, nor on any particular science or study; information of all kinds, and on all subjects, he grasped at with avidity.

At one time of his life, he read a great number of dramatic pieces, and had play-books constantly by him; even at that time, however it is not known that he spent any money in obtaining such works, or in attending theatrical entertainments. The fact is, he never spent any money on any luxury at any time when he could avoid it; but when he could obtain the loan of books or newspapers of any description, he failed not in adding to his store of knowledge. He is spoken of by all as an exceedingly quiet and unobtrusive man, who would not harm a fly, up to the time of giving up his regular business.

He never took up with his fellow-lodgers, and had few companions. There is one only, who was his bedfellow for about three years, with whom he was at all communicative. With him, and with the young man who succeeded him in the wood-turning business, he used to take long walks and frequent bathings in the river. So much was he devoted to the latter kind of enjoyment, that he is known to have bathed every morning for years, and even during the coldest days in winter. He had a very acute, retentive memory, not only in matters pecuniary, connected with his business, but also on the subjects of which he had been reading. The young man, his successor, says he was more than usually fastidious as to the getting in of his accounts at all times, frequently sending him fifty times for one account until it was obtained. Latterly he assigned, as a reason for this anxiety, his belief that some persons were disposed to do him an injury. His fellow-lodger says that his memory was so good that he does not think it possible he could have mistaken Mr. Drummond for Sir R. Peel, he having frequently seen the latter in the House of Commons after one of his trips to Paris. He mentioned to him, when last in Glasgow, that he had been frequently in the House of Commons; and he not only saw and heard the leading members, but made very shrewd remarks on their several oratorical displays. He said that Sir Robert Peel was a more polished orator than either Daniel O'Connell or Lord John Russell, although Dan was the ablest declaimer.

It is alleged by a contemporary, that M'Naughten was a keen politician, a violent Radical, and extremely anxious to enter into controversy with all and sundry. Now, this statement is altogether opposed to the experience of any of his friends and acquaintances. So far from this, he is spoken of as a man who anxiously avoided controversy, and even conversation with anyone. The extent of his violent Radicalism and hatred of Conservatism only amounted to his voting for Liberals at the Glasgow elections when his vote was called for, and expressing his dislike to Toryism and the income-tax (no very violent indication, we should think, either of furious Radicalism or insanity).

We have already hinted that M'Naughten had no very great care for the ministers or ordinances of religion, and this is fully corroborated by our further inquiries. It is a fact that he occasionally attended church, but it was more as a matter of taste or speculation than for reproof, correction, or instruction. He disliked prayers, and especially lengthy ones, and when he went to church (he preferred no church in particular) he always went when he expected the first prayer to be over. He also often expressed his belief that half an hour or 20 minutes was enough time for a sermon. If he had any religious opinions, nobody knew what they were.

When in London, he stated to an acquaintance who he called upon on his last visit to Glasgow, that he had made many applications for situations of different descriptions. In particular, he had attended closely to the advertisements of vacant situations in the London morning papers, but found after he called to offer himself as a candidate for any place, however humble, that hundreds of persons had applied before him. He wished a situation, he said, more as a means of employing his time than for any profit or emolument, having upwards of 1,000£ in bank, independent of other monies.

He also mentioned to his friend and former-fellow lodger, when last in Glasgow, that he had applied for a situation in the Excise many times, but never could get one, and a question suggested itself to his friend could M'Naughten have mistaken Mr. Drummond, secretary to Sir R. Peel, for Mr. Drummond, Chairman of the Board of Excise? It may or may not be possible. Those who knew him in Glasgow, however, seem quite satisfied, from their knowledge of his excellent memory, that he never could have mistaken Mr. Drummond for the Premier.

M'Naughten never gave indications of superior ability as a scholar, or superior genius in literary matters. His friends are aware that he sometimes wrote little bits of poetry and dabbled in acrostics, &c., which were amusing enough, but none of these showed anything very brilliant. From evidence taken by the parties appointed to investigate the subject here, we are able to state that none of his family showed any indications of insanity. M'Naughten never gave any reason why "devils in human shape" were hunting him. It was remarked by his landlady (to whom he paid 1s. 6d. weekly for a room) that about a year ago he became very incoherent in his manner, and that latterly she observed a peculiar wild appearance about his eyes.

He had also given signs of his altered disposition by attacking dishes and furniture when he came very near them. The old woman, his landlady, states that when in these fits he seemed as if in a palsy, and in great terror of something, and he had broken a great many dishes of hers of late. When asked by his successor, during a long walk he had with M'Naughten on a Sunday, and on one of the last occasions he had been in company with him in Glasgow, who were his persecutors, and of what country they were, he said they belonged to this city. When further asked if ever he had seen them, he said no, but if he could see them, they would not be long in the land of the living. He swore violently when this topic was alluded to.

On other subjects, during this walk with his apprentice, he talked very solidly and sensibly, gave him many good advices as to his future conduct and the management of the business; not till the old sore (his persecutors) was touched upon did he exhibit any violence of feeling. The apprentice says he took care, during the long walk in question, which occupied about five hours, to avoid introducing the subject of irritation and by this means it was made rather a pleasant affair. On the income-tax, the prevailing topic of public talk at the time, M'Naughten talked rationally, alluded to its effects upon the clergy, the farmers, and other persons with small salaries, but on this point exhibited no violence. Like the generality of insane people, whatever his conduct in other respects, he paid close attention to the interests of No.1 and in the transfer and sale of the business exhibited this virtue most pointedly.

There can be no doubt that M'Naughten's habits were out of the common track, but they were not sufficiently so to induce his friends to take personal charge of him. He is known sometimes to have thrown pieces of wood after people when going out of his shop, but this was considered by the spectators more in the light of diversion than otherwise. When he first purchased the pistols which were found in his possession, he rather alarmed the old woman with whom he lodged in Glasgow. She observed them on a shelf in his room, and, fearing that he either meditated shooting himself or her, she said to him. "In the name of God, Daniel, what are you doing with pistols!" He coolly replied, "I am going to shoot birds with them." She desired him at that time to take the pistols out of the house, which he did shortly afterwards, taking himself off along with them. She had not seen him since.

His after-conduct while in London is already before the public. His father, a decent, respectable man, has been called upon by the authorities. He recollects that his son had told him, about the beginning of last summer that he was going to call on Sir James Campbell, the Lord Provost. Application has been made to His Lordship, who calls to mind that about the end of May or beginning of June, M'Naughten did call at his residence in Bath-street. There he had some conversation in the hall with M'Naughten, who is described by the Lord Provost as a jolly-looking man, and as speaking very coolly, although evidently labouring under some hallucination of mind. He told the Provost with great earnestness that he had been incessantly watched and dogged by certain parties who had an ill-will to him. He said they had forced him from his home by their spiteful machinations, and on the very night before they had obliged him to fly to the fields in the suburbs for refuge.

Sir J. Campbell asked the name of the complainer, which he gave, as also the name of his father, and afterwards reasoned with him as to the folly of his notions. Sir J. Campbell likewise, inquired, pretty broadly, whether he had ever been treated, as if it had been suspected there was anything wrong with his (M'Naughten's) intellects, and being replied to in the negative, seriously advised him to consult his relations or some medical man as to the state of his health. On application to the superintendent of the Glasgow Asylum, we learn that he has had several of the name of M'Naughten under his charge, and in particular one Donald M'Naughten, who answers the description given of the assassin. The superintendent adds that he has one individual at present under his charge who has similar notions to those of M'Naughten – fortunately, however, he was secured before he did any mischief.

Anxious to be seen as taking an unprejudiced position in the M'Naughten proceedings, The *London Standard* weighed in on the side of caution:

Colonel Rowan, Mr. Hall (Chief Magistrate of Bow Street police-office), and Mr. Maule (Solicitor to the Treasury), had a long interview with Sir J. Graham at the Home-office yesterday morning; after which, we understand, that orders were given to bring up the miscreant M'Naughten for final examination at Bow-street today, at 12 o'clock. It is not supposed that the inquiry will be a long one, as the facts attending the late dreadful murders are so clear, and not disputed by the prisoner himself.

With respect to his state of mind, that will form a question for the jury to decide on his trial, and must depend upon the evidence then produced. We have heard that M'Naughten has, for three weeks previous to the assassination, been seen as many as 20 or 30 times a day walking in front of the public offices, but he never made any inquiry. On Saturday week he was observed in Downing-street, at the time the cabinet Ministers were assembling to hold a council; on that occasion several other persons were standing near him but with whom he did not appear to have any acquaintance or conversation.

On one occasion, we are informed, that his constant appearance about Whitehall induced one of the officers of the Board of the Trade to inquire whether he was a policeman in plain clothes, to which inquiry he answered that "he was." There are many other reports as to the prisoner's conduct for the last few weeks, but as we cannot ascertain their truth we forebear to allude to them.

At this point a rather rich description of M'Naughten is available through the press, cumulatively a rather obvious description of florid mental disorder. However, the various observations come from a variety of unrelated sources. The full picture does not appear to have ever been in the hands of a single observer. Had that occurred, perhaps the situation would have been sufficiently compelling to, as put by the press, *induce his friends to take personal charge of him.* As is so often the case with individuals suffering from circumscribed delusional thinking, they appear to be rather unremarkable until one steps into the ways of thinking of the subject of the delusion, at which point any aberrancy is abundantly clear.

Chapter Ten

ON JANUARY 30, ten days after the Drummond shooting, the story continued to be one of the most newsworthy in England, *The Times* affording its readers a glimpse of Queen Victoria's increasingly concerned interest:

THE COURT – WINDSOR, Sunday's Evening.

Sir Robert Peel left town yesterday, immediately after the conclusion of the examination of the assassin M'Naughten at Bow Street, for Windsor, proceeding to Slough by the Great Western Railway, and arrived at the Castle a few minutes before 3 o'clock. The right hon. baronet had an immediate audience of Her Majesty, and remained at the Castle for upwards of an hour. The Queen was informed yesterday, for the first time that the murderer of Mr. Drummond had admitted that he had imagined it was Sir Robert Peel whom he had shot, and not the unfortunate gentleman who had fallen victim to the murderous attack of the prisoner. Her Majesty, upon this circumstance being related to her, is said to have evinced the most gratifying emotions at the providential escape of the right hon. baronet, mingled with feelings of the deepest pain and regret for the melancholy fate of Mr. Drummond. Sir Robert Peel took his departure from the Castle for Slough shortly after 4 o'clock, and returned to town by the railway.

Elsewhere, in *The Observer*, a notice appeared regarding the funeral for "the late Mr. Drummond." A date had not yet been fixed, but his family had decided that the interment would take place in the church at Charlton, near Woolwich, of which his brother the Reverend Arthur Drummond was rector. Adding what was surely a grim touch, the notice pointed to the irony in Drummond's being laid to rest on the grounds in this particular churchyard, for "[i]t may be recollected, that Mr. Perceval, who was shot in the lobby of the House of Commons by Bellingham was interred in a vault in this church – a singular coincidence that two persons engaged in political affairs, who had fallen by the hands of assassins, should lie beside each other in death."

∾❀❀❀∾

UNDER THE HEADLINE "Final Examination of the Assassin M'Naughten," *The Times* announced to its readers that as a consequence of Drummond's death, it had been decided that M'Naughten, who was originally remanded till Monday, February 6th, should be finally examined without delay, in order that he could be brought to trial in the Central Criminal Court sessions that were about to commence. Details of the proceedings were given as follows:

> The determination of the authorities with respect to the prisoner having become generally known, the neighbourhood of Bow Street police-court was, long before the hour appointed for the examination to take place (12 o'clock), crowded with persons anxious to catch a sight of the prisoner when brought to the court, and shortly after 10 o'clock, when the doors were thrown open, the court became instantly densely thronged. The prisoner was brought from Tothill Fields, between 11 and 12 o'clock, in a hackney-coach, in the custody of the chief turnkey of the prison, and was locked up in one of the cells attached to the court till the hour appointed for his examination arrived.
>
> Shortly after 10 o'clock, Mr. Twyford took his seat upon the bench, and proceeded to dispose of the night charges till 12 o'clock, when he adjourned to one of the private rooms, and the court, by order of the chief magistrate, was immediately cleared in order that the witnesses and the professional gentlemen engaged in the case should not be inconvenienced. Precisely at half-past 12 o'clock, Magistrate Hall took his seat, at which time there were several other magistrates and gentlemen on the bench, anxious to hear the proceedings. The doors of the court were again thrown open, and the portion allotted to the public was immediately filled.
>
> Mr. Maule, solicitor to the Treasury, attended to conduct the prosecution, but no legal adviser appeared on behalf of the prisoner. The prisoner was then placed at the bar: he was dressed in the same

manner as at the former examination, and looked extremely well; his incarceration did not appear to have had the slightest effect upon his health. Throughout the whole of the examination, he seemed to pay extreme attention to what was going forward.

Mr. Maule said he attended to conduct the prosecution: he did not know the usual course of proceeding adopted in that court, but he thought the best course would be to have the depositions already taken read over, and then he would adduce some additional evidence, with which he was prepared.

Mr. Hall thought the course suggested would be most convenient.

Mr. Burnaby then proceeded to read over the depositions taken on the prisoner's previous examination, and which were reported at length in our columns of Monday last.

On the evidence of police constable Silver being read over, the witness, in answer to questions by Mr. Maule, said, he attended at the house of Mr. Drummond, No. 19, Lower Grosvenor Street on the evening of the 25th; he there saw the body of Mr. Drummond; it was that of the same person he saw the prisoner fire the pistol at and wound.

Mr. Hall (to the prisoner): "On the last occasion you refused to put any questions of this witness, but you may ask him anything now if you please."

Prisoner: "No."

The evidence of Benjamin Weston, a porter at the Ship Hotel, Charing Cross and Robert Hodge, a carpenter, was next read over; after which Mr. Maule put one or two questions to the witnesses, but they were of a merely formal nature.

The prisoner declined to ask these witnesses any questions.

Weston here said he wished to correct a portion of his evidence. The fact was, the second pistol was discharged in the struggle with the policeman, and before he (the witness) seized the prisoner.

The evidence of constable Partridge was next read, and passed without observation.

Mr. Bransby Cooper was then sworn, and after his former evidence had been read over, he was examined by Mr. Maule, and said: "I was present when the ball was extracted from Mr. Drummond's person."

Mr. Maule: "It was done, I believe, by Mr. Guthrie?"

Mr. Cooper: "It was done by both of us. Mr. Guthrie made the incision, and removed the ball."

Mr. Maule: "You were present, I believe, at the *post mortem* examination on Thursday last."

Mr. Cooper: "I was."

Mr. Maule: "Who attended it?"

Mr. Cooper: "Dr. Chambers, Dr. Hume, Mr. Guthrie, Mr. Jackson, myself, Mr. Guthrie, Jr., a gentleman who accompanied Mr. Guthrie, and a gentleman of the name of Cocks, who went with me."

Mr. Maule: "Is the ball now produced the same you took from the body?"

Mr. Cooper: "I believe it is. I marked the ball and I see a similar mark on this."

Mr. Maule: "You gave the ball to Miss Drummond?"

Mr. Cooper: "I offered it to her, but her maidservant took it."

Mr. Maule said he now proposed to put in the notes of the *post mortem* examination, signed by the respective medical gentlemen.

Mr. Cooper said the document he held in his hand was only a copy of the original, but having read it over, he declared that it was perfectly correct.

Mr. Hall thought Mr. Cooper had better read the document and then it could be entered on the depositions as his own evidence.

Mr. Maule: "You perfectly concur in that statement?"

Mr. Cooper: "Yes, certainly."

Mr. Maule: "I believe Mr. J. Guthrie, Jr., was the person who actually made the *post mortem* examination, but in the presence of yourself and the other gentlemen whose names are attached to the document?"

Mr. Cooper: "Mr. Guthrie, Jr., and Mr. Cocks; but Mr. Guthrie principally.

Mr. Cooper then read the result of the *post mortem* examination, a copy of which we gave in our report here of the inquest on Friday last.

Mr. Maule: "And you are also of opinion that the wound was the cause of Mr. Drummond's death?"

Mr. Cooper: "I am."

Mr. Hall: "Let me call your attention to one expression you made use of just now, viz. "that the absence of all that shock and alarm which almost invariably follows injury to the vital organs led to the hope that the ball had not passed directly across the body."

Mr. Cooper: "That is exactly what I meant to say."

Mr. Hall: "In your last examination you said that you believed the ball had traversed round the left half side of the body."

Mr. Cooper: "That was my impression then; and my belief also from the absence of those symptoms which I have described, that the ball had not penetrated either of the cavities of the chest. My impression as to the direction of the ball was different to what I found it upon the *post mortem* examination."

Mr. Hall said it was impossible to be too particular in this description of evidence.

In order to release Mr. Cooper from further attendance, he was at once bound over to appear and give evidence against the prisoner at the trial for willful murder.

Upon hearing the last words the countenance of the prisoner slightly changed and he appeared rather agitated, but he almost immediately regained his usual composed appearance.

Mr. Charles Drummond was next called, but Mr. Hall said that gentleman's evidence was unnecessary, as the body of the deceased had been identified by the officer.

Mr. Drummond was examined on the last occasion for want of better evidence.

Mr. Maule intimated that he did not propose to call Mr. Guthrie, Jr., as the evidence of Mr. Cooper had been so fully given.

Edward Howe was next examined, and said: "I am office-keeper at the Board of Trade in Whitehall. I know the prisoner by sight, in consequence of having seen him loitering about the neighbourhood of the public offices for about a fortnight previous to the 20th inst."

Mr. Maule: "What offices do you mean?"

Howe: "The Treasury, the Privy Council Office, the Home Office, and the Horse Guards. I have observed him standing at the top of the steps leading to the Privy Council-office, sometimes looking towards the Duke of Bucclauch's and sometimes the other way."

Mr. Maule: "Did you ever speak to him?"

Howe: "Yes, I addressed him on the day Mr. Drummond was shot: he was standing on the steps of the Privy Council-office, opposite the door. That was between 3 and 4 o'clock in the afternoon. I had understood that he was a policeman in plain clothes, and I said to him 'You will excuse me taking the liberty; I am employed in the next office, and I understand you are a policeman: are you or are you or not?'" To which he replied, 'Yes.' I observed, 'Oh! Very well, I suppose it is all right,' and then went away, but I only went into the adjoining street, and on my return found the prisoner in custody at Gardiner's Lane station-house."

William Parrott, servant to Miss Drummond, of 19 Lower Grosvenor Street, said: "Mr. Edward Drummond died at that house about half-past 10 o'clock on Wednesday morning last, and the corpse still remains there. He is the same person upon whom the inquest was held. I did not go into the room with the jury, but stood upon the top of the stairs. I know that during his illness he was attended by Mr. Bransby Cooper, Mr. Guthrie, Jr. and other medical gentlemen."

Sergeant Shaw, A 10, said: "I searched the prisoner's lodgings, No. 7, Poplar Row, Newington, on the evening of the 20th. I found in a drawer in the room five leaden balls, powder-flask containing a quantity of gunpowder, and a pistol key, all wrapped in a handkerchief (all produced). I have tried the balls, and find they fit the pistols, but they fit the larger better than the smaller pistol. When screwed into the small pistol a mark is made upon the ball."

At the conclusion of the examination of each of the above witnesses, the prisoner was asked whether he would ask them any questions, but he merely replied "No."

Inspector Tierney, A Division police, was then sworn, and deposed as follows:

"I saw the prisoner the evening he was apprehended, at the station-house in Gardiner's Lane. I first saw him between 4 and 6 o'clock, before the charge was entered upon the police-sheet. He was then standing in an ante-room."

Mr. Maule: "Had you any conversation with him then?"

Tierney: "Not at that time, but I had three or four times afterwards, when he was in the cell."

Mr. Maule: "State what passed between you; but first let me ask you, whether anything was said to induce him to make any communication?"

Tierney: "No. When I first entered the cell, I gave him strict caution not to say anything to me by which he might criminate himself;

and on that occasion, or at a subsequent interview with him, when I again cautioned him, he said that I acted very fairly towards him, and that fair-play was the character of the English."

Mr. Maule: "Now state what passed."

Tierney: "I first asked him where he came from, and he said from Glasgow, but had been from there about three months, and had remained at Liverpool seven days, on his road to London, where he had since remained. He said he had been in business at Glasgow, on his own account, as a turner; that he gave up that business, and was going into another line, but was prevented. I said, 'You have a good share of money,' to which he replied that he had, but he had wrought half of it; that he used to do the work of three ordinary men daily. I then told him that I had been in Glasgow three or four months previous, and had brought back with me a prisoner of the name of Ellis, and asked him if he knew Mr. Richardson, of the Gorbals police. He said he knew him, though not intimately, but he was considered a more clever man than Miller (meaning another officer). I said I did not recollect the name of the vessel I went over in, but thought it was the *British Queen*. He said, 'No, it must have been the *Princess Royal*.' I then recollected that, that was the name of the vessel, and told him so. I then asked him whether that was the same vessel he came over in, but he said it was not, he came in the *Fire-King*. I next asked him whether he had ever been at Paisley. He said he had. I remarked it was a great place for shawls, and he replied they were nearly all weavers there, but a great many of them were out of employ. I asked him whether he would take any food, and he expressed a wish to have some tea or coffee; and some coffee and bread and butter was supplied to him. In the course of the conversation I asked him whether Drummond was a Scotch name. He said it was, that it was the family name of the Earl of Perth, but the title had died away. Nothing further passed that evening."

Mr. Maule: "When did you see him again?"

Tierney: "About 9 o'clock on the following morning. I then asked him whether he had taken his breakfast, and he said he had. He also asked what o'clock it was, and I told him. He then asked if I would allow him to have some water to wash with, to which I consented, and sent the constable who had remained with him all night to get it. When the constable had left, I said to the prisoner, 'I suppose you will assign some reason to the magistrates this morning for the act you have committed.' He said he would – a short one. I then told him he might have said anything he pleased to me on the night previous after the caution I had given him."

Mr. Hall here asked the prisoner whether he heard all the witness was saying.

Prisoner: (nodding his head) "Yes, sir."

Tierney: (continuing) "The prisoner then said the Tories had adopted a system of persecution against him; they followed him from place to place; and continually persecuted him."

Mr. Hall: "The prisoner said that, I presume, in the first person, and not in the third?"

Tierney: "I am now speaking his own words; he said it in the first person."

Mr. Hall: "Then you ought to do so, too; you should give his exact words."

Tierney: "I then said, 'I suppose you are aware who the gentleman is you shot at.' He said, 'Sir Robert Peel, is it not?' I said, 'No' at the moment, but instantly recalled the word, and said, 'We are not aware exactly who it is yet; but recollect the caution I gave you last night, for anything you say may be used against you.' The prisoner, who was sitting down at the time, looked up at me, and said, 'But you won't use this or these words against me.' I said, 'I don't know; I gave you a proper caution.' I said nothing more, but immediately left him."

Mr. Maule: "That is all I believe, sir."

Mr. Hall: (to the prisoner) "You have heard what the witness has said, do you wish to put any questions to him?"

Prisoner: "No."

Mr. Hall: "You shall have the evidence read carefully over again, and then you can do as you please." He turned to the witness. "Have you told us everything that passed?"

Tierney: "I have, to the best of my recollection."

Mr. Maule: "That is the case on behalf of the prosecution, sir."

Mr. Hall: (to the prisoner) "When you were last brought before me, I told you, you might make any statement you thought proper, having previously given you a caution that whatever you said would be taken down in writing and used against you. You must consider that caution now repeated. Do you wish to say anything more?"

Prisoner: "No, sir."

Mr. Hall: "You have already made a statement, which was taken down in writing, do you wish to have that read over to you?

Prisoner: "No."

Mr. Hall: "For your information I must tell you that you will not be brought up again before me. I shall commit you today to take your trial; the sessions at which you will be tried will commence on Monday next, but I cannot say what day may be fixed for your trial."

The witnesses having signed their depositions, were bound over to give evidence upon the trial of the prisoner at the Central Criminal Court.

Mr. Hall: "Prisoner, you are entitled to have, if you please, a copy of the depositions given to you; therefore if you wish to have them, say so."

Prisoner: "Yes, I should like to have them."

Mr. Burnaby: "Prisoner, you stand committed to Newgate to take your trial for willful murder."

The prisoner M'Naughten, whose demeanour throughout had been extremely calm and collected, bowed respectfully to the court, and was removed from the bar.

Chapter Eleven

THE ANTI-CORN LAW League was formed in 1839 by members of the industrial classes to fight the government's enormously unpopular Corn Laws, first introduced in 1804, which were put in place to protect the profits of the wealthy land-owning farmers by setting inflated, rather than market-driven, prices on corn. The effect of the laws was to keep the price of wheat and therefore bread unconscionably high. This legislation was particularly hated by the people living in the large fast-growing urban centres who were offended by having to pay these exorbitant prices.

Enormous pressure was put upon the government of Sir Robert Peel who eventually was won over and repealed the laws in 1846 – three years after Drummond's murder. Some elements of the Anti-Corn Law League were not averse to violent displays of their dissatisfaction. At the time of Mr. Drummond's murder in 1843, Sir Robert Peel and his government were enduring constant pressure to repeal the laws. The anti-government attitude of the league and the suspicion that they were behind various nefarious events, caused some commentators to speculate that it may have been the proselytizing of the league that incited M'Naughten to attempt the murder of Sir Robert Peel.

In response to such speculation, *The Times* wrote in its issue of January 31 on the subject of Drummond's murder:

> This brings us to the consideration of a point, which we would handle with great delicacy; and we must begin by saying that we do not think even the least scrupulous of our political opponents so destitute of Christian and manly feeling as to promote or countenance assassination or any other act at all approaching it in the scale of criminality. The Anti-Corn Law League for instance, we have never ceased to

denounce as a combination dangerous in its tendency, and suspicious in its acts with reference to their effects upon the public tranquility; but, although we have found some of its agents and partisans so indiscreet as to retail idle stories about murderous plots and designs against Ministers, we have not charged it with being *particeps criminis* in intent.

Although we have found men emulating the blood-thirsty aspirations of the rabble in *Coriolanus* against the life of Caius Marcius, who go about exclaiming, "Let us kill him and we'll have corn at our own price," we have never for a moment harboured so much as a suspicion that the members of the League, as a body, contemplated the evil effects of such poison in the ears of the ignorant and violent.

Mr. Abel Heywood's celebrated story purporting the League's influence on M'Naughten was admitted to be an idle figment, but it was sufficiently mischievous nevertheless. A Reverend Mr. Bailey, at the League's "Convention of Delegates," in London, last summer, was reported to have said, "I heard a person say, in a private party, that he would not mind making one of a hundred to draw lots which should shoot Sir R. Peel, and," continued his reverence, "I will venture to assert this myself, that whenever Sir Robert dies, no tears will be shed over his grave."

Then we had Mr. Duffy, the journeyman tailor, in his tell-tale lecture against the League at the Corn Exchange, informing us that no less a personage than Mr. Villiers, the Anti-Corn Law *spes gregis*, had said, in his hearing, that "if a single handful of mud had then been thrown at the Minister" when his motion for the repeal of the Corn Laws was first proposed to the Legislature, "it would have been carried." We bear all these things in mind, and although we seek not to fix either act or intention upon the League, as a body, yet we cannot help cautioning respectable men against having any connexion with a society whose agents and partisans give the cue, it may be thoughtlessly, to the evil-disposed.

Who can pretend to say that the murderer of Mr. Drummond, sane or insane, may not have drawn his incentive to murder, in the first instance, from such hints as those we have quoted? We do not say that he was so influenced, but unless we had the power of seeing in particular events certain and unvarying consequences, the presumption that he was so influenced cannot he held to be either violent or unnatural. Let those connected with the League bestow some thought upon these suggestions. Their power as honest opponents of the Corn Laws will lose nothing, and in our judgment it would rather gain, as by secession from a combination the effect of whose operations is at the least suspicious.

The following day, *The Times* offered a story reprinted from the *Glasgow Herald* apparently with the intention of shedding further light both on its position and on the details of M'Naughten's life, more of which were emerging all the time.

The melancholy interest which attaches to this tragedy has increased, if possible, since the death of the amiable and unfortunate Mr. Drummond, and it may be said to occupy the public mind to the exclusion of every other topic. The feeling of indignation with which the act of the assassin is regarded, is universal in Glasgow, the place of his birth; but we are well aware that popular feeling, however strong it may be over the kingdom, will not, for one moment, be allowed to mar the course of justice, or to interfere with the right of the wretched man M'Naughten to a fair and dispassionate trial.

In our last we gave some statements regarding the intercourse of M'Naughten with Mr. A Johnston, M.P., Sir J. Campbell, the Rev. Mr. Turner, of Gorbals, Mr. Carlow, his successor in business, Mrs. Pattison, his landlady, and other parties, from which the only deduction that could be drawn was…that the man was insane. We have since made further inquiry into the character and conduct of this wretched person, but we do not find the opinion of his insanity so strongly supported by some as by others; and, indeed, it is perfectly plain that in his intercourse with many people during the last year or two his conduct was not only rational, but intelligent, though it must always be borne in mind that on the one point, the illusion that he was persecuted by devils or Tories, he has always shown strong symptoms of insanity.

The state of M'Naughten's mind will no doubt form the principal point for investigation at the trial, and, under these circumstances, it would be alike unfair and injudicious to make any reflections which might have an appearance of prejudging the case. We give the following facts, therefore, simply as they have come to our knowledge, and which, so far as they go, discountenance the plea that M'Naughten laboured under insanity to the extent of being generally observable.

It has now been clearly ascertained by the authorities here, that the pistols, one of which inflicted the fatal wound on Mr. Drummond, were purchased from Mr. Martin, Highs Street, Paisley. According to Mr. Martin's recollection, a person who answers as nearly as may be the description of Daniel M'Naughten called at his shop in the month of July last, and wished to purchase a pair of pistols. Amongst others, two were shown him, which did not match, the one being longer in the barrel than the other. M'Naughten expressed his liking for the long-barreled pistol, and wished to have another like it, stating that it would "look daft-like to have pistols that were not matched."

Mr. Martin had not its match, but he stated to his intended purchaser that he would send his son, who kept a shop in Argyll-street, Glasgow, and he would, in all likelihood, have it in readiness for him by the following day, at which time he was requested to call again. Mr. Martin's son had not the peculiar kind of pistol needed, which fact he communicated to M'Naughten a day or two afterwards, when he called in Paisley, at which time he resolved to take the two odd ones. At the same time he looked at a powder-flask, and some balls were cast for him to suit the caliber of both pistols – the amount of charge being about 17s, which the purchaser paid and departed.

The pistols were known by the name of "center-cock detonating." And upon one of them was engraved the words, "*Martin, Paisley.*" From his appearance, it was Mr. Martin's impression that M'Naughten was engaged in some small country trade, but nothing to countenance this opinion escaped him, nor did anything pass from which it could be guessed that he was a native of Glasgow, or had ever been in it; the only statement worth notice which he made being that he was about to leave the country in three weeks.

His demeanor throughout was composed and sensible. It is not a little curious that M'Naughten should buy the pistols in Paisley at all; but it is still more remarkable that when Mr. Martin said he would send to his son in Glasgow for a match to the long-barreled pistol he did not utter any sentiment to show that he was acquainted with Mr. Martin, Jr. in this city, for it has now been ascertained that he knew him perfectly well, and had been more than once employed by him in his profession as a wood-turner.

The description of the pistols in the London papers entirely corresponds with those sold in Paisley. It would be observed, from our statement last week, that when M'Naughten was challenged by his landlady here for having these instruments in his possession, he stated that he had got them for the purpose of shooting birds; and it is only fair to state, that a small quantity of "hail" or lead drops, which might be employed for this purpose, was found in his lodgings, though we have not heard of any person who was ever actually aware that he had used the pistols in bird shooting.

It seems to be the opinion of all who have known him, that M'Naughten was of a studious and inquiring turn of mind; and from a ticket found in his lodgings, it appears that he attended the lectures of Dr. James Douglas on practical anatomy, in the Medical School, Portland-street, during the session beginning May 1 and ending July 29, 1842. Dr. Douglas states, however, that in reality M'Naughten did not join the class till a fortnight after it had commenced; that he attended with regularity, and seemed anxious, by his assiduity, to make up for the time he had lost; he appeared much interested in the study, and displayed an anxiety to become acquainted with anatomy.

Although there was a dissecting-room connected with the school, M'Naughten did not himself dissect, but spent an hour a day in it reading anatomical works, and using steady efforts to make-up the lee-way caused by his not joining the class at the beginning. Dr. Douglas mentions that he conversed occasionally with M'Naughten on the subject of anatomy, and he found him always rational and composed, there being nothing unusual or *outré* about him, and he seemed to be acquiring as much knowledge as any of the other students.

He was quiet in his manners; and it was the Doctor's impression that his pupil had been left money, and in consequence, had taken it into his head to qualify himself for a medical practitioner, a little later in life than usual. He was particularly anxious to make himself acquainted with the structure of the bones of the human frame, and studied this subject at an hour separate from the lecture. He did not, however, attend the usual Saturday examinations, from the difficulty he felt in pronouncing the names in Latin, with which language he was unacquainted. Altogether, nothing occurred to raise in Dr. Douglas's mind the slightest suspicion as to M'Naughten's sanity; but, of course, it must always be born in mind, that their conversation never embraced the political point upon which the mind of the latter was understood to be unsettled.

It has also been ascertained that the assassin attended some of the classes in the Mechanics' Institution here during the session 1839-40; and we may state, on the authority of Mr. William Ambrose, who was then secretary, that there being at that time a movement among some of the students to effect an alteration in the constitution of the institute, M'Naughten interested himself much in this object, and was a member of a small committee which had been appointed to carry out their views. During this discussion he took a share in the business like the other members, and conducted himself, calmly and rationally. At the same time he was generally regarded as a person of retired and unsocial habits.

In testing the mind of this wretched person, however, by his sensible conduct at this period, it must be remembered that it was previous to the time when he appears to have become possessed by the illusion as to his persecution by devils or Tories. The library list of the institution at this time also shows that he was a great reader, the books used by him being almost entirely on practical subjects. We have not ascertained whether M'Naughten was a student at the Mechanics' Institute subsequent to this period. Indeed, we rather think not; but in May 1842, he procured what is called "A Summer Reader's Ticket," and continued to read upon it till the 16th of September 1842, having got out, and it is believed perused, about 40 different volumes.

By way of showing, to a certain extent, the bent of his mind during this comparatively recent period, we give the titles of a few of the books procured by him. Amongst them were: *Quain's Anatomy*, *Douglas's Anatomy of the Body*, *Animal Mechanics*, *Robertson on Spinal and Nervous Diseases*, *Logan's Scottish Banker*, *Lamartine's Travels in the East*, *Drinkwater's Siege of Gibraltar*, *Elements of Rhetoric*, *Juniua's Letters*, *Murray's Travels in America*, *Study of Mathematics*, *Dr Andrew Combes's 'Observations on Mental Derangement'*, *Whateley's Logic*, *Reid's Medical Botany*, *Italy and Italian Literature*, *Babbage's Bridgewater Treatise*, &c.

Among the articles found in Mrs. Pattison's lodgings, which had been used by the murderer, were a number of books, few or none of which were of the light-reading class, and altogether the collection might be considered to constitute a very decent little library for a journeyman tradesman. Amongst them were some French works, and some French exercises in his handwriting, which showed that he had made some little progress in the study of that language. There were also a pair of red sandals, such as are used by players, and we believe it is now ascertained that some years ago he did "fret his little hour", with a strolling company which visited Kilmarnook and other towns and villages in the west of Scotland. But by far the most curious article which has been found is an inventory, or rather a most minute description of his room, and all it contained, taken down in his own handwriting, but without any date. As it may possibly be considered to evince some of the peculiarities in M'Naughten's mind, it may not be amiss to give a few extracts from it.

He sets out by detailing the height of the room from the ceiling, and its length and breadth. He then states: "The walls were pretty thick, not very evenly plastered, and oil-painted of a dark cream colour; and the floor, a deal one, covered with two small pieces of carpet, for ornament as well as use; it being, in one sense, intended to prevent the feet coming in contact with the cold floor, it not being agreeable to do so when one jumps newly out of bed." He then describes the situation and size of a shelf in the room, and goes on to say: "On this shelf were placed a variety of dishes, evidently the manufacture of an adjoining country. Among the most prominent of them was a large tureen, a large bowl, both of blue pattern, an old China teapot, a pair of pourries," – milk-jugs, we presume, is meant – "and sundry old saucers, cups, and basins, all China. Several old bottles stood on the back side of the shelf, and two in the front, one of which was a neat little one, with a glass and crystal decanter beside it.

"On the extreme end of the shelf were placed two baskets, one an apparently pretty old one, and of nearly a square shape; the other much newer, and of a genteel modern cut." The narrator then describes the position of the door, and continues: "Close to the door stood an old-fashioned eight-day clock, with fir case, and painted in imitation of mahogany; at the side of it stood an old fir chest of the same colour, and at the end of the chest lay several bandboxes, a large tartan shawl, with one or two dirty gowns and shirts, sundry pairs of old boots and shoes, an old hat, and a new carpet bag, and on the top of the bandboxes lay a woman's check straw hat with dark brown ribbons. On the lid of the chest lay a silk pocket-handkerchief, a small piece of writing paper, and two odd volumes of books, and before it an old chair to sit upon.

"As you entered from the door, the bed lay on the left hand, of a considerable length and breadth, sufficient to hold two persons with ease, and three with a pinch. It was an excellent good feather bed, with bolsters, sheets, and pillows, in clean slips, a clean sheet, and a pair and a half of good blankets, with a capital thick mat. At the head of the bed two good clean hardwood posts were seen, connected at the top by a cross bar. At the bottom the posts were short, and not visible, rising only about three inches above the stock. Over the rail, which connected the top of the two head-posts, there lay an old stock, and close to that, hanging on a nail in the wall, was a gown, the hood of a woman's mantle, a pair of new tartan trousers, and a Mackintosh. On the back of the door was hanging an old "flannel" shirt. I forgot to mention that there were two umbrellas, suspended by the handles from the top of the clock-case."

We have only to close by mentioning that M'Naughten never was in the Glasgow Lunatic Asylum, as has been surmised. It is curious enough that a Donald or Daniel M'Naughten, a wood-turner, was at one time under treatment at the institution, but he is not the man who has now gained such a deplorable notoriety. We understand that M'Naughten's friends have engaged a highly respectable and intelligent agent here to prepare the defense, which must be one of insanity, and there is no doubt that every justice will be meted out to the wretched man."

Here the press set up in intricate detail the factual backdrop for the defence upon which M'Naughten would rely. That is, while in most respects M'Naughten appeared as a rather unremarkable character, when it came to the "illusion [*sic*] that he was persecuted by devils or Tories," he had always shown strong symptoms of insanity. With this, much of the work required to convince prospective jurors as to the merits of such a defence has been done by the press.

FUNERAL OF THE LATE MR. E. DRUMMOND

The mortal remains of the above lamented gentleman were yesterday consigned to their last resting place, in the churchyard of Charlton, near Woolwich, Kent. In accordance with the expressed desire of the deceased's relatives the funeral was conducted in the most private

manner, and the mourners consisted solely of the members of the
Drummond family. The mournful cavalcade left Grosvenor Street at
the early hour of 8 o'clock on its way to Charlton. The route taken was
over Vauxhall-bridge, by Kennington and Camberwell, to New Cross;
thence to Deptford, and over Blackheath to Charlton, at which place
the procession arrived about ten minutes past 11.

On arriving at the churchyard the body of the deceased gentleman
was met by the Hon. and Rev. Mr. Boscawen, vicar of Wotton, near
Dorking, Surrey, who commenced reading the service for the burial
of the dead. The church was fully attended by the most respectable inhabitants of the neighbourhood, all of whom appeared to be very much
affected by the melancholy scene. The coffin having been placed in the
centre aisle the mourners took their seats, and the service proceeded.

At the conclusion, the mourners moved towards the vault prepared
for the reception of the body at the eastern extremity of the churchyard. The circumstances under which the deceased met his death had
an evident effect on those assembled, and the greatest sympathy was
manifested by all present. The three brothers of the deceased were
very much affected, and when the coffin was lowered into the vault
the feelings of Colonel Drummond were completely overcome. The
prayers being ended, the brothers took their last look at the coffin
containing the remains of their deceased relative, and soon after left
the spot under feelings of the deepest emotion.

The coffin was covered with black furniture, and surmounted by a
brass plate, bearing the following inscription: – "Edward Drummond,
Esq., died 25th January, 1843, *antatis suro* 50." The very great respect
entertained for the deceased induced a large number of his friends to
request permission to pay the last tribute of respect to his remains by
attending the funeral, which was only prevented by the desire of the
family to conduct the ceremony in as private a manner as possible.

It was anticipated by many persons that Sir Robert Peel would
have attended, and it is understood that the right hon. baronet was
alone prevented from doing so by the solicitation of the friends of the
deceased. Several of the nobility and gentry wished their carriages to
follow, but for the same reason this mark of respect was also declined.
The vault in which the deceased is interred is a very ancient one, having been erected more than 200 years since. It had fallen into decay,
and was advertised some time since. No person coming forward to

own it, the vicar, Mr. Drummond, has appropriated it to his own use, and the deceased is the first member of his family whose body has been deposited therein.

Chapter Twelve

THE ENDORSEMENT MADE by a grand jury when they are satisfied with the truth of an accusation and find sufficient evidence to warrant a criminal charge, is known as a "true bill." If the grand jury is of the view that the allegations of the Crown do not support the charge, their response at the conclusion of the hearing would be "no bill" rather than a true bill. At New Court on the morning of February 1st, a grand jury, among other bills, returned a true bill against Daniel M'Naughten for murder. This prompted his appearance the following day in the Central Criminal Court; a solicitor named Clarkson had been instructed by M'Naughten to bring an application to the court on his behalf.

At the sitting of the court, before Lord Abinger and Mr. Justice Maule, the prisoner Daniel M'Naughten was placed at the bar, charged with the willful murder of Mr. Edward Drummond. Upon his name being called, M'Naughten immediately walked with a firm step to the front of the dock. He appeared perfectly calm and collected; he looked extremely well; and his general appearance was "very little altered from what it was when under examination at Bow Street; but if anything, he looked rather paler."

The Attorney General Mr. Waddington appeared on behalf of the Crown and Mr. Clarkson appeared for "the prisoner." Before Mr. Clarkson made application to their lordships as he had been instructed by the prisoner to do, he wished to ascertain their lordships' opinion whether, before he did so, the prisoner ought to be called upon to plead to the charge of murder against him.

Lord Abinger said that would entirely depend upon the nature of the application. If it were with respect to the incapacity of the prisoner to plead, in consequence of his state of mind, then the application must be made first; and a jury would be empanelled to determine whether he was in a fit state of mind to plead or not.

Mr. Clarkson offered that he was not instructed to make any application of such a nature, to which Lord Abinger responded that the prisoner "ought to be at once called upon to plead." Mr. Straight, the deputy clerk of arraignments, duly read the indictment, which was of a very considerable length. It alleged that the prisoner

> on the 20th of January, at the parish of St. Martin-in-the Fields, did feloniously assault Mr. Edward Drummond with a certain pistol, which he then and there held in his right hand, loaded with gunpowder and a leaden bullet, and which he of his malice aforethought discharged at and against the said Edward Drummond, thereby giving him a certain mortal wound, in and upon the left side of the back of the said Edward Drummond, a little below the blade-bone at his left shoulder, of the breadth of half an inch and of the depth of 12 inches, and of which wound the said Edward Drummond did languish until the 25th of January, and languishing did live, on which 25th of January he, of the said mortal wound so given in manner aforesaid by him, the said Daniel M'Naughten, died; and that he did willfully kill and murder the said Edward Drummond.[1]

Mr. Straight then turned and addressed M'Naughten. "How say you, prisoner, are you guilty of the charge, or not guilty?"

M'Naughten, who kept his eyes steadily fixed towards the bench, made no reply to the question.

Mr. Straight again asked him whether he was guilty or not guilty.

Mr. Cope, the Governor of the prison, here asked the prisoner whether he had heard the question.

Mr. Straight persisted: "Prisoner, you must answer the question, whether you are guilty or not."

The prisoner, after again hesitating for some time, said: "I was driven to desperation by persecution."

At this point Lord Abinger intervened: "Will you answer the question? You must say either guilty or not guilty."

M'Naughten, after another pause, said: "I am guilty of firing."

Lord Abinger: "By that do you mean to say you are not guilty of the remainder of the charge, that is, of intending to murder Mr. Drummond?"

M'Naughten: "Yes."

Lord Abinger: "That certainly amounts to a plea of "Not guilty." Therefore, such plea must be recorded."

The prisoner was then, upon the basis of the Coroner's inquisition, charged with the offence, and a plea of "Not guilty" was entered.

Mr. Clarkson then said that he had been instructed to apply to their Lordships on behalf of the prisoner to have the trial postponed until the next session, and he was instructed further to apply to have a certain paper, being a receipt for money, which had been taken from the prisoner at the time he was apprehended, restored to him; that receipt was for the sum of 750£, which had been lodged by the prisoner in the Glasgow and Shipping Bank.

A Mr. Humphries who had only been instructed to defend the prisoner several days earlier, held in his hand an affidavit which he told the Court would fully explain the grounds of his application. He felt he must, however, remind the Court that the prisoner had originally been remanded till the 6th of February, in order that the trial might not take place till the next session. But in consequence of the lamented death of Mr. Drummond, it was considered necessary to have the prisoner finally examined immediately and at once committed to take his trial.

The affidavit read as follows:

> "CENTRAL CRIMINAL COURT
> THE QUEEN *v.* DANIEL M'NAUGHTEN,
> INDICTED FOR WILFUL MURDER"

William Corne Humphries, of No. 119, Newgate Street, at the city of London, in partnership with George Perceval, solicitor, retained to defend the above-named prisoner, made oath, and said that the above-named prisoner was committed upon the above charge to Her Majesty's jail of Newgate on Saturday, the 28th of January last, and that this deponent was, in the afternoon of Monday, the 30th day of January last, instructed for the first time to act as solicitor in his defense.

That this deponent forthwith had an interview with the said prisoner, and found in his possession a copy of the depositions taken against him before the committing magistrate at Bow Street, and a copy also of certain other depositions, which appears to have been

taken at Glasgow, in Scotland, on oath, in the presence of Archibald
Allison, Esq., Advocate Sheriff of Lanarkshire, on the 24th of January last, which last-mentioned depositions set forth various acts and
circumstances having reference to the state of mind of the prisoner.

That this deponent was informed, that the said two sets of depositions were furnished to the said prisoner by some person in authority
at the Police Court, Bow Street, at the time when the said prisoner
was committed on last Saturday as aforesaid. And this deponent further said that from his communication with the said prisoner, and
from a letter which this deponent has seen, appearing to be written
from and bearing the postmark of Glasgow, respecting the prisoner,
and also from the perusal of the depositions so respectively taken at
Bow Street and before the advocate sheriff as aforesaid, this deponent
verily believes that it will be necessary for the full and fair defense of
the said prisoner that a number of witnesses should be procured from
Scotland, and that inquiry should be made for the purpose of procur-
ing, if possible, certain other witnesses from France, where the said
prisoner was some time since residing.

And this deponent further said, that he has been informed and
believes that a letter has been sent to Scotland with directions to
send some witnesses from there, who are expected to give important evidence in favour of the said prisoner upon the trial of the said
indictment, but from the shortness of the time since the prisoner's
committal this deponent is unable to say whether or not the said witnesses so sent for will arrive during the present session; and if the
said last-mentioned witnesses should so arrive, this deponent verily
believes that it would not even then be safe for the said prisoner to
take his trial until further and more extensive inquiry can be made
respecting him, extending as above said to the kingdom of France.

And this deponent further said, that very considerable outlay will
necessarily be incurred in traveling and other necessary expenses before the defense of the said prisoner can be so properly prepared as
to lay the same in a proper and satisfactory way before the jury who
is to try the said prisoner, as this deponent has been informed, and as
the deposition of James Silver, taken at Bow Street, states he has had
taken from him by the said James Silver the following notes, security,
and money – viz. two 5£ Bank of England notes, four sovereigns, four
half-crowns, one shilling, one four-penny piece, one penny piece, and

a receipt for 750£ from the Glasgow and Shipping Bank. And this deponent verily believes that the said prisoner is now personally without funds, and that if the said order for 750£ on the Glasgow Bank shall be restored to him it will take a very considerable time to transmit the said order and receive in return the cash in payment for the same in due course of post.

And this deponent further said, that after his interview with the said prisoner on Monday last, this deponent caused to be written a letter to Mr. George Maule, the solicitor for the Treasury, and who conducts this prosecution, of which letter the paper writing hereto annexed, marked "A" is a true copy, and which letter was sent by this deponent to the said Mr. Maule early on Tuesday morning, and to which letter this deponent received on the last-named day the answer hereto annexed marked "B."

And this deponent lastly said, that he verily believes that he cannot fairly and properly be prepared so thoroughly to defend the prisoner at the present session as he shall be at the session next coming, when this deponent verily believes, from the information aforesaid, that witnesses will be procured and produced from Scotland, and probably from France, who will give evidence most material and necessary for the defense of the said prisoner, and without which testimony it will be unsafe for the said prisoner to take his trial.

And this deponent, William Corne Humphries, further said, that from perusal of the said copies of depositions taken in Scotland as aforesaid, and from information furnished to this deponent, this deponent verily believes he shall by the next session be in a condition to lay before the Court and jury material evidence touching the unsoundness of mind of the said prisoner before and near to the time of the commission of the act with which he stands charged.

W.C. Humphries.

Sworn in court, at the Central Criminal Court, Justice Hall, Old Bailey, London, this 2nd day of February, 1843.

(Letter marked "A")
119, Newgate Street, Jan 31

Sir, – Yesterday afternoon, for the first time, we were consulted upon the case of the prisoner Daniel M'Naughten, and instructed to defend.

Upon seeing the prisoner it was found, that on his committal on Saturday last he was furnished, at Bow-street Police-court, with copies of depositions taken there upon that day and on some previous examinations, and he was also furnished at the same time with copies of depositions of witnesses, which appear to have been taken on oath, respecting him at Glasgow, on the 24th inst.; and we find that the prisoner's papers have been taken from him, and amongst them an accountable receipt for 750£, deposited by him in one of the banks at Glasgow.

From the matter contained in the voluminous depositions taken at Bow Street, as well as those taken at Glasgow, we think it utterly impossible to defend the prisoner if he be tried at the present session. The very recent committal, the means of evidence to be considered, and the detention of a security on the Glasgow Bank are all reasons which we respectfully submit may be fairly urged for a postponement; in addition to which we are instructed, that if time be allowed to make inquiry, evidence may, in all probability, be procured from Scotland, and, perhaps, from France, which may be most important to the interests of the prisoner, and we should hope, in the result, satisfactory to the public.

These inquiries, however, will require both time and funds, and on behalf of the prisoner we respectfully request that you will be pleased to consent to a postponement of his trial until the next session, and that you will direct that the order for money on the Glasgow Bank may be given to the prisoner's appointed agent; and that we may have inspection of the papers taken from him, and a restoration of such of them as you may deem unnecessary for the purposes of the prosecution.

We shall make application to the Central Criminal Court immediately on the indictment being returned; and we thus take leave to address you, in order that you may have the earliest possible notice on such intended application. Trusting that the same will be consented to, "we have the honour to be, &c."

Humphries and Perceval, G. Maule, Esq., Solicitor, Treasury.

(Letter marked "B")
Treasury, Jan. 31

Gentlemen, – I have to acknowledge the receipt of your letter of this date, and in answer thereto beg leave to acquaint you, that no direct consent can be given, as requested by you; but, on the part of the prosecution, it will be left to the Court to decide, upon the materials which may be produced on the part of the prisoner by affidavit. The accounting receipt and the papers taken from the prisoner cannot be delivered up, but there will be no objection to your inspecting them; and facility will be afforded for obtaining money for the necessary expenses of the defense upon the accountable receipt.

It is proposed to prefer the bill tomorrow; and, if it should be found, I shall be obliged by your acquainting me on what morning you will make your intended application to the Court, in order that the Attorney-General, or some counsel on the part of the Crown, may be present.

I am, &c.

G. Maule

Messrs. Humphries and Perceval,

119, Newgate Street

Mr. Clarkson added that as the receipt he had alluded to could not by any possibility have any connection with the charge against the prisoner, he hoped there would be no objection on the part of the prosecution to give it up.

Lord Abinger asked the attorney general whether he offered any opposition to the application. The attorney general said it would, certainly, have been more satisfactory if some of the depositions that had been returned from Scotland had been annexed to the affidavit, as it was only by the last part of it that it appeared any attempt would be made to show that the prisoner was not of sound mind; at the same time he felt bound in justice to say that he had seen the depositions alluded to, and they certainly contained matter that it would be very proper to lay before the jury who would have to try the prisoner. He would also add that those who conducted the prosecution were anxious that it should be conducted with the utmost fairness, both as regarded the prisoner and the public, whose interests were deeply involved in the result of the investigation.

Lord Abinger said, that after what had been stated by the learned attorney general, who had read the depositions referred to, and who considered they contained facts material to be proven on behalf of the prisoner, the court could not resist the application for the postponement of the trial; the depositions alluded to were certainly important, and without them he should not have considered the affidavit sufficient.

Mr. Clarkson again called his lordship's attention to the other part of his application, that is, the restoration of the bank receipt and the money taken from the prisoner. It was essentially necessary that he should have the means of properly getting up his defence, and as there was not the slightest pretence for saying either the one or the other had anything to do with the charge, he hoped there would be no objection to the property being handed over to the prisoner's solicitors.

Lord Abinger said it appeared that the prosecutor did not object to hand over to the prisoner a sufficient sum to meet the necessary expenses of getting up his defence; beyond that he thought he could not make any order.

The attorney general said that application had certainly been made to Mr. Maule for the restoration of the papers taken from the prisoner, but as they were considered important for the ends of the prosecution, an answer was sent back that they could not be returned; but at the same time an intimation was given that any reasonable amount would be handed over to the prisoner, upon the security of the receipt, for the purpose of preparing his defence. With respect to the receipt itself, he certainly could not consent to its being given up, because it might become a very important document in behalf of the prosecution. Lord Abinger said the trial would be allowed to stand over upon the understanding that sufficient funds should be supplied to the prisoner for the purpose of preparing his defence.

The attorney general begged to inform the court that the deposition alluded to had not been made by order of or under the authority of government, but by a public officer in the discharge of his duty and upon his own responsibility.

The prisoner was then removed from the bar.

∽∂∂∂∽

IN THE NEXT three weeks, the Glasgow witnesses as to M'Naughten's conduct in recent years were summoned to appear in London on Monday, the 27th of February, in preparation for his trial, which was expected to commence about the middle of the following week; the two lawyers retained by his friends expected to make the plea of insanity a very strong one. Witnesses for the defence were selected by Dr.

Hutchinson, physician to the Royal Lunatic Asylum, Glasgow, who would also come to London and speak in his defence, along with a Dr. Crawford, professor of medical jurisprudence at Anderson's University, Glasgow, who would act as medical counsel advising M'Naughten's legal counsel during the trial.

While awaiting trial M'Naughten was kept at Newgate Prison. Rebuilt after the Great Fire of London in 1666, it had stood on the same site since the twelfth century. Infamous as "an emblem of death and suffering," a place where unmentionable cruelty and disease plagued inmates, it was a legendary institution that over the years had inspired poems, dramas, and novels. In his book *London: The Biography*, Peter Ackroyd describes it thus:

> On arrival the prisoners were fettered and "ironed," passing under the gate to be led to their appropriate dungeon; they passed, on the left, the keeper's house beneath which was the "hold" for those condemned to death. A prisoner confined in this subterranean area, which did not perhaps differ very much from the dungeon before the Fire, is quoted in Anthony Babington's *The English Bastille* as saying there were "some glimmerings of light ... by which you may know that you are in a dark, opaque, wild room." Entered by a hatch, it was entirely constructed of stone with an open sewer running through the "middle" which diffused a "stench" that entered every corner. Fastened into the stone floor itself were hooks and chains to castigate and confine those who were "stubborn and unruly."[2]

There were different levels of comfort corresponding to the offender's means and status. It is likely that M'Naughten fared well here, because the celebrity of the case and his financial means led to his being kept in one of the most favourable sections of the jail. A piece in *The Times* of February 28th reported:

> [T]he prisoner M'Naughten passes a good deal of his time in walking about the yard and reading. Although supplied with the necessary articles for writing, he has scarcely availed himself of the privilege, and when he has, it appears to be without a motive. During the time he has been at Newgate he has enjoyed most excellent health, not the least change in his looks being apparent.

PART II

The Trial of
Daniel M'Naughten

Chapter Thirteen

ALTHOUGH FOR LONDONERS in the Victorian era the Old Bailey was, according to a writer of the time, associated with "ugliness, greasy squalor, crime of every description, in a cold, bleak-looking prison, with an awful little iron door, three feet or so from the ground," as well as "trial by jury, black caps, bullying counsel," a "visibly affected" judge, prevaricating witnesses, and a miserable, trembling, damp prisoner in the dock, the Old Bailey, or rather the Central Criminal Court held at the Old Bailey, was at the same time held to be

> *par excellence*, the criminal court of the country. In it all the excellences and all the disadvantages of our criminal procedures are developed to an extraordinary degree. The Old Bailey juries are at once more clear-sighted and more pig-headed than any country jury. The local judges, that is to say, the Recorder and the Common-Sergeant, are more logical, and more inflexible, and better lawyers, than the corresponding dignitaries in our sessions towns. The counsel are keener in their conduct of defenses than are the majority of circuit and session counsel; and at the same time the tone of their cross-examinations is not so gentlemanly, and altogether they are less scrupulous in their method of conducting the cases entrusted to them. The witnesses are more intelligent and less trustworthy than country witnesses. The officers of the court keep silence more efficiently, and at the same time are more offensive in their general deportment than the officers of any other court in the kingdom. And lastly, the degree of the prisoners' guilt seems to take a wider scope than it does in cases tried on circuit. More innocent men are charged with crime and more guilty men escape at the Old Bailey than at any other court in the kingdom; because the juries, being Londoners, are more accustomed to look upon

the niceties of evidence from a legal point of view, and in many cases
come into the jury-box with exaggerated views of what constitutes a
"reasonable doubt," and so are disposed to give a verdict for the prisoner, when a country jury would convict.

Known since 1834 as the Central Criminal Court, the Old Bailey
is England's most important Crown court. The court may try crimes
from any part of the country. The courthouse was originally built in
1539, rebuilt in 1774, and demolished in 1902. Today the Old Bailey sits
on the site of the Newgate Prison. The Central Criminal Court was
established in 1834 and empowered to try treasons, murders, felonies,
and misdemeanours, as well as offences committed on the high seas
and matters previously tried at the Admiralty sessions.

To get a feel for the courthouse and the courtroom, the following excerpt is particularly helpful. The depictions that follow, while
perhaps typical of the day-to-day operation of the court, would not
capture the greater solemnity attached to a trial of the importance
of M'Naughten's with the distinguished counsel and presiding jurists.
Nevertheless, it does give us an unusually colourful picture of the Old
Bailey as it was in Victorian London.

> The Old Bailey! Ugly words ... associated (in a Londoners' mind, at
> all events) with greasy squalor, crime of every description, in a cold,
> bleak-looking prison, with an awful little iron door, three feet or so
> from the ground, trial by jury, black caps, bullying counsel, a "visibly
> affected" judge, prevaricating witnesses, and a miserable, trembling,
> damp prisoner in the dock. The Old Bailey ... or rather the Central
> Criminal Court, held at the Old Bailey ... is, *par excellence*, the crim-
> inal court of the country. In it all the excellences and all the disadvan-
> tages of our criminal procedures are developed to an extraordinary
> degree. The Old Bailey juries are at once more clearsighted and more
> pig-headed than any country jury. The local judges ...that is to say, the
> Recorder and the Common-Serjeant ... are more logical, and more
> inflexible, and better lawyers than the corresponding dignitaries in
> our sessions towns. The counsel are keener in their conduct of de-
> fences than are the majority of circuit and session counsel; and at the
> same time the tone of their cross-examinations is not so gentlemanly,
> and altogether they are less scrupulous in their method of conducting
> the cases entrusted to them. The witnesses are more intelligent and

M'NAUGHTEN'S TRIAL AT CENTRAL CRIMINAL COURT, OLD BAILEY
SOURCE: ILLUSTRATED LONDON NEWS, 11 FEBRUARY 1843

less trustworthy than country witnesses. The officers of the court keep silence more efficiently, and at the same time are more offensive in their general deportment than the officers of any other court in the kingdom. And lastly, the degree of the prisoners' guilt seems to take a wider scope than it does in cases tried on circuit. More innocent men are charged with crime and more guilty men escape at the Old Bailey than at any other court in the kingdom; because the juries, being Londoners, are more accustomed to look upon the niceties of evidence from a legal point of view, and in many cases come into the jury-box with exaggerated views of what constitutes a "reasonable doubt," and so are disposed to give a verdict for the prisoner, when a country jury would convict. The Old Bailey, although extremely inconvenient, is beautifully compact. You can be detained there between the time of your committal and your trial . . . you can be tried there, sentenced there, condemned-celled there, and comfortably hanged and buried there, without having to leave the building, except for the purpose of going on to the scaffold. Indeed, recent legislation has removed even this exception, and now there is no occasion to go outside the four walls of the building at all . . . the thing is done in the paved yard that separates the court-house from the prison. It is as though you were tried in the drawing-room, confined in the scullery, and hanged in the back garden.

The court-house contains, besides ample accommodation for the judges, alder men, common-councilmen, sheriffs, and under-sheriffs, two large courts, called the Old Court and New Court, and two or three secondary courts, which are only used when the pressure of business is rather heavy. The gravest offences are usually tried in the Old Court on the Wednesday or Thursday after the commencement of the session, on which days one or two of the judges from Westminster sit at the Old Bailey. The arrangement of the Old Court may be taken as a tolerably fair sample of a criminal court. The bench occupies one side of the court, the dock faces it. On the right side of the bench are the jury-box and the witness-box; on the left are the seats for privileged witnesses and visitors, and also for the reporters and jurymen in waiting. The space bounded by the bench on one side, the dock on another, the jury-box on a third, and the reporters' box on the fourth, is occupied by counsel and attorneys, the larger half being assigned to counsel. Over the dock is the public gallery, to which admission was formerly obtained by payment of a fee to the warder. It is now free to about thirty of the public at large at one time, who can see nothing of the prisoner except his scalp, and hear very little of what is going on.

The form in which a criminal trial is conducted is briefly as follows: The case is submitted to the grand jury, and if, on examination of one or more of the witnesses for the prosecution, they find a *prima facie* case against the prisoner, a "true bill" is found, and handed to the clerk of arraigns in open court. The prisoner is then called upon to plead; and, in the event of his pleading "guilty", the facts of the case are briefly stated by counsel, together with a statement of a previous conviction, if the prisoner is an old offender, and the judge passes sentence. If the prisoner pleads "not guilty", the trial proceeds in the following form. The indictment and plea are both read over to the jury by the clerk of arraigns, and they are charged by him to try whether the prisoner is "guilty" or "not guilty." The counsel for the prosecution then opens the case briefly or at length, as its nature may suggest, and then proceeds to call witnesses for the prosecution. At the close of the "examination in chief" of each witness, the counsel for the defence (or, in the absence of counsel for the defence, the prisoner himself) cross-examines. At the conclusion of the examination and cross-examination of the witnesses for the prosecution, the counsel for the prosecution has the privilege of summing up the arguments that support his case. If witnesses are called by the defence, the defending counsel has, also, the right to sum up; and in that case the counsel for the prosecution has a right of reply. The matter is then left in the hands of the judge, who "sums up," placing the facts before the jury, pointing out discrepancies in the evidence, clearing the case of all superfluous matter, and directing them in all the points of law that arise in the case. The jury then consider their verdict, and, when they are agreed, give it in open court, and the prisoner at bar is asked whether he has anything to say why the sentence of law shall not be passed upon him. This question is little more than a matter of form, and the judge rarely waits for an answer, but proceeds immediately to pass sentence on the prisoner.

A visitor at the Old Bailey, to whom the courts of Westminster of Guildhall are familiar, will probably be very much struck with the difference between the manner in which Nisi Prius and the criminal barristers are treated by the officials of their respective Courts. At Westminster the ushers, who are most unpleasant in their demeanour towards the public at large, are as deferential in their tone to the bar as so many club servants. Like Kathleen's cow, though vicious to others, they are gentle to them. Indeed, at Westminster the bar are treated by all the officials as gentlemen of position have a right to expect to be. But at the Old Bailey it is otherwise. They appear to be on familiar terms with criers, ushers, thieves' attorneys, clerks and police serjeants. Attorney's clerks, of Israelitish aspect, buttonhole them; bumptious criers elbow them right and left, and the policemen on duty at the bar-entrance chaffs them with haughty condescension. Of course there are many gentlemen at the criminal bar whose professional position overawes even this overbearing functionary; but it unfortunately happens that there are a great many needy and unscrupulous practitioners at the Old Bailey, who find it to their advantage to adopt conciliatory policy towards everybody in office; for it is an unfortunate fact, that almost everybody in office has it in his power, directly or indirectly, to do an Old Bailey barrister a good turn. "Dockers", or briefs handed directly from the prisoner in the dock to counsel, without the expensive intervention of an attorney, are distributed pretty well at the discretion of the warder in the dock, or of the gaoler to whose custody the prisoner has been entrusted since his committal; and there are a few needy barristers who are not ashamed to allow their clerks to tout among prisoners' friends for briefs for half fees. It is only fair to state, that the counsel who resort to these ungentlemanly dodges form but a small proportion of the barristers who practise at the Old Bailey; but still they are sufficiently numerous to affect most seriously the tone that is adopted by Old Bailey officials towards the bar as a body.

The conventional Old Bailey barrister, however, is a type that is gradually dying out. The rising men at the criminal bar are certainly far from being all that could be desired; but their tone, in cross-examination, is more gentlemanly than that commonly in vogue among the Old Bailey barristers of twenty years since. There are a few among them who occasionally attempt to bully, not only the witnesses, but even the judge and jury; but they always get the worst of it. As a rule, cross-examinations are conducted more fairly than they were, and a determination to convict at any price is rarer on the part of a prosecuting counsel than of yore. If some means could be adopted to clear the court of the touting counsel, or, at all events, to render their discreditable tactics inoperative, a great change for the better would be effected in the tone adopted towards the bar by the officials about the court. As it is, it is almost impossible for a young counsel to retain his self-respect in the face of the annoying familiarities of the underlings with whom he is brought into contact. On the occasion of our last visit to the Old Bailey, during a trial of Jeffrey for the murder of his son, we happened to witness a dispute between an insolent policeman stationed at the bar-entrance, and a young barrister in robes, who was evidently not an *habitué* of that court. The barrister had a friend with him, and he wanted to get a place for his friend, either in the bar seats, or in the seats set aside for friends of the bench and bar. The policeman in question placed his arm across the door, and absolutely refused to allow either the barrister or his friend to enter, on the ground that the court was quite full. The barrister sent his card to the under-sheriff, who immediately gave directions that both were to be admitted to the bar-seats, which were occupied by about a fourth of the number which they could conveniently accommodate, about half the people occupying them being friends of counsel who, we suppose, were on more intimate terms with the discourteous functionary than was the barrister in question. On another occasion it came to our knowledge that a barrister, who did not habitually practice at the Old Bailey, was refused admission at the bar entrance to the court-house by the police-sergeant stationed there. He showed his card, but without avail, and eventually he expressed his intention of forcing his way past the policeman, and told that official that if he stopped him he would do so at his peril. The policeman allowed him to pass, but actually told another constable to follow him to the robing-room, to see whether he had any right there or not. The barrister, naturally annoyed at being thus conveyed in custody through the building, complained to one of the under-sheriffs for the time being, but without obtaining the slightest redress. Of course his system of impertinence has the effect of confining the Old Bailey practice to a thick-skinned few; but it does not tend to elevate the tone of the bar (of which the Old Bailey barrister is unfortunately generally taken as a type); and those who are jealous for the honour of the profession should take steps to do away with it.

To a stranger, a criminal trial is always an interesting sight. If the prisoner happens to be charged with a crime of magnitude, he has become quite a public character by the time he enters the dock to take his trial; and it is always interesting to see how far a public character corresponds with the ideal which we have formed for him. Then his demeanour in the dock, influenced, as it often is, by the fluctuating character of the evidence for and against him, possesses a grim interest for the unaccustomed spectator. He is witnessing a real sensation drama, and as the case draws to a close, if the evidence has been very conflicting, he feels an interest in the issue akin to that with which a sporting man would take in the running of a great race. Then the deliberations of the jury on their verdict, the sharp, anxious look which the prisoner casts ever and anon towards them, the deep breath that he draws as the jury resume their places, the trembling anxiety, or, more affecting still, the preternaturally compressed lips and contracted brow, with which he awaits the publication of their verdict, and his great, deep sigh of relief when he knows the worst, must possess a painful interest for all but those whom familiarity with such scenes has hardened. Then comes the sentence, followed, perhaps, by a woman's shriek from the gallery, and all is over, as far as the spectator is concerned. The next case is called on, and new facts and new faces soon obliterate any painful effect which the trial may have had upon his mind.

Probably the first impression on the mind of a man who visits the Old Bailey for the first time is that he never saw so many ugly people collected in any one place before. The judges are not handsome men, as a rule, the aldermen on the bench never are; barristers, especially Old Bailey barristers, are the ugliest of professional men, excepting always solicitors; the jury have a bull-headed look about them that suggests that they have been designedly selected from the most stupid of their class; the reporters are usually dirty, and of evil savour, the understrappers have a bloated, overfed, Bumble-like look about them, which is always a particularly annoying thing to a sensitive mind; and the prisoner, of course, looks (whether guilty or innocent) the most ruffianly of mankind, for he stands in the dock. We remember seeing a man tried for burglary some time since, and we came to the conclusion that he had the most villainous face with which a man could be cursed. The case against him rested on the testimony of as nice-looking and ingenious a lad as ever stepped into a witness-box. But, unfortunately for the ingenious lad, a clear *alibi* was established, the prisoner was immediately acquitted, and the nice boy, his accuser, was trotted into the dock on a charge of perjury. The principal witness against him was the former prisoner, and we were perfectly astounded at the false estimate we had formed of their respective physiognomies. The former prisoner's face was, we found, homely enough; but it absolutely beamed with honest enthusiasm in the cause of justice, while the nice lad's countenance turned out to be the very type of sly, insidious rascality. It is astounding how the atmosphere of the dock inverts the countenance of any one who may happen to be in it. And this leads us to the consideration how surpassingly beautiful must the ballet-girl have been, who, even in the dock, exercised so extraordinary a fascination over a learned deputy-judge at the Middlesex sessions not long ago. We remember once to have heard a well-known counsel, who was defending a singularly ill-favoured prisoner, say to the jury, "Gentlemen, you must not allow yourselves to be carried away by any effect which the prisoner's appearance may have upon you. Remember, he is in the dock; and I will undertake to say, that if my lord were to be taken from the bench upon which he is sitting, and placed where the prisoner is now standing, you, who are unaccustomed to criminal trials, would find, even in his lordship's face, indications of crime which you would look for in vain in any other situation!" In fairness we withhold the learned judge's name.

There was no doubt in anyone's mind that M'Naughten's was to be an interesting trial. He was charged with a crime of great magnitude and, as so often happened to defendants whose cases were tried at the Old Bailey, he had become quite a well-known character by the time he entered the dock on March 3rd, only six weeks after shooting Edward Drummond. Therefore, many in the courtroom were anxious to see how well this public character corresponded with the image they had formed while devouring stories in all the London papers about "M'Naughten the Assassin." The prestigious reputation of the counsel assembled for the Crown and for M'Naughten's defence also contributed to the enormity and celebrity of the trial.

Leading the defence team was a rising star in British legal circles, the thirty-nine-year-old Sir Alexander Cockburn. A highly regarded lawyer who had been made Queen's Counsel two years before (and who would go on to become attorney general then Lord Chief Justice of England), Cockburn was known to be a very colourful and unorthodox figure (fond of socializing and carousing but never compromising the integrity of his position) who had distinguished himself by the exceptionally detailed manner of his preparation for cases. He was renowned for acquainting himself thoroughly with the subject matter at issue, and was much in demand as a lawyer for he was recognized as a brilliant orator and tenacious advocate – a hard fighter but a fair one. There was probably no barrister in England at the time more suited to a *cause célebre* trial than Alexander Cockburn.

Not having been represented by counsel in his various appearances leading up to the trial, M'Naughten, being in possession of considerable funds, was able to pay a significant retainer for a top-notch lawyer and very wisely it seems, settled on one of the best the English legal world had to offer. While M'Naughten was able to pay what were surely hefty legal fees, there was also no doubt that Cockburn would have had a tremendous interest in becoming involved in a trial of such notoriety.

Prosecuting for the Crown, was the solicitor general of England, Sir William Follett. At forty-five, Follett was a slightly older man than

SIR ALEXANDER COCKBURN, 1802—1880, LORD CHIEF JUSTICE OF
ENGLAND (FROM 1859) SOURCE: PORTRAIT BY A.D. COOPER,
NATIONAL PORTRAIT GALLERY, LONDON

Cockburn, but was also an eminent and accomplished lawyer who dif-
fered in style, manner, and personal appearance yet who had risen early
in his legal career to a position of considerable prominence through his
gifts as a public speaker. Not that it would have much if any bearing on
the outcome of the case, but whereas Follett had most recently been
practising law almost exclusively in London, Cockburn was a barrister

of the Western Circuit and had travelled from New Sarum (Salisbury) specifically to represent M'Naughten. The news that Cockburn was to represent M'Naughten was favourably received by Follett (and indeed by the press corps too) for there was a sense at the time that the quality of the bar at the Old Bailey had been declining in recent years, lawyers being seen as rather rough and rude, hostile to outsiders. It would have been somewhat of a rarity, therefore, to see a barrister of Cockburn's calibre in the Central Criminal Court.

At ten o'clock M'Naughten was placed at the bar. He walked to the dock with a firm step, and bowed respectfully to the court. There was "nothing very striking in the personal appearance of the man," wrote *Town and Country* magazine. He was a decently dressed, fair-haired, fair-skinned, smooth-faced Scotsman, above average height, with a mournful expression on his face. "His air was sad, subdued and list-- less." Though pensive and pale, there appeared a strange and vacant glare about his eyes as he alternately surveyed the judges and the eager, attentive crowd. In all his wandering looks and floating gaze, there was not the slightest attempt at, or appearance, of acting. He firmly yet mildly pleaded "[n]ot guilty" to the indictment.

At five minutes past eleven Solicitor General Sir William Follett rose to state the case on behalf of the Crown.[1] As he began, there was an anxious restlessness about his manner, and as he spoke of the amiable character of Mr. Drummond and his untimely and undesired fate, his lips quivered, his eyes moistened, and he gave free scope and vent to his feelings:

> "May it please you, my Lord, gentlemen of the jury, you are assembled here to-day to discharge a most solemn and important duty. You will have to decide whether the prisoner at the bar be guilty or not guilty of the awful crime with which he stands charged; and I feel, gentlemen, that I shall best discharge my duty to the Crown and to the public, on whose behalf I appear here to-day, if I proceed at once to state, as calmly and dispassionately as I can, all the facts and circumstances connected with this melancholy case.
>
> "Mr. Drummond, whose death we are to inquire into this day, was, as you all know probably, the private secretary of Sir Robert Peel, and was on terms of friendship and intimacy with him. By virtue of his office he occupied apartments in the official residence of the Prime

M'NAUGHTEN SKETCH WITH SIGNATURE
SOURCE: SCOTCH REFORMERS GAZETTE, 4 MARCH 1843

Minister of this country. He was in the constant habit of passing from those rooms to the private residence of Sir R. Peel, in Whitehall Gardens; and it will be proved to you that the prisoner at the bar, for many days before the fatal occurrence took place, was seen loitering about those spots, and watching the persons who went in and out of the public offices and the houses in Whitehall Gardens.

"This conduct had attracted attention, and he was spoken to by some soldiers, who had observed him, as well as by the police; but, unfortunately, no steps were taken to remove him. On Friday, January 20, Mr. Drummond left his apartments in Downing Street, and went to the Treasury, and thence to the Admiralty, in company with Lord Haddington, whom he left at the Admiralty, and proceeded alone to Drummond's banking-house, at Charing Cross; on his return from which, when near the 'Salopian' coffee-house, the prisoner at the bar – for there can be no doubt of his identity – came behind him, and discharged a pistol almost close to him.

"After discharging that pistol, the prisoner drew another from his breast, presented it at Mr. Drummond, and was in the act of firing it at him when a policeman, who had observed him from the opposite side of the street, ran across the road and threw his arms about him; and other persons also assisted the policeman to secure the prisoner, who, in struggling with them, discharged the second pistol, but luckily without doing any mischief. The prisoner was then seized and taken to the police station-house, in Gardner's Lane, where he was searched, and there were found on his person two five pound notes, four sovereigns, and a deposit receipt for 745£ from the Glasgow Bank.

"Among some other trifling articles that were found in his pockets, were ten copper percussion caps, which fitted the nipples of the pistols he had discharged in the manner I have described; and afterwards, upon searching his lodgings, bullets were also found to match the barrels of those very pistols. Mr. Drummond, after the pistol which wounded him was fired, staggered from the effect of the shot, but did not fall. He walked, I believe, almost without assistance, back to the banking-house. A medical gentleman in the neighbourhood was sent for, and after a short time Mr. Drummond was removed in his own carriage to his private residence. For some time hopes were entertained of his recovery, and that the wound would not prove fatal; but, unfortunately, those hopes were abortive. He lingered in great pain for some days, and died on Wednesday, January 25.

"Gentlemen, his death is deeply, and I may say permanently, regretted; for he was beloved, esteemed, and valued by all who knew him. He was of a disposition so amiable that it was impossible he could have had any personal enemies. You will naturally ask, then, gentlemen, who was the prisoner at the bar, and what could induce him to deprive of life a being so unoffending? Mr. Drummond was not only without any personal enemies, but he did not fill any prominent situation before the public. He did not hold that situation in public life which would render him obnoxious to political enemies, but he was the private secretary of the principal Minister of the Crown, often an inmate of his house, and constantly passing therefore to the public offices in Downing Street and the neighbourhood, about which the prisoner was observed to be loitering and watching. You will be satisfied, from the facts of the case, from the threats used by the prisoner before he committed his crime, and his declarations afterwards, that it was not the life of Mr. Drummond that he sought. You will be satisfied that it was the life of Sir Robert Peel that he desired to take, and that it was his life that he believed he was destroying when he discharged the fatal pistol against the person of Mr. Drummond.

"Gentlemen, the nature of his crime is not altered by this circumstance, but it affords a reason for it. I need not tell you that he is guilty of murder, although he might have mistaken the person against whom he discharged the pistol. Of the guilt of the prisoner – of the fact of his having deprived Mr. Drummond of life – it is impossible I can suggest a doubt; it is impossible that any doubt can be suggested that the crime was committed, and that that crime was murder. But I cannot conceal from you, because I know, from applications which have been made to this Court, and the depositions which have been made on behalf of the prisoner, that it is intended to rest the defense on the plea, that he was insane at the time he committed the crime; and, gentlemen, it will be your painful duty – for painful it must be – to decide whether he was in that degree of insanity at the time he committed that crime which would render him not a responsible agent, and not answerable to the laws of his country for the offence of which he has been guilty. This defense is a difficult one at all times; for while, on the one hand, everyone must be anxious that an unconscious being should not suffer, yet, on the other hand, the public safety requires that this defense should not be too readily listened to; and, above all, the public safety requires that the atrocious nature of the act itself, and the circumstances under which it was committed, should not form any ingredient in that defense.

"There are few crimes that are committed, and, above all, crimes of an atrocious nature like this, that are not committed by persons

labouring under some morbid affection of the mind; and it is difficult for well-regulated minds to understand the motives which lead
to such offences in the absence of that morbid affection of the mind.
I believe that the truth of this remark will be more especially proved
when attacks are directed to persons holding high and important stations in the nation. If you look back upon the pages of history, and
consider the facts connected with the death of persons whose lives
have been destroyed by the hands of assassins, you will be satisfied, in
one moment, of the truth of that proposition.

"But we need not look far back; occurrences of our own times furnish us with sufficient instances for illustration. If you look at a neigh-
bouring country, you will see there that persons in broad day, in the
crowded streets of the metropolis of France, without any precaution
for their own safety, without any attempt to escape, in the midst of the
people, close to the armed guards of the King, have discharged their
weapons at the person of the sovereign of the country. What motive
had they? We know of none but that of an ill-regulated mind, worked
upon by morbid political feeling. We have seen other instances in
France of parties, having laid plans to assist themselves in their escape,
discharging infernal instruments in the streets of Paris, regardless of
how many and what lives they destroyed, provided they could reach
the person of the sovereign.[2] I refer to these things, gentlemen, to
show that the circumstances attendant upon the crime itself afford no
grounds for holding that the parties committing it are not responsible
to the laws of their country.

"But I know that in this case the defense on the part of the prisoner will not rest upon this, but that evidence will be offered to show
that the prisoner was not in a sane state of mind at the time he committed the crime; and knowing that, I feel that I ought, in this stage
of the case, to refer to some authorities, and state my view of the
principles of the English law. It will be open to my learned friend,
whose powerful assistance I am happy to see the prisoner will have, to
comment upon that, and to differ from me if he thinks I am wrong. It
has been the custom in these cases to refer to proceedings of authority, and to the *dicta* of judges who have tried similar questions; not
that I mean to say for one moment that it is a question of law; on
the contrary, the question to be decided by you is a question of fact,
a question of common sense and belief. The whole question will turn

upon this: if you believe the prisoner at the bar at the time he committed this act was not a responsible agent; if you believe that when he fired the pistol he was incapable of distinguishing between right and wrong; if you believe that he was under the influence and control of some disease of the mind which prevented him from being conscious that he was committing a crime; if you believe that he did not know he was violating the law both of God and man: then, undoubtedly, he is entitled to your acquittal.

"It is my duty, subject to the correction of my Lord and to the observations of my learned friend, to tell you that nothing short of that will excuse him upon the principle of the English law. To excuse him it will not be sufficient that he laboured under partial insanity upon some subjects – that he had a morbid delusion of mind upon some subjects, which could not exist in a wholly sane person; that is not enough, if he had that degree of intellect which enabled him to know and distinguish between right and wrong, if he knew what would be the effects of his crime, and consciously committed it, and if with that consciousness he willfully committed it. I shall be able to show you, gentlemen, with regard to the authorities upon this point that observations have been made to the effect that they have attempted to define the law too strictly; but such observations were made without regard to the object of those authorities.

"It is impossible beforehand to lay down any definition of the kind of madness which will excuse the crime of murder; the disease assumes such different forms and such various shapes, and acts in such opposite ways, that you cannot define it. But you may lay down the principles of law which are applicable to it; and they are laid down, and uniformly laid down in the same way, that it is a question for the jury to take into their consideration whether the party was a responsible agent when he committed the crime, whether he then knew right from wrong, whether he was conscious that he was offending against the law of his country and nature, and whether he did it willfully.

"Gentlemen, the public safety is the object of all law; the public safety is entrusted solely to the protection of courts of criminal judicature, and to juries who administer justice under the law; and it is with a view to the public safety that the law is laid down by legal authorities principally for the guidance of juries who have to decide upon questions of this nature."

In support of his opening remarks, Fowlett then cited passages from earlier notable cases, those of Hale and Arnold, Leblanc and Bowler, and of Lord Ferrer in 1760:

"If there be a total permanent want of reason, it will acquit the prisoner; if there be a total temporary want of it when the offence was committed, it will acquit the prisoner; but if there be only a partial degree of insanity mixed with a partial degree of reason not a full and complete use of reason, but (as Lord Hale carefully and emphatically expresses himself) a competent use of it sufficient to have restrained those passions which produced crime – if there be thought and design, a faculty to distinguish the nature of actions, to discern the difference between moral good and evil; then, upon the fact of the offence proved, the judgment of the law must take place."

He continued:

"There is certainly one other case to which I should refer. It is not the authority of a judge; but it is one of the most celebrated cases of the kind. I allude to the trial of Hadfield,[3] on a charge of high treason, for firing at King George the 3rd. He was defended by Lord Erskine, who made one of the most eloquent and able speeches, probably, that was ever delivered at the bar; and he entered at that time much into the law of insanity, and the nature of the insanity that would excuse the prisoner.

"In that case, I believe, no doubt could be entertained of the insanity of the prisoner, and the Court upon that ground, stopped the trial. But in the course of that trial Lord Erskine said the prisoner must be shown to labour under some delusion, that it must also be shown that he committed the act in consequence of that delusion. That was the ground upon which Lord Erskine put the defense. But, as was remarked by the present Lord Chief Justice of the Court of Queen's Bench,[4] the counsel for the prisoner would only state so much of the law as was applicable to the defense of the prisoner; and I cannot help thinking that there may be many cases in which the prisoner may be excused from the consequences of a crime that would not fall under the description of Lord Erskine.

"A party may have that state of mind which would render him wholly unconscious of right and wrong; he may have that state of mind which makes him not aware that he is committing a crime, and yet the crime may not be the offspring of any delusion he labours under; nor do I think it is right in another point of view. I think that parties may be liable to be punished under the law, although they did labour under a delusion, and although the act may have been committed under that delusion. I think, therefore, the doctrine of Lord Erskine is not true in either way to its fullest extent.

"I will put one case, that which Lord Erskine refers to in that celebrated speech. He speaks of two brothers – one of whom laboured under the morbid delusion that the other was his enemy, and conspiring against him; and in consequence of that delusion he made a will, in which he disinherited that brother. The question arose as to whether that will could be set aside; and it was held that the will was made under circumstances which rendered it invalid. Now, I cannot help thinking that, upon the principles of the English laws, if that brother was aware of the consequences of what he did; if he knew the difference between right and wrong and with that knowledge and consciousness had deprived his brother of life, he would have been guilty of murder. I own that in that case the ground laid down does not appear satisfactory either in favour of, or against the principle.

"The next case, gentlemen, is that which took place here in the year 1812, when Bellingham was tried for the murder of Mr. Perceval, and convicted of that offence. He was tried in this Court before Lord Chief Justice Mansfield, Sir James Mansfield, who laid down the law in this way:

> In another part of the prisoner's defense, which was not, however, urged by himself, it was attempted to be proved that at the time of the commission of the crime he was insane. With respect to this the law was extremely clear. If a man were deprived of all power of reasoning, so as not to be able to distinguish whether it was right or wrong to commit the most wicked transaction, he could not do an act against the law. Such a man, so destitute of all power of judgment, could have no intention at all.
>
> In order to support this defense, however, it ought to be proved, by the most distinct and unquestionable evidence, that the criminal was incapable of judging between right and

wrong. It must, in fact, be proved beyond all doubt that, at the time he committed the atrocious act with which he stood charged, he did not consider that murder was a crime against the laws of God and nature. There was no other proof of insanity which would excuse murder or any other crime. There were various species of insanity. Some human creatures were void of all power of reasoning from their birth; such could not be guilty of any crime.

There was another species of madness, in which persons were subject to temporary paroxysms, in which they were guilty of acts of extravagance; this was called lunacy. If these persons were to commit a crime when they were not affected with the malady, they would be, to all intents and purposes, amenable to justice. So long as they could distinguish between good from evil, so long would they be answerable for their conduct.

There was a third species of insanity, in which the patient fancied the existence of injury, and sought an opportunity of gratifying revenge by some hostile act. If such a person were capable in other respects of distinguishing right from wrong, there was no excuse for any act of atrocity which he might commit under the description of insanity.[5]

"Now from the last observation of the learned judge who tried that cause, it appears to me, gentlemen, that a party may labour under the delusion of having received injury, but if he be able to distinguish between right and wrong, and if he be conscious of the nature of the crime, the delusion will not excuse him from punishment for that crime."

Here Follett referred to the case of *R. v. Oxford*,[6] in which Lord Lyndhurst approved of the direction in Bellingham's case, and told the jury that "they must be satisfied, before they could acquit the prisoner on the ground of insanity, that he did not know, when he committed the act, what the effect of it, if fatal, would be, with reference to the crime of murder." The question was, did he know that he was committing an offence against the laws of God and nature?

"I have referred to these authorities for the purpose of enabling you, gentlemen of the jury, to judge of the evidence which will, beyond doubt, be produced on behalf of the prisoner, that you may compare the circumstances and consider whether the prisoner at the bar was in that state of mind which rendered him not responsible for the crime he committed. But, knowing the nature and object of that evidence, I think I should not discharge my duty to the public or to the Crown, if I did not lay before you on my part what is known respecting the history of the prisoner and what is known of his conduct directly before his apprehension.

"It is right I should tell you, at least, that I do not mean to go into any observations which persons may have particularly directed to the state of mind of individuals in similar circumstances, but to show in what way the prisoner has conducted himself in his past life, the way in which he managed his business, the mode and manner of his living, what care he took of himself, and how he was left by all his connections to manage his own affairs, and continued to do so down to the very hour of his defense.

"It appears that he has carried on the business of a wood-turner in Glasgow, and that his father had carried on the same business before him. They did work together, but he left his father in consequence of some dispute between them, and set up on his own account as a wood-turner in Glasgow. He continued carrying on that business down to the end of the year 1840. He then left that business, and went and took lodgings in Glasgow with a person of the name of Patterson. He seems to have been of very sober, prudent, and saving habits, and had, during the time he was in business in Glasgow, saved a considerable sum of money by the time he retired at the close of the year 1840.

"He afterwards occasionally came to London, and it appears that he has been upon the continent. While in London he resided with a Mrs. Dutton, who lives at No.7, Poplar Row, Newington, and he was residing there when he committed the crime with which he now stands charged. While at Glasgow he attended lectures on natural philosophy at the Mechanics' Institution in that city, and he took an active part in various alterations which were made in the rules of that institution, and also in the arrangement of the rooms and the conveniences of the building.

"He was in the habit of getting books from the library; he was known to all the persons who frequented that institution, and, moreover, he afterwards attended lectures on anatomy, and made considerable progress in that science. I shall call one of the persons whose lectures he attended. He came first to London in July 1841, when he went to the house of Mrs. Dutton and lodged there continually, therefore she has had an opportunity of seeing him and noticing his habits for the last year and a half. He had been ill in her house, and she attended him, and she will be examined as a witness. She will tell you, gentlemen, that, as far as she could see, there was nothing extraordinary in his conduct.

"On the morning of the day on which the crime was committed she spoke to him, and assisted him in putting on part of his dress, but neither then nor when he left the house did she observe anything extraordinary in his manner or demeanor, and she had no reason at any time to consider him insane. Gentlemen, I stated that he came here in July 1841. Before that he had opened an account with the Bank of Glasgow, upon what is called a deposit receipt. He afterwards shifted that to the London Joint Stock Bank, and he had applied to the persons in London to give him 5£ on the deposit, which was for about 750£. They said it was contrary to usage to do it, and he then drew out the 750£, and obtained the 5£ he wanted, and then, when he got that sum of money, he paid the other back. But on the 23rd May of last year, desiring to transfer his account to the Glasgow Bank again, he wrote this letter:

I hereby intimate to you that I will require the money, ten days from this date, which I deposited in the London Joint Stock Bank, through you. The account is for 745£; the account is dated August 28, 1841, but is not numbered. As it would put me to some inconvenience to give personal intimation, and then remain in London till the eleven days' notice agreed upon had expired, I trust this will be considered sufficient. Yours, &c, Daniel M'Naughten.

"Well, upon that, gentlemen, the account was transferred to the Bank of Glasgow, and he received a deposit receipt from the Bank of Glasgow for the larger sum, specified in the deposit receipt found upon him at the time of his apprehension. Another letter was written by him in July 1842, which will be read to you, as it will be proved that he went to the shop of a gunsmith in the neighbourhood of Glasgow, where he bought the pistols, and bargained with the man for them, expressing a wish to have them of the same size, and desiring the man, if he had not them himself, to get them for him. In that month, he bought the pistols, and in that month he came to London, and again in the September following.

"But on the 19th of July he wrote the letter relating to his entering into some business or partnership in London, in consequence of an advertisement published in a London newspaper – the *Spectator* – of the 16th of that month as follows:

OPTIONAL PARTNERSHIP – Any gentleman having 1,000£ may invest them, on the most advantageous terms, in a very genteel business in London, attended with no risk, with the option, within a given period, of becoming a partner, and of ultimately succeeding to the whole business. In the meantime, security and liberal interest will be given for the money. – Apply by letter to "B.B.," Mr. Hilton's, bookseller, Penton Street, Pentonvllle.

"On the 21st of July the advertiser received from the prisoner the following letter:

Sir, my attention has been attracted to your advertisement in the *Spectator* newspaper, and as I am unemployed at present, and very anxious to obtain some, I have been induced to write, requesting you to state some particulars regarding the nature of the business which you are engaged. If immediate employment can be given or otherwise, what sort of security will be given for the money, and how much interest? I may mention that I have been engaged in business on my own account for a few years, am under 30 years of age, and of very active and sober habits. The capital which I possess has been acquired by the most vigilant industry, but unfortunately does not amount to the exact sum specified in your advertisement. If nothing less will do, I will be sorry for it, but cannot help it; if otherwise, have the goodness to write me at your earliest convenience, and address "D.M.M.," 90 Clyde Street, Anderton's, Frontland, top flat.

"He then came to London in that same month, and I shall call before you some of his friends and acquaintances who had known him in Glasgow, and who met with him and had various conversations with him, and with whom he walked by the house of Sir Robert Peel;

particularly, evidence will be given with regard to a conversation with the prisoner in the month of November 1842. He remained in London from that time down to the time when he committed the offence, in the month of January, and still lodged in Mrs. Dutton's house.

"Other persons at that time were acquainted with the prisoner; these persons I will put into the witness-box – persons conversant with his manners and habits, as well as his landlady, in order that you may form an opinion whether or not the prisoner was a responsible agent at the time he committed the offence. On the other side, no doubt evidence will be offered to prove his insanity; and certainly it is some consolation to me, in the discharge of a painful duty, to know that the interests of the prisoner will be most ably and powerfully attended to; but it will be your duty, and no doubt your desire also, to most attentively listen to the evidence on both sides, and to weigh the one against the other.

"What the precise nature or the details of the evidence on the part of the prisoner may be, I cannot say. I know not the exact nature of it, nor its extent; but when it is adduced, you will say, upon that evidence, are you or are you not satisfied that the prisoner was, at the time he committed this crime, a responsible agent, that he did know right from wrong, and that he was aware of the consequences of the act which he committed? If you think he was not, he ought to be acquitted. If that should be the result of the evidence he will be entitled to your acquittal. But if it fall short of that, if you think he was a responsible agent, I need not say to you that public justice requires a different verdict. It is a painful duty, gentlemen, but it is a duty which must be faithfully discharged; and I am perfectly satisfied that when you have heard the witnesses, when you have maturely deliberated upon and considered the evidence, your verdict will be one of justice between the public and the prisoner."

Follett's account of what constitutes "insanity" in this opening address was, in a legal sense, rather confused. Clearly, what the prosecution was suggesting was that unless the accused was fully incompetent in all aspects of his thinking, he was to be considered "sane." As we shall see, the law requires a more nuanced determination. In addition to the argument as to the state of the law, it is clear that the Crown tactic was intended to show that all who observed M'Naughten up to the date of the offence noted nothing conspicuous in his behaviour such that one could infer that he was insane. This, it will be recalled, was the approach taken by the press in the early days of reporting upon the case. However, as the information continued to pour in, the press abandoned this position and was of the view that M'Naughten was clearly insane at the time of the killing.

Chapter Fourteen

THE TWENTY-SIX WITNESSES called by the Crown to give evidence were, for the most part, the same as had testified previously at the hearing before the grand jury and then again before the coroner's inquest. Police constable James Silver described his apprehension of the accused and explained how, during the course of struggling with M'Naughten at the time of his arrest, the second pistol was discharged. The items seized upon his arrest were catalogued as before and Cockburn, rightly, declined to examine this witness in cross-examination other than to ask an innocuous question about the timing of the event.

Benjamin Weston, the office porter who heard M'Naughten's first pistol shot and turned to witness what happened in the following few minutes, confirmed what was reported by Silver, and again drew very little in the way of cross-examination from Cockburn. Richard Jackson the apothecary, Bransby Blake Cooper the physician, and George James Guthrie the surgeon once more described the immediate treatment of Drummond after the shooting and through to the ultimate cause of his death.

But after these requisite preliminaries, the proceedings took a somewhat dramatic turn when John Tierney, police inspector at A Division where M'Naughten was held following his arrest, took the stand. Tierney described his encounter with M'Naughten during his first night in custody:

"On the evening of the 20th of January I went to the station-house in Gardener's Lane, where I found the prisoner in custody. Between the hours of five and eleven o'clock I visited the prisoner in his cell several times, and conversed with him. When I first went to him, I gave him a caution that in any conversation we might have together he should say nothing to criminate himself, as it might be used in evidence against him. I cautioned him in the same manner on other occasions, when he said I acted fairly towards him, and that fair play was the English character.

"He said that he had left Glasgow about three months before; that he stayed at Liverpool seven days, and then came to London, where he had remained ever since; he then said that he was in business at Glasgow as a turner, but left that, and was going into another business, but was prevented. I observed that he had a good share of money, to which he replied that he had worked hard for it, that he generally did the work of three ordinary men daily.

"I told him I had been in Glasgow three or four weeks before. He then asked the name of the ship I went in. I said I had forgotten, but thought it was the *British Queen*. He said I must have been mistaken, it must have been the *Princess Royal*, and I then recollected that was the name of the vessel. I then asked him whether he knew Mr. Richardson, the superintendent of the Gorbals police. He said he did, and added that he was considered a more clever man than Miller (another police officer).

"I then asked him whether he came over in the *Princess Royal*. He said he did not; he came over in the *Fire King*. I asked him whether there was a railway from Edinburgh to Glasgow. He told me there was, and, as far as I recollect, said they were thirty or forty miles apart. He also mentioned the fares. I told him that when I was going to Glasgow I went through Paisley. I asked him whether he had ever been there. He said he had. I remarked that it was a great place for shawls. He admitted that it was; that nearly all the inhabitants were weavers, but he was sorry to say there were a great many of them out of employ.

"I then asked him whether he would take any refreshment, when he expressed a wish to have some coffee, with which he was supplied. In the course of conversation I asked him whether Drummond was a Scotch name. He answered that it was; that it was the family name of the Earl of Perth, but the title had become extinct.

"On the following morning I again saw the prisoner, between eight and nine o'clock. On entering his cell I asked him whether he had had his breakfast. He replied in the affirmative, and asked to have some water to wash himself with. I then sent the constable, who had been sitting up with him, for some water and when he had left the cell, I said to the prisoner – "I suppose you will assign some reason to the magistrate this morning for the crime you have committed?" He said, "I shall give a reason – a short one." I then said, "You might have stated anything you thought proper to me last night after the caution I gave you."

"He then told me that he was an object of persecution by the Tories, that they followed him from place to place with their persecution. He seemed inclined to go on with his statement, when I said, 'I suppose you are aware who the gentleman is you shot at? He said, 'It is Sir Robert Peel, is it not?' I at first said 'No,' but in a moment recollecting myself, said, 'We do not exactly know who the gentleman is yet.' Then turning round, I said, 'Recollect the caution I gave you last night, not to say anything to criminate yourself, as it may be used in evidence against you' to which he immediately replied, 'But you will not use this against me?' I said, 'I make you no promise; I gave you the caution.' I then left the cell, and in the course of the same day took him to the police court at Bow Street."

As one might imagine, this drew a blistering cross-examination from Cockburn.

"What was your purpose in going to the prisoner's cell?"

"It is my duty to visit all the cells in the course of the night."

"Is it your duty to put questions to the prisoners?"

"As long as I do not interfere with the case in point, I do not see any harm in putting questions to prisoners."

"Did anyone direct you to put such questions?"

"Certainly not."

"What was your object then in putting them?"

"I wanted to get all the information I could about his former life."

"In order to give it in evidence against him?"

"I never intended to give in evidence against him anything he told me till he mentioned the name of Sir Robert Peel."

"But what was your motive for wishing to get information respecting his former life?"

"Nothing that I know of but the anxiety of human nature, under such revolting circumstances, to know who and what he was."

"Now, do you mean to swear that you ever intended to suppress the evidence you have given?"

"Not to suppress it, no, but I had no intention to mention it till he mentioned the name of Sir Robert Peel. I cannot give you the precise conversation which took place at each interview, but I have stated the substance of them all. A constable, of the name of Edwards, was present when the conversations took place, but he is not here to-day. As I did not intend to mention the conversations I did not make any notes of them, but I did make a memorandum of the conversation in which Sir Robert Peel's name was mentioned."

"Why did you not have the morning conversation in the presence of the constable?"

"I wish he had been present. I had no motive for the conversation taking place in his absence. I first mentioned the conversation at Bow Street."

"Do you mean to swear that you had no motive lurking in your mind when you asked him whether he intended to make any statement before the magistrate?"

"I had no particular motive, but I imagined the responsibility was off my shoulders after the caution I gave him on the previous night."

"Was not the object of that interview to induce him to make that statement?"

"I did it for the purpose of letting him know that I was ready to receive any communication he thought proper to make."

"When did you first mention these circumstances?"

"I first mentioned them to Mr. Burnaby at Bow Street on the morning of the prisoner's first examination, before the examination took place; and to Mr. Hall, the chief magistrate, afterwards; but I believe he was aware of it before the examination. I was not examined on the first occasion."

"Did you mention the conversation to anyone else?"

"Yes, I mentioned it to the Commissioners of Police, but I cannot say whether I mentioned it to Colonel Rowan. I sent a private report in writing to the Commissioners."

"Now, perhaps you will tell me upon your solemn oath, whether, when you made that observation to him, you did not do so with the intention of extorting a confession from him?"

"The remark was thoughtlessly made. I wanted to turn the conversation, as I thought he was going to make a full confession, and I did not wish to hear it."[1]

Quick to take the jury's attention off the matter of Tierney's patently inappropriate behaviour and redirect it to M'Naughten and his grounds for having shot Sir Robert Peel, the solicitor general asked Inspector Tierney about the statement he had taken from M'Naughten the morning after their conversation in the prison cell:

"I was subsequently examined at Bow Street, and I then heard the prisoner make a statement. That statement was taken in writing by the clerk and signed by the prisoner."

"This is the statement?" He held up a copy.

"It is."

Follett then had the clerk read the statement:

"The Tories in my native city have compelled me to do this. They follow and persecute me wherever I go, and have entirely destroyed my peace of mind. They followed me to France, into Scotland, and all over England; in fact, they follow me wherever I go. I cannot get no rest for them night or day. I cannot sleep at night in consequence of the Course they pursue towards me. I believe they have driven me into a consumption. I am sure I shall never be the man I formerly was. I used to have good health and strength, but I have not now. They have accused me of crimes of which I am not guilty; they do everything in their power to harass and persecute me; in fact, they wish to murder me. It can be proved by evidence. That's all I have to say."

In support of its contention that M'Naughten had been "loitering" in and around Whitehall for weeks prior to the shooting in preparation for an attack on Sir Robert Peel at some suitable opportunity, the Crown called several witnesses. The office keeper of the Board of Trade in Whitehall, Edward Howe, testified that for two weeks prior to the shooting he had seen M'Naughten walking up Downing Street to Sir Robert Peel's official residence. "I saw him almost daily, either on the Privy Council Office steps or in the neighborhood of the Treasury. Sometimes I have seen him twice in one day."

James Partridge, a police constable in Whitehall, confirmed what Howe had said, adding that he had frequently noticed the prisoner in the neighbourhood of Whitehall between the 5th and 20th of January:

"On the 13th I spoke to him, and asked him whether he was waiting
for any person, when he replied that he was waiting for a gentleman,
and immediately walked away in the direction of the Horse Guards.
On the 20th I again spoke to him, about ten o'clock in the morning;
he was standing on the last step leading to the Privy Council Office,
where he remained for about twenty minutes. I asked him whether he
had seen the gentleman he had previously told me he was waiting for?
He quickly replied 'No,' and instantly walked away. He did not appear
inclined to answer any questions. About twelve o'clock the same day I
again saw the prisoner standing near Lady Dover's residence, eating a
piece of bread. Lady Dover's is opposite Gwydyr House, at the back of
which is the residence of Sir Robert Peel; but it cannot be seen from
Lady Dover's."

Some telling and, for the defence, potentially damaging testimony
was provided by John Gordon, an acquaintance of M'Naughten's for
about six years, who said that he had never noticed anything to suggest
that his mind was disordered. Yet he told the court of an encounter
with M'Naughten that couldn't help but strengthen the Crown's position that political motives were behind his shooting of Drummond:

"I came to London in November last, when I met the prisoner in
St. Martin's Lane. Prisoner said, 'I am in search of employment.' He
asked me where I was going, and I told him to Mr. Hedge's, in Great
Peter Street. We then walked on together and passed by the Horse
Guards and down Parliament Street. I know Sir Robert Peel's house.
I mentioned to him that that (I pointed to the house) was where
Sir Robert Peel stopped. He said, "D—n him, sink him," or something like that. When we passed the Treasury, he said, 'Look across
the street, there is where all the treasure and worth of the world is,' or
something like that. When we got to Westminster Hall, we entered
some of the courts, and afterwards we went to the Abbey. He said,
'You see how time has affected that massive building,' or something
like that. We then went to Great Peter Street."

A variety of other witnesses with whom M'Naughten had had dealings over the years all failed to observe anything remarkable or particular
about "his conversation or manner." It is noteworthy that without exception these people were mere acquaintances; M'Naughten appeared

to have had no close friends. John Caldwell and James Thompson, who worked with M'Naughten in Glasgow, both observed nothing of a peculiar nature. Nor did Alexander Martin, the gunmaker from Paisley who sold M'Naughten the pistols used at the time of the shooting, nor William Ambrose, a Glasgow writer who was secretary of the Mechanics' Institute where M'Naughten had attended lectures in 1840: "I never observed any thing strange in his behaviour ... neither do I have any recollection of his ever bursting out into a loud fit of laughter without any cause for it." This was likely offered as evidence of M'Naughten's soundness of mind in light of what another witness from the Mechanics' Institute had said under cross-examination "that the prisoner once burst out laughing in the middle of a speech when there was no reason for it."

One witness said of M'Naughten that "he never expressed any opinion of his own," another that he had a habit "of rolling his eyes and knitting his brow." His landlady Mrs. Dutton added to her previous testimony regarding his Spartan habits and reserved manners by noting that "he was not in the habit of looking people in the face, but always hung his head down." She attributed the sullenness of which many people spoke "to his difficulty in obtaining a working situation." A doctor, James Douglas, who had given lectures on anatomy that M'Naughten had attended, declared that he "never observed anything to lead me to suppose his mind was disordered." When directed by the Treasury solicitor Maule to identify M'Naughten at the time he was taken into custody, Douglas expressed his surprise at seeing him there. M'Naughten made "some monosyllabic reply, but I could not tell what." Under cross-examination by Cockburn, Douglas again said he thought there was nothing particular about the man, except his being one of little education.

"There was a want of polish about him. I think he was capable of understanding what was said to him."

"Now, sir, do you mean to say you had an opportunity of forming a judgment as to the man's sanity or insanity?"

Douglas came back: "No, I merely mean that he appeared to understand what he heard of my lectures."

A slight touch of levity was introduced to the proceedings by the testimony of Joseph Forrester, a hairdresser in Glasgow who had known M'Naughten for eighteen months:

SIR NICHOLAS TINDAL, 1776—1846, CHIEF JUSTICE OF THE
COMMON PLEAS, SOURCE: PORTRAIT BY T. PHILIPS, R.A.,
NATIONAL PORTRAIT GALLERY, LONDON

"I never saw anything in [the prisoner's] manner which led me to
think he was not in his right senses, or that he was wrong in his intellect. I used to stay with him sometimes half an hour, sometimes two
hours. I never suspected there was anything wrong in his mind. But
then it never occurred to me that I should like to come to London as
a witness. I am not aware how the attorneys for the prosecution found

me out. I never offered myself as a witness to anyone else. I never told Mrs. Patterson that I wished to come as a witness for the prisoner, neither did I ever tell Wilson, the baker, that M'Naughten was a 'daft' man. I have spoken to Mrs. Patterson on several occasions respecting the prisoner. One night she told me she wondered I said he was right, as I had once said he was wrong, but I denied having said anything of the sort. She then said that I was tipsy. I am quite sober now."

By late afternoon, with his evidence presented and his witnesses examined, William Follett rose and announced the conclusion of his case on behalf of the Crown to Chief Justice Tindal. Alexander Cockburn rose immediately after and asked the court if he might be allowed till the next morning before presenting his case for the defence. He confessed to be suffering from a severe cold and sore throat, and from the length to which evidence on behalf of the prisoner might run, he felt it would be impossible "to close the proceedings that night."

The Chief Justice wondered if they did adjourn at that point, whether it was certain the remainder of the case could be dealt with the following day. Cockburn replied that he hoped it would, but that would depend mainly upon the course pursued by the counsel for the Crown.

"If there is a probability of its being concluded tomorrow," Tindal said, "the Court will accede to the learned counsel's request and adjourn at once," to which Cockburn replied that "rather than make any statement which might mislead the Court, I will go on till a late hour tonight." But Tindal had made up his mind that whatever might be the consequences, the Court would be adjourned at once "since the learned counsel had intimated that he did not feel he could in his present state do justice to the prisoner." Cockburn assured the court that he not only spoke with great pain, but he felt that if he proceeded he should not be able to address the jury at the length the importance of the case required.[2]

⁣᯽᯽᯽

IT IS CLEAR that the Crown's tactic, anticipating the evidence of the defence, was to show M'Naughten as a "sane," "competent," "inoffensive," "studious," "sober" individual who, while perhaps eccentric, was certainly not a lunatic. This tactic was, as we shall come to see, completely anticipated by the defence who went on to show that notwithstanding an unremarkable superficial appearance of normalcy, an accused may still be "insane" in a rather circumscribed manner, to an extent that would render him blameless. Of importance is the fact that while the Crown was able to call many people who "had nothing to say," there were no witnesses called who had any sort of an intimate relationship with M'Naughten. Today, M'Naughten's presentation, as we shall see in the next chapter, surely would attract a diagnosis of "paranoia" of one sort or another. With this contemporary diagnosis it is common for patients to appear, apart from their delusional thinking, in virtually every other respect, "normal."

Worthy of note here is the blistering pace at which the trial was progressing. During the first day of the trial the court had heard the Crown's opening address and the testimony of twenty-six witnesses. While it is true that many had very little to say, nevertheless by today's standards this pace is unheard of: the Crown's entire case presented in one day! This was unusual even for its time – it had been calculated that the average length of a trial at the Old Bailey was a mere eight-and-a-half minutes.

It is clear that the reason for the fast pace is that counsel wasted no time with needless cross-examination. The evidence of the witnesses was pithy and to the point. Unfortunately, the same cannot always be said of present-day advocacy. Estimates of trial time are now usually based on an assumed rate of four to six witnesses per day where the evidence is fairly straightforward. Key witnesses in serious cases may now take several weeks to be directly examined and cross-examined.

In any event, the trial was postponed until nine o'clock the following morning. An officer was sworn to take charge of the jury and they were promptly escorted to a nearby coffeehouse where they were to remain for the night. This too was unusual for the time. Juries often deliberated in open court, huddling together to go over their opinions, delivering their verdict when done, often within a few minutes of the last defence witness having spoken.

Chapter Fifteen

SHORTLY AFTER NINE o'clock the next day, a Saturday, Lord Chief Justice Tindal, Mr. Justice Williams, and Mr. Justice Coleridge, accompanied by the lord mayor, the sheriffs, and other official persons, entered the Old Court and took their seats upon the bench, which on the right and left of the learned judges was soon afterwards crowded with both ladies and gentlemen. There were several ladies in the boxes usually reserved for members of the City corporation and jurors-in-waiting, and the courtroom was completely occupied, *The Times* reported, "by attentive listeners, amongst whom was a large number of young barristers," to whom, very naturally, the case was a subject both of curiosity and study. "The galleries," it was noted, "were not as full of visitors as they had been the previous day," which, according to *The Times*, was a result of "the extreme rudeness, in some degree approaching ruffianism" shown by the guards stationed at the court entrances to the influx of extra reporters and curious spectators on the opening day of the trial.

The jury was then called, the prisoner was placed at the bar, where he stood some minutes, and then, as on the previous day, was given a chair. He maintained the same quiet attitude and listless demeanour as he had all along, not looking over at his lawyer until Cockburn had begun his speech for the defence:

"May it please your Lordships and gentlemen of the Jury, I rise to address you on behalf of the unfortunate prisoner at the bar, who stands charged with the awful crime of murder, under a feeling of anxiety so intense – of responsibility so overwhelming – that I feel almost borne down by the weight of my solemn and difficult task. Gentlemen, believe me when I assure you that I say this, not by way of idle or common-place exordium, but as expressing the deep emotions by which my mind is agitated.

"I believe that you – I know that the numerous professional brethren by whom I see myself surrounded – will understand me when I say that of all the positions in which, in the discharge of our various duties in the different relations of life, a man may be placed, none can be more painful or more paralyzing to the energies of the mind than that of an advocate to whom is committed the defense of a fellow being in a matter involving life and death, and who, while deeply convinced that the defense which he has to offer is founded in truth and justice, yet sees in the circumstances by which the case is surrounded, that which makes him look forward with apprehension and trembling to the result.

"Gentlemen, if this were an ordinary case – if you had heard of it for the first time since you entered into that box – if the individual who has fallen a victim had been some obscure and unknown person, instead of one whose character, whose excellence, and whose fate had commanded the approbation, the love, and the sympathy of all, I should feel no anxiety as to the issue of this trial. But alas! Can I dare to hope that even among you, who are to pass in judgment on the accused, there can be one who has not brought to the judgment-seat a mind imbued with preconceived notions on the case which is the subject of this important inquiry?

"In all classes of this great community – in every corner of this vast metropolis, from end to end, even to the remotest confines of this extensive empire, has this case been already canvassed, discussed, determined, with reference only to the worth of the victim, and the nature of the crime, not with reference to the state or condition of him by whom that crime has been committed; and hence there has arisen in men's minds an insatiate desire of vengeance, nay there has gone forth a wild and merciless cry for blood, to which you are called upon this day to minister!

"Yet do I not complain. When I bear in mind how deeply the horror of assassination is stamped on the hearts of men, above all, on the characters of Englishmen, and believe me, there breathes no one on God's earth by whom that crime is more abhorred than by him who now addresses you, and who, deeply deploring the loss, and acknowledging the goodness – dwelt upon with such touching eloquence by my learned friend – of him who in this instance has been its victim, would fain add, if it may be permitted, an humble tribute to the memory of him who has been taken from us – when I bear in mind, I say, these things – I will not give way to one single feeling, I will not breathe one single murmur of complaint or surprise at the passionate excitement which has pervaded the public mind on this unfortunate occasion.

"But I shall, I trust, be forgiven if I give utterance to the feelings of fear and dread by which, on approaching this case, I find my mind borne down, lest the fierce and passionate resentment to which this event has given rise may interfere with the due performance of those sacred functions which you are now called upon to discharge.

"Yet, gentlemen, will I not give way to feelings of despair, or address you in the language of despondency. I am not unmindful of the presence in which I am to plead for the life of my client. I have before me British judges, to whom I pay no idle compliment when I say that they are possessed of all the qualities which can adorn their exalted station and ensure to the accused a fair, a patient, and an impartial hearing. I am addressing a British jury, a tribunal to which truth has seldom been a suppliant in vain. I stand in a British court, where Justice, with Mercy for her handmaid, sits enthroned on the noblest of her altars, dispelling by the brightness of her presence the clouds which occasionally gather over human intelligence, and awing into silence by the holiness of her eternal majesty the angry passions which at times intrude beyond the threshold of her sanctuary, and force their way even to the very steps of her throne. In the name of that eternal justice – in the name of that God, whose great attribute we are taught that justice is – I call upon you to enter upon the consideration of this case with minds divested of every prejudice, of every passion, of every feeling of excitement. In the name of all that is sacred and holy, I call upon you calmly to weigh the evidence which will be brought before you, and to give your judgment according to that evidence. And if this appeal be not, as I know it will not be, made to you in vain, then, gentlemen, I know the result, and I shall look to the issue without fear or apprehension.

"Gentlemen, my learned friend the Solicitor-General, in stating this case to you, anticipated, with his usual acuteness and accuracy, the nature of the defense which would be set up. The defense upon which I shall rely will turn, not upon the denial of the act with which the prisoner is charged, but upon the state of his mind at the time he committed the act. There is no doubt, gentlemen, that, according to the law of England, insanity absolves a man from responsibility and from the legal consequences which would otherwise attach to the violation of the law. And in this respect, indeed, the law of England goes no further than the law of every other civilized community on the face of the earth. It goes no further than what reason strictly prescribes; and, if it be not too presumptuous to scan the judgments of a higher tribunal, it may not be too much to believe and hope that Providence, when in its inscrutable wisdom and its unfathomable councils it thinks fit to lay upon a human being the heaviest and most appalling of all calamities to which, in this world of trial and suffering, human nature can be subjected – the deprivation of that reason, which is man's only light and guide in the intricate and slippery paths of life – will absolve him from his responsibility to the laws of God as well as to those of man.

"The law, then, takes cognizance of that disease which obscures the intellect and poisons the very, sources of thought and feeling in the human being – which deprives man of reason, and converts him into the similitude of the lower animal – which bears down all the motives which usually stand as barriers around his conduct, and bring him within the operation of the Divine and human law – leaving the unhappy sufferer to the wild impulses which his frantic imagination engenders, and which urge him on with ungovernable fury to the commission of acts which his better reason, when yet unclouded, would have abhorred.

"The law, therefore, holds that a human being in such a state is exempt from legal responsibility and legal punishment; to hold otherwise would be to violate every principle of justice and humanity. The principle of the English law, therefore, as a general proposition, admits of no doubt whatsoever. But at the same time, it would be idle to contend that, in the practical application of this great principle, difficulties do not occur. And therefore it is that I claim your utmost attention whilst I lay before you the considerations which present themselves to my mind upon this most important subject.

"I have already stated to you that the defense of the accused will rest upon his mental condition at the time when the offence was committed. The evidence upon which that defense is founded will be deserving of your most serious attention. I will content myself in the present stage by briefly stating its general character. It will be of a two-fold description. It will not be such as that by which my learned friend the Solicitor-General has sought to anticipate the defense, and to establish the sanity of the prisoner. It will not be of that naked, vague, indefinite, and uncertain character; it will be testimony positive and precise, and I say, from the bottom of my heart, that I believe it will carry conviction to the mind of everyone who shall hear it.

"It will be the evidence of persons who have known the prisoner from his infancy – of parties who have been brought into close and intimate contact with him – it will be the evidence of his relations, his friends, and his connections; but as the evidence of near relations and connections is always open to suspicion and distrust, I rejoice to say that it will consist also of the statements of persons whose testimony will be beyond the reach of all suspicion or dispute.

"Gentlemen, I will call before you the authorities of his native place, to one and all of whom this unfortunate calamity with which it has pleased Providence to afflict the prisoner at the bar was distinctly known – to all of whom he has from time to time, and again and again, applied for protection from the fancied miseries which his disordered imagination produced; all of them I will call, and their evidence will leave no doubt upon your minds that this man has been the victim of a fierce and fearful delusion, which, after the intellect had become diseased, the moral sense broken down, and self-control destroyed, has led him on to the perpetration of the crime with which he now stands charged.

"In addition to this evidence I shall call before you members of the medical profession – men of intelligence, experience, skill, and undoubted probity – who will tell you upon their oaths that it is their belief, their deliberate opinion, their deep conviction, that this man is mad, that he is the creature of delusion, and the victim of ungovernable impulses, which wholly take away from him the character of a reasonable and responsible being. I need not point out to you the great importance and value of the latter description of testimony.

"You will not, I am sure, think that what I say is with the view, in the slightest degree, of disparaging your capacity, or of doubting your judgment, when I venture to suggest to you that, of all the questions

which can possibly come before a tribunal of this kind, the question
of insanity is one which (except in those few glaring cases where its
effects pervade the whole of a man's mind) is the most difficult upon
which men not scientifically acquainted with the subject can be called
upon to decide, and upon which the greatest deference should be paid
to the opinions of those who have made the subject their peculiar
study.

"It is now, I believe, a matter placed beyond doubt that madness
is a disease of the body operating upon the mind, a disease of the cerebral organization; and that a precise and accurate knowledge of this
disease can only be acquired by those who have made it the subject of
attention and experience, of long reflection, and of diligent investigation. The very nature of the disease necessitates the seclusion of those
who are its victims from the rest of the world. How can we, then,
who in the ordinary course of life are brought into contact only with
the sane, be competent to judge of the nice and shadowy distinctions
which mark the boundary line between mental soundness and mental
disease?

"I do not ask you, gentlemen, to place your judgment at the mercy,
or to surrender your minds and understanding to the opinions, of any
set of men, for after all, it must be left to your consciences to decide. I
only point out to you the value and importance of this testimony, and
the necessity there is that you should listen with patient attention to
the evidence of men of skill and science, who have made insanity the
subject of their especial attention. My learned friend the Solicitor-
General has directed your attention to the legal authorities; and, perhaps, when those authorities shall have been minutely examined, no
great difference will be found to exist between my learned friend and
myself.

"But lest any confusion should be produced in your minds to the
detriment of justice, you will forgive me if I pray your attention to the
observations which I deem it my duty to make on this branch of the
subject. I think it will be quite impossible for any person, who brings
a sound judgment to bear upon this judgment, when viewed with the
aid of the light which science has thrown upon it, to come to the opinion that the ancient maxims, which, in times gone by, have been laid
down for our guidance, can be taken still to obtain in the full force of
the terms in which they were laid down.

"It must not be forgotten that the knowledge of this disease in all its various forms is a matter of very recent growth. I feel that I may appeal to the many medical gentlemen I see around me, whether the knowledge and pathology of this disease has not within a few recent years first acquired the character of a science? It is known to all that it is but as yesterday that the system of treatment, which in past ages – to the eternal disgrace of those ages – was pursued towards those whom it had pleased Heaven to visit with the heaviest of all human afflictions, and who were therefore best entitled to the tenderest care and most watchful kindness of their Christian brethren – it is but as yesterday, I say, that that system has been changed for another, which, thank God, exists to our honour, and to the comfort and better prospect of recovery of the unfortunate diseased in mind!

"It is but as yesterday that darkness and solitude – cut off from the rest of mankind like the lepers of old – the dismal cell, the bed of straw, the iron chain, and the inhuman scourge, were the fearful lot of those who were best entitled to human pity and to human sympathy, as being the victims of the most dreadful of all mortal calamities. This state of things has passed, or is passing fast away. But in former times when it did exist, you will not wonder that these unhappy persons were looked upon with a different eye. Thank God, at last – though but at last – humanity and wisdom have penetrated, hand in hand, into the dreary abodes of these miserable beings, and whilst the one has poured the balm of consolation into the bosoms of the afflicted, the other has held the light of science over our hitherto imperfect knowledge of this dire disease, has ascertained its varying character, and marked its shadowy boundaries, and taught us how, in gentleness and mercy, best to minister to the relief and restoration of the sufferer!

"You can easily understand, gentlemen, that when it was the practice to separate these unhappy beings from the rest of mankind and to subject them to this cruel treatment, the person whose reason was but partially obscured would ultimately, and perhaps speedily, in most cases, be converted into a raving madman. You can easily understand, too, that when thus immured and shut up from the inspection of public inquiry, neglected, abandoned, overlooked: all the peculiar forms, and characteristics, and changes of this malady were lost sight of and unknown, and kept from the knowledge of mankind at large, and therefore how difficult it was to judge correctly concerning it.

"Thus I am enabled to understand how it was that crude maxims and singular propositions founded upon the hitherto partial knowledge of this disease, have been put forward and received as authority, although utterly inapplicable to many of the cases arising under the varied forms of insanity. Science is ever on the advance; and, no doubt, science of this kind, like all other, is in advance of the generality of mankind. It is a matter of science altogether; and we who have the ordinary duties of our several stations and the business of our respective avocations to occupy our full attention, cannot be so well informed upon it as those who have scientifically pursued the study and the treatment of the disease.

"I think, then, we shall be fully justified in turning to the doctrines of matured science rather than to the maxims put forth in times when neither knowledge, nor philanthropy, nor philosophy, nor common justice had their full operations in discussions of this nature. My learned friend the Solicitor-General has read to you the authority of Lord Hale upon the subject-matter of this inquiry. I hold in my hand perhaps the most scientific treatise that the age has produced upon the subject of insanity in relation to jurisprudence – it is the work of Dr. Ray, an American writer on medical jurisprudence, and a professor in one of the great national establishments of that country."

Here, Cockburn read from Dr. Ray's[1] criticisms of the test for criminal responsibility based on mental disorder as suggested by Sir Matthew Hale in his 1736 book *A History of the Pleas of the Crown*. Hale's definition was widely adopted and came to be known as "the child of fourteen years test": "Such a person as labouring under melancholy distempers hath yet ordinarily as great understanding as ordinarily a child of fourteen years hath, is such a person as may be guilty of treason or felony."

"On this Dr. Ray observes: 'That in the time of this eminent jurist insanity was a much less frequent disease than it is now, and the popular notions concerning it were derived from the observation of those wretched inmates of the mad-houses whom chains and whips, cold and filth, had reduced to the stupidity of the idiot, or exasperated to the fury of a demon. Those nice shades of the disease in which the mind – without being wholly driven from its propriety, pertinaciously clings to some absurd delusion – were either regarded as something

very different from real madness, or were too far removed from the
common gaze, and too soon converted by bad management into the
more active forms of the disease, to enter much into the general idea
entertained of madness. Could Lord Hale have contemplated the
scenes presented by the lunatic asylums of our own times, we should
undoubtedly have received from him a very different doctrine for the
regulation of the decisions of after generations.'

"This is not the first time, gentlemen, that this doctrine of Lord
Hale has been discussed, with the view to ascertain its true interpretation. One of those master minds whose imperishable productions
form part of the intellectual treasure and birthright of their country – the great Lord Erskine, whose brilliant mind never shone forth
more conspicuously than upon the occasion to which I am about to
allude, and whose sentiments it would be presumption and profana-
tion to give in other than the language which fell from his own gifted
lips at the celebrated trial to which allusion was made by my learned
friend – put the true interpretation upon the doctrine of Lord Hale.

"I will read the passage, and I know you will pardon me the time I
occupy, for who would not gladly spare the time to listen to observations coming from such a man on so momentous an inquiry?"

He then read from Erskine's speech in defence of James Hadfield,
charged with treason for shooting at King George III at the Drury
Lane Theatre in 1800, concluding as follows:

"Delusion, therefore, when there is no frenzy or raving madness, is the
true character of insanity; and when it cannot be predicated of a man
standing for life or death for a crime, he ought not, in my opinion, to
be acquitted, and if courts of law were to be governed by any other
principle, every departure from sober, rational conduct would be an
emancipation from criminal justice. I shall place my claim to your
verdict upon no such dangerous foundation. I must convince you, not
only that the unhappy prisoner was a lunatic within my own definition
of lunacy, but that the act in question was the immediate, unqualified
offspring of the disease.

"You perceive, therefore, gentlemen, that the prisoner, in naming
me for the counsel, has not obtained the assistance of a person who
is disposed to carry the doctrine of insanity in his defense so far as
even the books would warrant me in carrying it. He alone can be so

emancipated whose disease (call it what you will) consists not merely in seeing with a prejudiced eye, or with odd and absurd particularities, differing, in many respects, from the contemplations of sober sense upon the actual existence of things; but he only whose whole reasoning and corresponding conduct, though governed by the ordinary dictates of reason, proceed upon something which has no foundation or existence.[2]

"Such gentlemen, is the language of this great man, and in this doctrine is the true interpretation of the law to be found. Gentlemen, that argument prevailed with the Court and jury in the case of the person on behalf of whom it was urged. Upon that argument I take my stand this day. I will bring this case within the scope of the incontrovertible and unanswerable reasoning which it comprises, and I feel perfectly confident that upon you, gentlemen, this reasoning will not be lost, but that the same result will follow in this as did in that memorable case.

"My learned friend, the Solicitor-General, has cited to you one or two other cases which I will dispose of in a very few words. A prominent case in his list is that of Earl Ferrers. Here, too, I am glad that my learned friend has referred to the celebrated case of Hadfield, because that case furnishes me with some valuable observations of Lord Erskine's made on Hadfield's trial, which will enable me to show how that great authority disposed of two of the cases relied on by my learned friend. I prefer to read to you gentlemen, those observations rather than trouble you with any of my own. After stating Lord Ferrers' case and drawing the distinction between the species of insane delusion which produces erratic acts, and that species of insanity which I trust I shall be able to prove to you possessed the prisoner now at the bar, Lord Erskine says:

'I have now lying before me the case of Earl Ferrers. Unquestionably there could not be a shadow of doubt, and none appears to have been entertained, of his guilt. I wish, indeed, nothing more than to contrast the two cases; and so far am I from disputing either the principle of that condemnation, or the evidence that was the foundation of it, that I invite you to examine whether any two instances in the whole body of the criminal law are more diametrically opposite to each other

than the case of Earl Ferrers and that now before you. Lord
Ferrers was divorced from his wife by Act of Parliament; and
the person of the name of Johnson, who had been his steward, had taken part with the lady in that proceeding, and had
conducted the business in carrying the Act through the two
Houses. Lord Ferrers consequently wished to turn him out of
a farm which he occupied under him; but his estate being in
trust, Johnson was supported by the trustees in his possession.
There were also some differences respecting coal mines, and
in consequence of both transactions Lord Ferrers took up the
most violent resentment against him.'

Erskine continues:

'Let me here observe, that this was not a resentment founded
upon any illusion; not a resentment forced upon a distempered
mind by fallacious images, but depending upon actual circumstances and real facts; and acting like any other man under the
influence or malignant passions, he repeatedly declared that
he would be revenged on Mr. Johnson, particularly for the part
he had taken in depriving him of a contract respecting the
mines.

'Now, suppose that Lord Ferrers could have showed that
no difference with Mr. Johnson had ever existed regarding his
wife at all, that Mr. Johnson had never been his steward, and
that he had only, from delusion, believed so when his situation in life was quite different. Suppose, further, that an illu-
sive imagination had alone suggested to him that he had been
thwarted by Johnson in his contract with these coal mines,
there never having been any contract at all for coal mines; in
short, that the whole basis of his enmity was without any foundation in nature, and had been shown to have been a morbid
image imperiously fastened upon his mind.

'Such a case as that would have exhibited a character of insanity in Lord Ferrers, extremely different from that in which
it was presented by the evidence of his peers. Before them he
only appeared as a man of turbulent passions, whose mind was
disturbed by no fallacious images of things without existence,
whose quarrel with Johnson was rounded upon no illusions,

but upon existing acts, and whose resentment proceeded to the fatal consummation with all the ordinary indications of mischief and malice, and who conducted his own defense with the greatest dexterity and skill.

'Who then could doubt that Lord Ferrers was a murderer? When the act was done, he said, "I am glad I have done it. He was a villain and I am revenged"; but when he afterwards saw that the wound was probably mortal, and that it involved consequences fatal to himself, he desired the surgeon to take all possible care of his patient; and, conscious of his crime, kept at bay the men who came with arms to arrest him, showing, from the beginning to the end, nothing that does not generally accompany the crime for which he was condemned. He was proved, to be sure, to be a man subject to unreasonable prejudices, addicted to absurd practices, and agitated by violent passions; but the act was not done under the dominion of uncontrollable disease; and whether the mischief and malice were substantive or marked in the mind of man whose passions bordered upon, or even amounted to insanity, it did not convince the lords that, under all the circumstances of the case, he was not a fit object of criminal justice.'

"Thus gentlemen, Lord Erskine showed the greatest possible contrast between the two cases; and I shall, in the case now before you, do the same thing."

From this, Cockburn went on to quote Erskine's reference to Arnold's case and Dr. Ray's arguments, to show that Arnold was insane.[3] Though Arnold was convicted, Lord Onslow, at whom he fired, thought he was insane, and procured a reprieve.

"Gentlemen, I will now go on to another case cited by my learned friend the Solicitor-General. I allude to the case of Bowler, which is reported in Collinson on Lunacy.[4] I trust, gentlemen, I shall not be considered open to the imputation of arrogance, or as traveling out of the line of my duty on the present occasion, if I say that I cannot bring myself to look upon that case without a deep and profound sense of shame and sorrow that such a decision as was there come to should ever have been resolved upon by a British jury, or sanctioned by a

British judge. What, when I remember that in that case Mr. Warburton, the keeper of a lunatic asylum, was called and examined, and that he stated that the prisoner Bowler had, some months previously, been brought home apparently lifeless, since which time he had perceived a great alteration in his conduct and demeanour; that he would frequently dine at nine o'clock in the morning, eat his meat almost raw, and lie on the grass exposed to rain; that his spirits were so dejected that it was necessary to watch him lest he should destroy himself.

"When I remember that it was further proved in that case that it was characteristic of insanity occasioned by epilepsy for the patients to imbibe violent antipathy against particular individuals, even their dearest friends, and a desire of taking vengeance upon them, from causes wholly imaginary, which no persuasion could remove, and yet the patient might be rational and collected upon every other subject – when I also recollect that a commission of lunacy had been issued and an inquisition taken upon it, whereby the prisoner was found to have been insane from a period anterior to the offence – when all these recollections cross my mind, I cannot help looking upon that case with feelings bordering upon indignation.

"But, gentlemen, I rejoice to say – because it absolves me from the imputation of presumption or arrogance in thus differing from the doctrines laid down in that case by the learned judge and adopted by the jury – that in the view which I have taken of it I am borne out by the authority of an English judge now living amongst us – a judge who is, and I trust will long continue to be, one of the brightest ornaments of a profession which has, through all times, furnished such shining examples to the world. I refer, gentlemen, to Mr. Baron Alderson, and the opinion that learned judge pronounced upon Bowler's case on the recent trial of Oxford in this Court;⁵ and I must say that I think, if the attention of my learned friend the Solicitor-General had been drawn to that case, if he had heard or read the observations made by Mr. Baron Alderson on that occasion, he would not now have pressed Bowler's case upon your notice.

"The Attorney-General of that day, the present Lord Campbell, in conducting the prosecution against Oxford for shooting at Her Majesty, had, in his address to the jury, cited the case of Bowler. When he came to the close of it, Mr. Baron Alderson interrupted him with this observation, 'Bowler, I believe, was executed, and very barbarous it was!' Such was the expression of Mr. Baron Alderson upon the mention of Bowler's case, and I rejoice to be able to cite it. I reverence the strength of feeling which alone could have given rise to that strength of expression; and I am sure that if the attention of my learned friend had been directed to such an observation coming from so high an authority, I know my learned friend's discretion and sense of propriety too well to think he would have cited Bowler's case for your guidance.

"Gentlemen, you will therefore, I am sure, dismiss that case from your minds after so clear and decided an exposition of the fallacious views which led to that decision. Let the error in that case – I implore you – operate as a warning to you not to be carried away headlong by antiquated maxims or delusive doctrines. God grant that never in future times may any authority, judicial or otherwise, have reason in this case to deplore the consequences of a similar error; never may it be in the power of any man to say of you, gentlemen, that you agreed to a verdict which in itself, or in its execution, deserved to be designated as barbarous.

"I pass now, gentlemen, to the next case cited by my learned friend the Solicitor-General, the case of Bellingham. All I can say of that case is, that I believe, in the opinion of the most scientific men who have considered it, there now exists no doubt at all that Bellingham was a madman. Few, I believe, at this period, unbiased by the political prejudices of the times, and examining the event as a matter of history, will read the report of Bellingham's trial without being forced to the conclusion that he was really mad, or, at the very least, that the little evidence which did appear relative to the state of his mind was strong enough to have entitled him to a deliberate and thorough investigation of his case. The eminent writer I have already quoted – I mean Dr. Ray – in speaking of Bellingham's case, says:[6]

'It appeared from the history of the accused – from his own account of the transactions that led to the fatal act, and from the testimony of several witnesses – that he laboured under many of those strange delusions that find a place only in the brains of a madman. His fixed belief that his own private grievances were national wrongs; that his country's diplomatic agents in a foreign land neglected to hear his complaints and assist him in his troubles, though they had in reality done more than could have reasonably been expected of them; his conviction, in which he was firm almost to the last, that his losses would be made good by the Government, even after he had been repeatedly told, in consequence of repeated applications in various quarters, that the Government would not interfere in his affairs; and his determination, on the failure of all other means to bring his affairs before the country, to effect this purpose by assassinating the head of the Government, by which he would have an opportunity of making a public statement of his grievances and obtaining a triumph, which he never doubted, over the Attorney General; these were all delusions, as wild and strange as those of seven-eighths of the inmates of any lunatic asylum in the land. And so obvious were they, that though they had not the aid of an Erskine to press them upon the attention of the jury, and though he himself denied the imputation of insanity, the Government, as if virtually acknowledging their existence, contended for his responsibility on very different grounds.'

"Gentlemen, it is a fact that Bellingham was hanged within one week after the commission of the fatal act, while persons were on their way to England who had known him for years, and who were prepared to give decisive evidence of his insanity. He was tried, he was executed, notwithstanding the earnest appeal of Mr. Alley, his counsel, that time might be afforded him to obtain evidence as to the nature and extent of the malady to which Bellingham was subject. Moreover, on the occasion of the trial of Oxford in this Court, the then Attorney General, Sir John Campbell, now Lord Campbell, after Bowler's case had been disposed of by the emphatic observation of Mr. Baron Alderson, expressed himself in these words: 'I will not refer to Bellingham's case, as there are some doubts as to the correctness of the mode in which that case was conducted.'

"I would that my learned friend the Solicitor-General had taken on this occasion the same course, and had exercised the same wise forbearance; because the doubts expressed by the late Attorney-General as to the propriety of the conduct of that case are not confined to that learned person, it being notorious that very serious doubts as to

the propriety of that trial are commonly entertained among the profession at large. Under such circumstances, gentlemen, I feel that it
would have been much better if your attention had not been directed
to that trial as it has been. I turn now to a very recent treatise on criminal law, which I am the more entitled to cite as an authority, because
its learned author, Mr. Roscoe, has been snatched from us by the hand
of death,[7] while his career was full of that promise which his great
attainments and varied learning held out to us. Referring to the rule
laid down in the case of Bellingham, and which you have been told
was adopted by Lord Lyndhurst in Rex *v.* Oxford, Mr. Roscoe says:
'The direction does not appear to make a sufficient allowance for the
incapacity of judging between right and wrong upon the very matter
in question, as in all cases or monomania.'[8]

"Mr. Roscoe quotes some remarks by an eminent writer on the
criminal law of Scotland. Now I may here observe, that I have the
authority of the present Lord Campbell, when Attorney General, in
Oxford's case, for saying that there is no difference between the law of
Scotland and that of England in this respect; so that all which I may
have to cite with respect to the law of Scotland will be quite applicable
to the case in hand.

"Gentlemen, Mr. Roscoe goes on to say: 'The following observations of an eminent writer on the criminal law of Scotland (Mr. Alison) are applicable to the subject: "Although a prisoner understands
perfectly the distinction between right and wrong, yet if he labours,
as is generally the case, under an illusion and deception in his own
particular case, and is thereby incapable of applying it correctly to his
own conduct, he is in that state of mental aberration which renders
him not criminally answerable for his actions. For example, a mad
person may be perfectly aware that murder is a crime, and will admit
it, if pressed on the subject; still he may conceive that the homicide
he has committed was nowise blamable, because the deceased had
engaged in a conspiracy, with others, against his own life, or was his
mortal enemy, who had wounded him in his dearest interests, or was
the devil incarnate, whom it was the duty of every good Christian to
meet with weapons of carnal warfare."'

"These observations of Mr. Roscoe and Mr. Alison, when applied
to the cases of Bellingham, of Arnold, and of Oxford, show that they
are not cases to be relied upon as perfect – that the doctrine laid down

in them cannot be taken as an unerring criterion by a jury. Unless you attend to all the circumstances of the particular case, you may be led into disastrous results, which it must be your most anxious wish to avoid."

Cockburn next referred to Oxford's case, and read the report[9] to the jury, informing the court that the verdict was "not guilty. I think my learned friend did not state to you the verdict." Follett, the solicitor general, said, "I beg your pardon; I did."
Cockburn conceded:

"If so, I was in error, and on my learned friend's statement, I withdraw at once the observation I made. I am sorry that I made it; and here let me take the opportunity of expressing my sense – and I am sure my learned friend will not object to receive such a tribute from me – of the forbearance and merciful consideration with which he opened and has conducted this case. I am bound also to say, that whatever facilities could be afforded to the defense, have been readily granted to the prisoner's friends by those who represent the Crown on this occasion.

...

"But to resume. With respect, then, to Oxford's case, I have only to remind you that Oxford was acquitted on the ground of insanity. Here, gentlemen, I shall prove a much stronger case; and when I have done so, you will, I feel confident, have no hesitation in following the precedent set you by the jury in that case. So much, gentlemen, for the legal authorities cited by my learned friend the Solicitor-General; but, after all, as was observed by him, this is not so much a question of law as of fact. That which you have to determine is, whether the prisoner at the bar is guilty of the crime of willful murder. Now, by 'willful' must be understood, not the mere will that makes a man raise his hand against another; not a blind instinct that leads to the commission of an irrational act, because the brute creation, the beasts of the field, have, in that sense, a will; but by will, with reference to human action, must be understood the necessary moral sense that guides and directs the volition, acting on it through the medium of reason.

"I quite agree with my learned friend, that it is a question – being, namely, whether this moral sense exists or not – of fact rather than of law. At the same time, whatever right legal authorities may afford on the one hand, or philosophy and science on the other, we ought to avail ourselves of either with grateful alacrity. This being premised, I will now take the liberty of making a few general observations upon what appears to me to be the true view of the nature of this disease with reference to the application of the important principle of criminal responsibility.

"To the most superficial observer who has contemplated the mind of man, it must be perfectly obvious that the functions of the mind are of a twofold nature – those of the intellect or faculty of thought alone, such as perception, judgment, reasoning – and again, those of the moral faculties – the sentiments, affections, propensities, and passions, which it has pleased Heaven, for its own wise purposes, to implant in the nature of man. It is now received as an admitted principle by all inquirers, that the seat of the mental disease termed insanity is the cerebral organization; that is to say, the brain of man.

"Whatever and wherever may be the seat of the immaterial man, one thing appears perfectly clear to human observation, namely that the point which connects the immaterial and the material man, is the brain; and, furthermore, it is clear that all defects in the cerebral organization, whether congenital – that is to say, born with a man – or supervening either by disease or by natural and gradual decay, have the effect of impairing and deranging the faculties and functions of the immaterial mind. The soul is there as when first the Maker breathed it into man; but the exercise of the intellectual and moral faculties is vitiated and disordered.

"Again, a further view of the subject is this – it is one which has only been perfectly understood and elucidated in its full extent by the inquiries of modern times. By anyone of the legion of casualties by which the material organization may be affected, anyone or all of these various faculties of the mind may be disordered – the perception, the judgment, the reason, the sentiments, the affections, the propensities, the passions – any one or all may become subject to insanity; and the mistake existing in ancient times, which the light of modern science has dispelled, lay in supposing that in order that a man should be mad – incapable of judging between right and wrong, or of exercising that self-control and dominion, without which the knowledge of right and wrong would become vague and useless – it was necessary that he should exhibit these symptoms which would amount to total prostration of the intellect; whereas modern science has incontrovertibly established that anyone of these intellectual and moral functions of the mind may be subject to separate disease, and thereby man may be rendered the victim of the most fearful delusions, the slave of uncontrollable impulses impelling or rather compelling him to the commission of acts such as that which has given rise to the case now under your consideration.

"This is the view of the subject on which all scientific authorities are agreed – a view not only entertained by medical, but also by legal authorities. It is almost with a blush that I now turn from the authorities in our own books, to those which I find in the works of the Scottish writers on jurisprudence. I turn to the celebrated work of a profound and scientific jurist, I allude to Baron Hume. He treats on the very subject which is now, gentlemen, under your consideration, namely, the test of insanity as a defense with reference to criminal acts, and he says:[10]

'To serve the purpose, therefore, of an excuse in law, the disorder must amount to absolute alienation of reason, "*ut continua mentis alienatione, omni intellectu cureat*" – such a disease as deprives the patient of the knowledge of the true disposition of things about him, and of the discernment of friend from foe, and gives him up to the impulse of his own distempered fancy, divested of all self-government or control of his passions. Whether it should be added to the description that he must have lost all knowledge of good and evil, right and wrong, is a more delicate question, and fit, perhaps, to be resolved differently, according to the sense in which it is understood.

'If it be put in this sense in a case for instance, of murder – did the panel[11] know that murder was a crime? Would he have answered on the question, that it is wrong to kill a neighbour? This is hardly to be reputed a just criterion of such a state of soundness as ought to make a man accountable in law for his acts. Because it may happen to a person, to answer in this way, who yet is so absolutely mad as to have lost all true observation of facts, all understanding of the good or bad intention of those who are about him, or even the knowledge of their persons. But if the question is put in this other and more special sense, as relative to the act done by the panel, and his understanding of the particular situation in which he conceived himself to stand. Did he at that moment understand the evil of what he did? Was he impressed with the consciousness of guilt and fear of punishment? It is then a pertinent and a material question, but which cannot, to any substantial purpose, be answered, without taking into consideration the whole circumstances of the situation.

'Every judgment in the matter of right and wrong supposes a case, or state of facts, to which it applies. And though the panel may have that vestige of reason which may enable him to answer in the general, that murder is a crime, yet if he cannot distinguish his friend from his enemy, or a benefit from an injury, but conceive everything about him to be the reverse of what it really is, and mistake the illusions of his fancy for realities in respect of his own condition and that of others, those remains of intellect are of no use to him towards the government of his actions, nor in enabling him to form a judgment on any particular situation or conjunction of what is right or wrong with regard to it; if he does not know the person of his friend or neighbour, or though he do know him, if he is possessed with the vain conceit that he is come there to destroy him, or that he has already done him the most cruel injuries, and that all about him are engaged in one foul conspiracy to abuse him, as well might he be utterly ignorant of the quality of murder.

'Proceeding as it does on a false case of conjuration of his own fancy, his judgment of right and wrong, as to any responsibility that should attend it, is truly the same as none at all. It is, therefore, only in this complete and appropriated sense as relative to the particular thing done, and the situation of the panel's feelings and consciousness on that occasion, that this inquiry concerning his intelligence of moral good or evil is material, and not in any other or larger sense.'

"This, gentlemen, I take to be the true interpretation and construction of the law. The question is not here, as my learned friend would have you think, whether this individual knew that he was killing another when he raised his hand to destroy him, although he might be under a delusion, but whether under that delusion of mind he did an act which he would not have done under any other circumstances, save under the impulse of the delusion which he could not control, and out of which delusion alone the act itself arose. Again, gentlemen, I must have recourse to the observations of that eminent man, Lord Erskine. I am anxious, most anxious on this difficult subject, feeling deeply my own incapacity, and that I am but as the blind leading the blind (you will forgive me the expression); I am, I repeat, anxious to avail myself as much as possible of the great light which others have thrown upon the subject, and to avoid any observations of my own by referring to the remarks of much greater minds. I turn again, therefore, to the remarks of Lord Erskine on the subject of delusion, in the case which has so often been mentioned. The case here is one of delusion – the act in question is connected with that delusion out of which, and out of which alone, it sprung."

At this point in his opening address, Cockburn sets us up for the specifics of his defence and more nuanced view of what constitutes insanity. He will rely most heavily upon the construction of insanity accepted by the court in *Hadfield's Case* (1800).

Chapter Sixteen

FORTY-FIVE MINUTES INTO his opening address – five times longer than it took to try the "average" Old Bailey case – Cockburn proceeded to set up a more specific and nuanced view of what he wanted the jury to regard as constituting insanity, directing them now to consider Erskine's construction of it, which was accepted by the court in *Hadfield's Case*, in 1800.

"'Delusion, therefore,' says Lord Erskine, 'where there is no frenzy or raving madness, is the true character of insanity, and where it cannot be predicated of a man standing for life or death for a crime, he ought not, in my opinion, to be acquitted; and if the courts of law were to be governed by any other principle, every departure from sober rational conduct would be emancipation from criminal justice. I shall place my claim to your verdict upon no such dangerous foundation.'

"*And*, gentlemen, I, following at an immeasurable distance that great man, I, too, will place my claim to your verdict on no such dangerous foundation. 'I must convince you,' said Lord Erskine, 'not only that the unhappy prisoner [Hadfield] was a lunatic within my own definition of lunacy, but that the act in question was the immediate unqualified offspring of this disease.' I accept this construction of the law: by that interpretation, coupled with and qualified by the conditions annexed to it, I will abide. I am bound to show that the prisoner was acting under a delusion, and that the act sprung out of that delusion, and I will show it. I will show it by evidence irresistibly strong; and when I have done so I shall be entitled to your verdict.

"On the other hand, my learned friend the Solicitor-General told you yesterday that in the case before you the prisoner had some rationality, because in the ordinary relations of life he had manifested ordinary sagacity, and that on this account you must come to the conclusion that he was not insane on any point, and that the act with which he now stands charged was not the result of delusion. I had thought that the many occasions upon which this matter had been discussed would have rendered such a doctrine as obsolete and exploded in a court of law as it is everywhere else. Let my learned friend ask any of the medical gentlemen who surround him, and whose assistance he has on this occasion, if they will come forward and pledge their professional reputation, as well as their moral character to the assertion that shall deny the proposition that a man may be a frenzied lunatic on one point, and yet on all others be capable of all the operations of the human mind, possessed of a high degree of sagacity, in possession of full rational powers, undisturbed by evil or excessive passions. On this point Dr. Ray,[1] in the following observations (the result of his long experience), disposes of the very objection which my learned friend has put forward on the present occasion:

> 'The purest minds cannot express greater horror and loathing of various crimes than madmen often do, and from precisely the same causes. Their abstract conceptions of crime, not being perverted by the influence of disease, present its hideous outlines as strongly defined as they ever were in the healthiest condition; and the disapprobation they express at the sight arises from sincere and honest convictions. The particular criminal act, however, becomes divorced in their minds from its relations to crime in the abstract; and being regarded only in connection with some favourite object which it may help to obtain, and which they see no reason to refrain from pursuing, is viewed, in fact, as of a highly laudable and meritorious nature.
>
> 'Herein, then, consists their insanity, not in preferring vice to virtue, in applauding crime and ridiculing justice, but in being unable to discern the essential identity of nature between a particular crime and all other crimes, whereby they are led to approve what, in general terms, they have already condemned. It is a fact not calculated to increase our faith in the march of intellect, that the very trait peculiarly characteristic of insanity

has been seized upon as conclusive proof of sanity in doubtful cases; and thus the infirmity that entitles one to protection, is tortured into a good and sufficient reason for completing his ruin.'

"I trust, gentlemen, that these observations, proceeding from a man of the most scientific observation, having all the facilities of studying everything connected with the subject, will not be lost upon you. I could mention case after case – I could continue till the sun should go down on my uncompleted task – I could, as I say, cite case after case in which the intellectual faculty was so impaired that the insanity upon one point was beyond all doubt, and yet where there was upon all others the utmost sagacity and intelligence. You will see that all the evidence of my learned friend the Solicitor-General relates to the *ordinary* relations of a man's life. That does not affect the real question. It may be that this man understood the nature of right and wrong on general subjects – it may be that he was competent to manage his own affairs, that he could fulfill his part in the different relations of life, that he was capable of transacting all ordinary business. I grant it. But admitting all this, it does not follow that he was not subject to delusion, and insane.

"If I had represented this as a case of a man altogether subject to a total frenzy – that all traces of human reason were obliterated and gone – that his life was one perpetual series of paroxysms of rage and fury, my learned friend might well have met me with the evidence he has produced upon the present occasion; but when I put my case upon the other ground, that of partial delusion, my learned friend has been adducing evidence which is altogether beside the question. I can show you instances in which a man was, on some particular point, to all intents and purposes mad – where reason had lost its empire – where the moral sense was effaced and gone – where all control, all self-dominion, was lost for ever under one particular delusion; and yet where in all the moral and social relations of life there was, in all other respects, no neglect, no irrationality, where the man might have gone through life without his infirmity being known to any except those to whom a knowledge of the particular delusion had been communicated.

"My learned friend has also remarked upon the silent design and contrivance which the prisoner manifested upon the occasion in question, as well as upon his rationality in the ordinary transactions of life. But my friend forgets that it is an established fact in the history of this disease, perhaps one of its most striking phenomena, that a man may be mad, may be under the influence of a wild and insane delusion – one who, all barriers of self-control being broken down, is driven by frenzied impulse into crime – and yet, in carrying out the foul purposes which a diseased mind has suggested, may show all the skill, subtlety, and cunning, which the most intelligent and sane would have exhibited. Just so in the case of Hadfield; it was urged against Lord Erskine that Hadfield could *not* be mad, because he had shown so much cunning, subtlety, deliberation, and design, in the whole of the circumstances which led to the perpetration of the act with which he was charged.

"In the present case, my learned friend the Solicitor-General has told you that the prisoner watched for his victim, haunted the neighbourhood of the Government offices, waited for the moment to strike the blow, and throughout exhibited a degree of design and deliberation inconsistent with insanity. The same in Hadfield's case; Hadfield went to the theatre, got his pistol loaded, and took his position in a place to command the situation in which he knew the King would sit; he raised the pistol, he took deliberate aim, and fired at the person of the King. All these circumstances were urged as evidence of design, and as inconsistent with the acts of a madman.

"What then, gentlemen, is the result of these observations? What is the practical conclusion of these investigations of modern science upon the subject of insanity? It is simply this: that a man, though his mind may be sane upon other points, may, by the effect of mental disease, be rendered wholly incompetent to see some one or more of the relations of subsisting things around him in their true light, and though possessed of moral perception and control in general, may become the creature and the victim of some impulse so irresistibly strong as to annihilate all possibility of self-dominion or resistance in the particular instance; and this being so, it follows, that if, under such an impulse, a man commits an act which the law denounces and visits with punishment, he cannot be made subject to such punishment, because he is not under the restraint of those motives which could alone create human responsibility.

"If, then, you shall find in this case that the moral sense was impaired, that this act was the result of a morbid delusion, and necessarily connects itself with that delusion; if I can establish such a case by evidence, so as to bring myself within the interpretation which the highest authorities have said is the true principle of law as they have laid it down for the guidance of courts of law and juries in inquiries of this kind, I shall feel perfectly confident that your verdict must be in favour of the prisoner at the bar.

"With these observations I shall now proceed to lay before you the facts of this extraordinary case. My learned friend the Solicitor-General has already given you some account of the prisoner at the bar, and I will now fill up the outline which my learned friend has drawn. The prisoner, as you have been told, is a native of Glasgow. At an early age he was apprenticed to his father, who carried on the business of a turner in that city; at the end of the apprenticeship he became a journeyman to his father, having been disappointed in not being taken by him as a partner. The prisoner, I should observe, is a natural son, and probably did not meet with that full measure of kindness which is usually shown to legitimate offspring.

"Whatever might have been the predetermining cause, he appears to have been from the commencement a man of gloomy, reserved, and unsocial habits. He was, moreover, as you will hear, though gloomy and reserved in himself, a man of singularly sensitive mind – one who spent his days in incessant labour and toil, and at night gave himself up to the study of difficult and abstruse matters; but whose mind, notwithstanding, was tinctured with refinement.

"As one trait of his character, I would mention that he was extremely fond of watching children at play, and took infinite delight in their infantine and innocent ways. I will prove, also, that he was a man of particular humanity towards the brute creation, and that when he went out he was in the habit of carrying crumbs in his pocket to distribute to the birds. If in the course of their walks his companions discovered a bird's nest, he would interfere, and not allow them to approach it. These things are striking indications of character, and certainly do not accord with the ferocity of an assassin.

"I mention these things to show that, from the earliest period, the prisoner had a predisposition to insanity. I shall prove to you, gentlemen, that the man and his wife with whom he lodged in 1837, became so alarmed at his behaviour that they gave him notice to quit, and forced him to leave, despite his wish to remain, from an apprehension that all was not right within his mind. I shall next carry him on to the time when he relinquished his business. When he quitted his lodgings in 1837 he went to live in his own workshop, and there he lived alone, without friend or associate, without recreation or amusement, save that which was found in turning from severe toil to severer studies. He then began to believe that persons persecuted him; he then began to act more strangely than before.

"With these moral phenomena must be coupled certain physical accompaniments. The unhappy prisoner would complain of pain; he would sit for hours, aye, even for days, holding his head within his hands, and uttering ejaculations descriptive of the tortures he endured. Often has he been known to hasten out, under the influence of these agonies, and throw himself into the waters of the Clyde in order to seek some relief from the torturing fever by which his brain was consumed. These facts I shall prove to the court and jury. They do not amount to insanity, but they will show what was going on within. They will show his predisposition to the disease which has since assumed so terrible a shape.

"It appears that in the beginning of 1841 he gave up his business from which he was deriving considerable gain. Why? – Doubtless because at that time the fearful phantasms of his own imagination rendered his existence miserable. He was wretched, because he was constantly harassed by the terrible images his disordered mind conjured up. These terrifying delusions had become associated with the place of his abode, haunting him at all hours of the day and night. You will hear from one of the witnesses, to whom he explained himself that he gave up business 'on account of the persecution by which he was pursued.' Yet it appears that all this time his business was prosperous and thriving, and, in addition, the great tendency of his mind seemed still to be a desire to earn money and to save it.

"That these phantasms long existed in that man's mind there is no doubt, before he at length sought relief by flight from this hideous nightmare, which everlastingly tortured his distracted senses. No doubt these delusions existed in his mind before, but it was not until he left his business that they were revealed to others in anything like a definite shape. And, gentlemen, you will learn from the medical authorities that it was natural for him, who became at last borne down by these delusions to struggle against them as long as he could; to resist their influence, and to conceal their existence; until, at last, the mind, overwrought and overturned, could contain itself no longer, and was obliged to give form, and shape, and expression, 'a local habitation and a name,' to the fantasies against which it had struggled at first, believing, it may be, for a time, that they were delusions, until their influence gradually prevailing above the declining judgment, they at last assumed all the appearance of reality, and the man became as firmly persuaded of the substantiality of these creations of his own fevered brain as of his very existence.

"Wherever he was, these creatures of his imagination still haunted him with eager enmity, for the purpose of destroying his happiness and his life. Nothing, then, could be more natural than that a man under such a persuasion should attempt to escape from the persecution which he erringly imagined to exist, and to seek in some change of place and clime a refuge from the tortures he endured. Alas! Alas! In this man's case the question put by the poet of old received a melancholy response: '*Patriae quis exul / Se quoque fugit?* – What exile from his country's shore can from himself escape?'

"When he left his own country he visited England, and then France; but nowhere was there a 'resting-place for the sole of his foot.' Wherever he went, his diseased mind carried with him the diseased productions of its own perverted nature. Wherever he was, there were his fancies; there were present to his mind his imaginary persecutors. When he planted his foot on the quay at Boulogne, there he found them. No sooner was he landed on a foreign soil than there were his visionary enemies around him. Again he fled from them, and again returned to his native land. Feeling the impossibility of escape from his tormentors, what course did he pursue? When he found it was impossible to go anywhere by night or by day to effect his escape from those beings which his disordered imagination kept hovering around him, what does he? What was the best test of the reality of the delusion? That he should act exactly as a sane man would have done, if they had been realities instead of delusions.

"And there is my answer to the fallacious test of my learned friend the Solicitor-General. He did so act; he acted as a sane man would have done, but he manifested beyond all doubt the continued existence of the delusions. He goes to the authorities of his native place, to those who could afford him protection, and with clamours entreats and implores them to defend him from the conspiracy which, he told them, had been entered into against his happiness and his life. Are we to be told that a man acting under such delusions, on whose mind was fixed the impression of their existence, and who was goaded on by them into the commission of acts which but for them he never would have committed – are we to be told that such a man is to be dealt with in the same way as one who had committed a crime under the influence of the views and motives which operate upon the minds and passions of men under ordinary circumstances?"

Here, Cockburn referred to M'Naughten's requests to his father, to Mr. Wilson, the sheriff substitute, and to the lord provost of Glasgow for protection from those he claimed were persecuting him.

"That these delusions afterwards took a political bias is possible; they may have done so. But such was not the first morbid impression of the prisoner's mind. The first was, according to his own complaint to Mr. Wilson, that the Catholic priests and Jesuits were engaged in persecuting him, and he stated that the annoyance he had experienced from them was such that he had been obliged to leave the country, and had gone to France, but that on landing at Boulogne he found he was watched by them still, and therefore it was useless to go further. Mr. Wilson endeavoured to soothe him and to disabuse his mind, and he went away, apparently somewhat quieted.

"At the end of three or four days he comes back and says that there are spies all around him, and that the Church of Rome and the police and all the world is against him. Here you have in addition to the Church of Rome, the 'police' and 'all the world.' Mr. Wilson spoke to him of the folly of supposing the Church of Rome to be against him, and assured him that if the police did anything against him, he, Mr. Wilson, would find it out.

"He comes again in the course of a few days, and then, in addition to his former complaints, he says, 'The Tories are now persecuting me on account of a vote I gave at a former election.' You will at once comprehend gentlemen that the delusion arose not from any part he had individually taken in politics – it was the form which was assumed by a diseased mind, believing itself to be the victim of persecution by anybody and everybody. First it was the 'Catholic priests,' then it was 'the Church of Rome, the police, and all the world,' and then it was 'the Tories.'

"After that he called again upon Mr. Wilson to know what had been done for him, when Mr. Wilson, to soothe him, told him that he had made inquiries; and promised to speak to Captain Miller, a super-intendent of police. Again he called, and was told that Captain Miller said there were no such persecutors, if there were, he should know of it. The prisoner said that Captain Miller was deceiving Mr. Wilson, as he knew that his persecutors were more active than ever; that they gave him no rest day or night; that his health was suffering, and that the persecutions he endured would drive him into a consumption.

"Mark that statement, gentlemen; couple it with the declaration he made after he was apprehended, and it will enable you to judge of the state of the man's mind at the time he made that declaration. Again he goes away; he does not come back again for some months, when he returns to talk again of his persecutors. This was in the sum-mer, and the time was drawing nigh to the period of this unhappy deed. Mr. Wilson will tell you, gentlemen, that when he saw him at that time his conduct had become more strange and his conversa-tion more incoherent; doubtless as time progressed his disorder was becoming worse. Having got rid of him, Mr. Wilson does that which affords the best test of the sincerity of the conviction he will express to you, namely, that he believed the man to be insane. He goes to the man's father and tells him that, in his opinion, it was unfitting for his son any longer to be left at large. He applies also to Mr. Turner, who gives the same advice to his father.

"Would to God that advice had been listened to! Would to God that warning voice had produced the effect which was intended! Then this melancholy catastrophe might have been prevented! By judicious medical treatment the man might have been restored to reason, or, at all events, such means might have been resorted to as the law allows for the protection of society. Oh, then, what different results would have been produced! The unhappy prisoner might have been spared the horror of having imbrued his hand in the blood of a fellow crea-ture; he would have been spared the having to stand to-day at that bar on his trial for having committed the worst crime of which hu-man nature is capable; as it now is, his only trust must be in your good sense, judgment, and humanity, in the opinion of which you may form upon the evidence which those who come from a distant part to throw a light on the subject will give you, and in such aid as my humble capacity enables me to afford him. So much, gentlemen, for the evidence I shall give with respect to the origin of this wretched assassination.

"The evidence called by the Solicitor-General does not in the slightest degree negate the case of insanity which the witnesses will clearly establish. It is that sort of negative testimony which can only spring either from the absence of all opportunity of observation, or from want of attention to the matter in question.

"I now come, gentlemen, to the act itself, with which the prisoner now stands charged. The Solicitor-General has said that you are not from the nature of the act itself, to draw an inference as to the state of mind of the person committing it. My learned friend put the proposition rather vaguely, but I can scarcely suppose that he meant what I have just said to the full extent of the terms. He might have meant either that you were not necessarily to infer from the nature of the act, from its atrocity and the absence of all probable impelling motives, the insanity of the person committing it, that is to say, that you were not to infer it conclusively from those circumstances alone, or he might have meant that the nature of the act itself ought not all to be an ingredient in forming a judgment of the state of the party committing it.

"Now, if my learned friend could have meant this last proposition, I must say, that with all my respect for him, I should be compelled boldly to differ from him, and to dissent altogether from a proposition so monstrous as that would seem to be. If it be found that an act is done, for which he who committed it was without any of those motives which usually actuate men in a state of sanity to wickedness and crime, if the whole circumstances connected with the perpetration of that act tend to show that it was one wholly inconsistent with the relation towards the surrounding world of the party committing it, am I, in such a case, to be told that I am to draw no inference at all from the nature of the act itself? I am sure, gentlemen, you will not allow your minds to be influenced and misled by any such proposition.

"You must look to the act, not conclusively, indeed, but in connection with the other leading circumstances of the case. What is the act?

In the broad face of day, in the presence of surrounding numbers, in one of the great and busy thoroughfares of this peopled metropolis, with the certainty of detection, and the impossibility of flight, with the inevitable certainty of the terrible punishment awarded to such a deed, a man takes away the life from one who (in any view of the case) had never, in thought, word, or deed, done to the perpetrator of that act the faintest vestige of an injury, from one who, as my learned friend yesterday described him, was of so mild a nature that he would not injure any being that had life, does this in the total absence of all motive, with the certainty of inevitable detection, and of equally inevitable punishment; yet you are told by my learned friend that you are not to let the nature and the circumstances of such an act enter into your judgment as to whether the person so committing it was sane or not.

"Who is there who, not having his judgment overclouded by the indignation which the very mention of such a deed is calculated to excite, could bring for a single moment his dispassionate reason to bear upon the nature of the case whose mind would not suggest that the act must be that of a frenzied lunatic and not of one possessed of his senses? My learned friend says that, nevertheless, you are not to look to the question of motive, and he appeals to history for instances where fanaticism and enthusiasm have operated on ill-regulated minds to induce them to commit similar crimes.

"I might possibly object that these instances are not strictly in evidence before you, but I will not adopt such a course. I admit that in order to understand the nature of insanity aright we must look beyond the evidence in the particular case. I will travel, therefore, with my learned friend beyond the facts now before you, and will turn to history in order to aid our judgment. I concede to him that fanaticism and enthusiasm operating on ill-regulated minds have produced similar disastrous results on former occasions. But look at the mode in which those motives operated on the minds of the criminals. The religious fanatic sharpened his steel against his sovereign's life, because he was told by a fanatical priesthood that he was doing a service to God, and to religion, that he was devoting himself by that act to the maintenance of God's religion, and that, while incurring an earthly martyrdom, he was also ensuring to himself an everlasting reward.

"Again, I admit that political enthusiasm has urged on others to similar crimes. Why? Because they acted under the belief that in some great emergency, while they were sacrificing the moral law, they were ensuring the welfare of their country. They were impelled by fanaticism in another form, by political enthusiasm, by misdirected and ill-guided notions of patriotism; Political enthusiasm! Where in this case is there a single trace of the existence of such a sentiment in the mind of the assassin? Where has the evidence for the prosecution furnished you with a single instance of political extravagance on the part of this man? Is he shown to have taken a strong and active part in political matters? Did he attend political meetings? Is he shown to have been a man of ill-guided, strong, and enthusiastic political sentiments? There is not a tittle of evidence on that subject.

"Many among us entertain strong political opinions. I do not disclaim them myself. I entertain them, and most strongly too; but if I believed that they would make me love, cherish, esteem, or honour any human being the less on account of his holding different opinions I would renounce politics for ever, for I would rather live under the most despotic and slavish government than forego aught of those feelings of humanity which are the charm of human life, and without which this world would be a wilderness. The prisoner had no animosity against Sir Robert Peel, for whom he is said to have mistaken Mr. Drummond. There is no evidence to show that he did intend to *shoot* Sir Robert Peel, save that of the policeman – I hardly know whether I am not throwing away time in devoting a single observation to the evidence of a man whose own statement justifies me in saying that he was acting a thoroughly treacherous part; a man who now shows himself in his true colours, an inquisitor and a spy; but who then, in the garb of fairness and honesty, sought to worm himself into the secrets of the unhappy man at the bar.

"I allude to the statement made before the magistrate as to the conversation he had with the prisoner. Having gently insinuated himself into the man's confidence, he asks a question as to the identity of the individual who had been shot. The answers he says the prisoner gave may be true or false; the statement of that witness may be consistent with truth, or it may be a fabrication; I know not, care not. Sure I am of this, that whatever may be the nature of the crime with which a man may stand charged, a British jury will hesitate to admit any one single fact which is an essential ingredient in the proof of the case, on the unsupported testimony of an individual who has manifested so much black perfidy, which will remain indelibly stamped upon his character. If the statement were true, why should it rest upon the evidence of that policeman only, when it is clear that at part of the conversation at least there was also a constable present? But I really waste time upon this part of the case, and I will proceed at once to a more important point, namely, the conduct of the prisoner himself after he had been brought before the magistrates.

"And this brings me to the question, whether or not the delusion under which the prisoner previously laboured existed in his mind at the time the act was done with which he now stands charged, and in truth was the cause of that act? I have already laid before you circumstances (and they will be proved in evidence) which establish beyond all controversy the existence of a delusion, exercising a blind and imperious influence over the man; and I have only further to establish, that the delusion led to the act, and was subsisting at the time that act was done. But surely it would be most monstrous and unjust to say that the same degree of delusion which prevailed eighteen months or two years before did not exist at the time of his committing the act. What was his statement before the magistrate? He said: 'The Tories in my native city have compelled me to do this. They follow and persecute me wherever I go, and have entirely destroyed my peace of mind. They followed me to France, into Scotland, and all over England; in fact, they follow me wherever I go. I can get no rest for them night or day. I cannot sleep at night in consequence of the course they pursue towards me. I believe they have driven me into a consumption. I am sure I shall never be the man I formerly was. I used to have good health and strength, but I have not now. They have accused me of crimes of which I am not guilty; they do everything in their power to harass and persecute me; in fact, they wish to murder me. It can be proved by evidence; that's all I have to say.'

"Save only that the enemies he spoke of and their persecution were the phantoms of a disordered mind, his statement was true. True it was that he was a different man, in health of body, and in health of mind, quite different in the regulation of his passions and propensities; he that at home had been a quiet, calm, inoffensive man, one who never raised his hand against a human being or created thing, had been converted by the pressure of imaginary evils into a shedder of human blood. This statement of the prisoner which doubtless was at first received with suspicion, shows in a totally different light when coupled with his previous history, and so now cannot be regarded otherwise than as the true and genuine expression of the feelings which were alive in his breast.

"No wonder that in the first excitement of popular feeling such a statement should be unfavourably received; the people had seen an innocent and unoffending man perish by the hand of an assassin; they were justified in viewing with distrust manifestations of insanity, which might be only assumed; but now, when the fearful delusions under which this man has so long laboured are made clearly known to you, the whole matter will, I am sure, be regarded by you under a totally different aspect. But then the Solicitor-General speciously asks, whether this is not the case of a man feigning and simulating insanity in order to avoid the consequences of his crime?

"It is not so; it is the case of a man who manifested, after the deed was done, the same delusion, which will be proved to have been present in his mind for months, nay, years before the act was committed. But I shall not leave this part of the case upon the prisoner's statement alone, for I am enabled to lay before you evidence that will satisfy your minds of the prisoner's insanity since he has been confined within the walls of a prison. He has been visited by members of the medical profession, of the highest intelligence and the greatest skill, not chosen by the prisoner himself, but some of them selected by his friends, and others deputed by the Government which my honourable and learned friend the Solicitor General represents on the present occasion. They visited the prisoner together several times; they together heard the questions put to him, and noted the answers he gave.

"My learned friend has accurately told you the nature of the defense I have to offer; he has sought to anticipate it by evidence to establish the prisoner's sanity. How is it, then, that the medical men employed by the Crown have not been called? Why, my learned friend has now beside him, within his arm's reach, two of the medical gentlemen sent by the Government, and he has not dared to call them. My learned friend knew (because their opinions have been communicated to the Government and to my learned friend) that the man was mad, and in justice to the public and to the prisoner those gentlemen ought

to have been brought forward. I was astonished when the case for
the prosecution was closed without those two witnesses being called.
They sat within my learned friend's call, and yet my learned friend, in
the exercise of the discretion which is his characteristic, dared not put
them in the witness-box. Their testimony is, however, upon record;
it requires not their delivery by their own mouths of the opinions I
know them to entertain; their absence from the witness-box speaks
trumpet-tongued as to the opinions they were ready to pronounce;
and when I call before you the medical gentlemen who have attended
at the request of the friends of the prisoner, and have communicated
with this poor deluded maniac, and it is found that their opinions
correspond in all particulars, there will not be left a shadow of doubt
that this was no simulated insanity, but a real delusion, by which the
prisoner was deprived of all possibility of self-control, and which left
him a prey to violent passions and frenzied impulses.

"I know there has been much said of the danger of admitting a
defense of this kind. I do not dispute it; it is a defense of what it is
the province of a court and jury to look with care. True, it is a defense
easily made, but it is a defense which the sagacity of courts and juries
prevents being too easily established. If an offender should first suggest insanity as a defense after the perpetration of a crime, the eye of
suspicion would naturally rest upon such a defense. Here, however,
there can be no pretence for saying there is the slightest reason to believe that this was a case of feigning and simulation, when I shall have
proved the existence of the delusion for the space of two long years
before, as well as its continuance since, the act was committed.

"When I have proved this, my learned friend will not dream of
contending that this is a case of simulation. Again, I ask, is there no
distinction between the manner in which the common murderer who
acts under the impulse of ordinary motives executes his purpose, and
that of the unhappy maniac who, in self-defense as he thinks, slays
one who in his delusion he fancies is attacking him? There is every
distinction. The ordinary murderer not only lays plans for the execution of his designs; not only selects time and place best suited to his
purpose; but when successful, he either flies from the scene of his
enormities, or makes every effort to avoid discovery.

"The maniac, on the contrary, for the most part, consults none of
the usual conveniences of crime; he falls upon his victim with a blind

fury, perhaps in the presence of a multitude, as if expressly to court observation, and without a thought of escape or flight; not infrequently he voluntarily surrenders himself to the constituted authorities. When, as is sometimes the case, he prepares the means, and calmly and deliberately executes his project, his subsequent conduct is still the same as in the former instance. The criminal often has accomplices, and always vicious associates; the maniac has neither. What was the case in the present instance? The prisoner does not attempt to escape; he acts coolly and deliberately; he shows himself to be a maniac seeking only the gratification of his involuntary impulse; he made no attempt to secure his own safety by flight or escape, though he knew that the noise of his first pistol must have attracted attention to the spot; though he saw Mr. Drummond's coat in flames, and his victim staggering under the shot, though he must have known that his purpose was effected, instead of thinking of himself, he drew forth the other pistol, with a deliberate intent he passed it from one hand to the other, he leveled it at his victim, and when the policeman had even seized him, still the struggle was not to escape, but to raise his arm and to carry out the raging impulse of his burning and fevered brain.

"A common murderer would have acted in a different manner; he would have chosen a different time, a different place; he would have sought safety by escape.

"Gentlemen, I have mentioned that I shall call medical men of the highest rank in the profession; men who have frequently been employed by the Government in cases of this nature, and upon whose characters the stamp of the highest approbation has thus been placed. They will state the result of their examinations of the prisoner, and their evidence upon the whole will be such as to leave no other than a firm conviction that he is insane. I shall also call the surgeon of the jail, whose duty it has been to see him daily, and whose facilities of observation have therefore been such as to enable him to come to a sound conclusion, and who, besides, was directed to pay particular attention to the state of the prisoner's mind. My friend has not thought fit to call him. I will call him. You will hear from that gentleman the result of his deliberate and impartial judgment, which is that the prisoner is labouring under morbid insanity, which takes away from him all power of self-control, and that he is not responsible for his acts.

"When I have proved these things, I think the defense will be complete. I do not put this case forward as one of total insanity; it is a case of delusion, and I say so from sources upon which the light of science has thrown its holy beam. I have endeavoured to show the distinction between partial delusion and complete perversion and prostration of intellect. I may, however, perhaps be allowed to refer to one more author on this subject. I allude to M. Marc, physician to the King of the French, and one of the most profound investigators of this disease. I will translate the passage as I proceed. M. Marc, in his treatise 'De la Folie,' says:[2]

'Homicidal monomania is a partial delusion characterized by an impulse, more or less violent, to murder; just as suicidal monomania is a partial delusion characterized by a disposition, more or less voluntary, to destroy oneself. This monomania presents two very distinct forms. In some cases the murder is provoked by an internal but raving conviction, by the excitement of a wandering imagination, by a false reasoning, or by the passions in delirium. The monomaniac is impelled by some motive obvious but irrational; he always exhibits sufficient signs of partial delirium, of the intelligence or of the affections. Sometimes his conscience makes him turn with horror from the act which he is about to commit; but his will is overcome by the violence of his impulse; the man is deprived of his moral liberty; he is a prey to a partial delirium; he is a monomaniac; he is mad. In the other cases the homicidal monomaniac does not present any alteration of the intelligence or affections; he is carried away by a blind instinct, by something indefinable, which impels him to kill.'

"I think, gentlemen, I have sufficiently dwelt upon the authorities which can throw light upon this inquiry. I trust that I have satisfied you by these authorities, that the disease of partial insanity can exist – that it can lead to a partial or total aberration of the moral senses and affections, which may render the wretched patient incapable of resisting the delusion, and lead him to commit crimes for which morally he cannot be held to be responsible, and in respect of which, when such a case is established, he is withdrawn from the operation of human laws. I proceed now to lay the evidence before you. In doing so I shall give my learned friend the Solicitor-General the opportunity of a reply. In this case it will be of considerable advantage, for he will have the opportunity of addressing you, and commenting on the evidence after it all shall have been given; whereas I can only anticipate what it may be.

"Many facts may be spoken to by the witnesses – many important observations may fall from them – on which I shall be deprived of all comment.[3] The arguments which my friend's profound experience and his great legal acquirements may suggest are yet within his own mind: I can but dimly anticipate them. If any advantage should exist in such a case, surely it should not be on the part of the prosecution, but of the prisoner. And my learned friend, moreover, will have the immense advantage resulting from that commanding talent before which we all bow down. But I know that he will prolong to the end of this eventful trial that calm and dispassionate bearing, that dignified and appropriate forbearance which sat so gracefully on him yesterday.

"Gentlemen, my task is at an end. I have received at your hands, and at the hands of the Court, a degree of considerate attention for which I owe you my most grateful acknowledgments. I ought to apologize to my lords and to you for the length of time that I have detained you; but you know the arduous and anxious duty which I have had to perform, and you will pardon me. From the beginning to the end I have felt my inadequacy to discharge it; but I have fulfilled it to the best of my poor ability. The rest is with you. I am sure that my observations in all that deserves consideration will be well weighed by you, and I am convinced that the facts of this case, and the evidence adduced in support of them, will be listened to by you with the most anxious and scrupulous attention.

"You can have but one object: to administer the law according to justice and to truth; and may that great Being from whom all truth proceeds guide you in this solemn inquiry, that when hereafter the proceedings of this memorable day, and their result shall be scanned by other minds, they may bear testimony that you have rightly done your duty; and, what to you is far more important, that when hereafter in the retirement of your own homes, and the secrecy of your own thoughts, you revert to the part you have taken in the business of this day, you may look back with satisfied consciences and tranquil breasts on the verdict you will this day have given.

"Gentlemen, the life of the prisoner is in your hands; it is for you to say whether you will visit one on whom God has been pleased to bring the heaviest of all human calamities – the most painful, the most appalling of all mortal ills – with the consequences of an act which most undoubtedly, but for this calamity, never would have been committed. It is for you to say whether you will consign a fellow being under such circumstances to a painful and ignominious death. May God protect both you and him from the consequences of erring reason and mistaken judgment!

"In conclusion, let me remind you, that though you do not punish the prisoner for an offence committed at a time when he was unconscious of wrong, you have, on the other hand, the power of causing him to be placed in an asylum provided by the mercy of the law, where he will be protected from the consequences of his own delusions, and society will be secured from the danger of his acts. With these observations I trust the case in your hands, with the full conviction that justice will be upheld in the verdict to which you shall come."

With the conclusion of his opening address, Cockburn's case for the defence began. It would require certain findings of fact and an interpretation of the law that would permit a defence based upon a circumscribed delusion. "Partial Insanity" of this sort was apparently accepted by the court in *Hadfield's Case* (1800), which Cockburn relied upon heavily.

Cockburn first of all had to adduce evidence from which the jury could make the finding that M'Naughten suffered from a mental disorder (at the time the distinction between the legal concept and the medical concept was not at all clear and were often seen as synonymous and referred to as "insanity" or "lunacy"). Secondly, it was incumbent on Cockburn to show that, if his construction of the law was accepted, that M'Naughten's partial insanity caused him to be "legally insane." For "medical insanity" or lunacy to amount to legal insanity, it must take the accused over a particular threshold or legal test.

Now, it was here that the state of the law governing insanity was rather murky in 1843. Must the mental condition render the accused incapable of knowing right from wrong? Was it a lack of "self-control" that must be produced? Was it a "prostration of intellect"? Or, was it a misperception of reality caused by a delusion? All these possibilities were alluded to by Cockburn in his address. The law with respect to insanity was indeed in a very unsatisfactory state. It was not articulated in a statutory form and judicial decisions were, as we saw earlier, less than consistent.

Whatever the test, of great significance and tactical importance was Cockburn's clear information to the jury that a finding of insanity would not result in M'Naughten "getting off." This is always an important message for defence counsel to convey to the jury who may be under the misapprehension that a successful insanity defence would have the accused walk out on to the street. It was clearly left with the jury that M'Naughten would, if successful, be delivered to an asylum so that the public would be safe from future behaviour driven by his lunacy.

Chapter Seventeen

WITHOUT DELAY, COCKBURN then commenced presenting the witnesses he had assembled for the defence, starting with M'Naughten's father, also named Daniel M'Naughten. After affirming that he presently resided in Glasgow and worked in the wood-turning business, he described for the court his relationship with the accused:

"The prisoner, who is a natural son of mine, was apprenticed to me, and after he had served about four years and a half became my journeyman, in which capacity he continued for about three years. When he left me he went into business as a turner on his own account, and was always a very steady, industrious young man, and exceedingly temperate in his habits.

"After he went into business I did not see him so often, although I saw him then frequently. He seemed to me more distant than formerly; but I knew of no reason for his being so. He would frequently pass me in the street and not speak to or notice me.

"About two years ago I recollect the prisoner calling at my house, and, upon seeing me, he expressed a wish to have an interview in private. We went into a room alone, and he then told me that various prosecutions [*sic*] had been raised against him, and begged that I would speak to the authorities of the town upon the subject, in order to have a stop put to them. He particularly mentioned the name of Mr. Sheriff Alison as one of the persons I was to speak to.

"I asked who the persons were that persecuted him, and he told me that Mr. Sheriff Alison knew all about it. I told him I was extremely sorry to hear that he was so persecuted, and endeavoured to persuade him that he was labouring under some mistake. I told him that I was not aware of any person being persecutive in Glasgow.

"Finding that he was labouring under some delusion, I said nothing more upon the subject, but tried to turn the conversation. We then talked upon other subjects, upon all of which he spoke rationally enough. He then asked me to get him a situation in some counting house in Glasgow. I promised him that I would endeavour to do so, but told him that I thought he had, in the first instance, better go to some respectable teacher, and learn writing and arithmetic. He said he would do so, and we then parted.

"About a week after that interview he again called upon me, and inquired whether I had, according to my promise caused the authorities to take any measures to prevent the persecution which was going on against him? I told him that I thought after our last interview he would have gone to school, and banished all such ideas from his mind.

"He then said that the persecution still continued, and that he was followed night and day by spies; wherever he went they followed him. I asked him who the spies were, whether he knew any of them, or whether he could point them out. To which he replied that it would be quite useless to point them out, as they were always in his presence; wherever he might be, whenever he turned round, there they were.

"I asked him whether he ever spoke to them, or they to him. He said they never spoke to him, but whenever he looked at them they laughed at him and shook their fists in his face, and those who had sticks shook them at him.

"He also said that one of the men, whenever he looked at him, threw straws in his face. I asked him whether, if I went out with him, he could point out any of the spies to me. He said, 'Oh, no; if they see anyone with me they will not follow at all; it is only when I am alone that they follow and annoy me.'

"I then asked him what he thought they meant by showing him straws? To which he replied, he presumed it meant that he was to be reduced to a state of beggary by them. I told him that if he really saw a person with straws, in all probability it must be some person out of his mind.

"After some further conversation in the same strain, he begged of me, nay, insisted upon my calling on Mr. Sheriff Bell. I then promised him that I would see Sheriff Bell upon the subject.

"In about a week he called upon me a third time, and asked whether I had seen Sheriff Bell. I told him I had not. He then said the persecution still continued, and inquired why I had not seen Sheriff Bell according to my promise, as he knew all about the matter.

"I saw nothing more of him for a considerable time, and I then accidentally met him on the road, a short distance (about four miles) from Glasgow. We had a conversation for upwards of an hour, and the chief topic was the persecution he was enduring; he said he had left Glasgow, and had gone to England, and even to France, to get rid of the spies, but they still followed him; the moment he landed in France there they were also.

"After that interview he called upon me again, and requested that I would prevail upon the authorities, particularly Sheriffs Alison and Bell, to put an immediate stop to the persecution. On that occasion I reasoned with him for some time upon the folly and absurdity of supposing that such a conspiracy existed against him, and assured him that such was not the case; and I then thought that the impression was effaced. He again spoke to me about getting him a situation, and I promised I would do so.

"Between that interview and the month of September he called upon me several times, and always requested me to see the authorities upon the subject. I never saw any of the civil authorities, as I saw that he was labouring under some extraordinary delusion, and therefore considered it quite unnecessary."

Solicitor General Follett, in cross-examination for the Crown, asked when last he had had dealings with his son.

"The last interview I had with him was in August last, shortly before he came to London. When he was apprenticed to me he lived in my house, but whilst a journeyman he went into lodgings. I do not know his reason for leaving my house, but it certainly was not on account of any quarrel. He did not go into business for himself before he left my house, nor till some time afterwards. I believe he went into business for himself because he felt dissatisfied at my not letting him have a share of my little business."

"Did he ask you to take him into partnership?"

"Yes, he did; but I refused, because I had some younger children to provide for. After he went into business we very seldom spoke. For a long time I think he fancied that I was annoyed because he took some of my business from me, which was not the case. I know that his shop was in Stockwell Street, but I never went there. He carried on business in Stockwell Street for about five years, and disposed of it two years ago. We were not at all upon the terms that a father and son usually are. At times party politics run very high at Glasgow."

"At the time the conversations you have been mentioning occurred, what was your opinion with respect to your son's mind?

"It certainly was my impression that his intellects were impaired."

"Did you consult any medical gentleman?

"I did not, because I thought the delusions under which he was labouring would eventually pass away."

"Then am I to understand that upon all other subjects he conversed rationally?"

"Yes, upon all subjects except the one I have mentioned."

The lawyer Clarkson, Cockburn's co-counsel for the defence, in cross-examination, questioned M'Naughten's father further as to their relationship: "The prisoner continued to work at my shop after he left my house. He frequently passed me in the street without taking the slightest notice; it was his own act to do so, not mine. He was always a very harmless, inoffensive youth, and appeared harmless when labouring under these delusions. I never heard of his having evinced any disposition to do any injury either to himself or anyone else."

William Gilchrist, a Glasgow printer, spoke of having known M'Naughten the prisoner since 1834:

"I lodged with him at Gorbals. We slept in the same bed. The prisoner used frequently to get up in the night and walk about the room, uttering incoherent sentences, and making use of such ejaculations as 'By Jove,' 'My God.' He uttered them in a very serious manner, but not in a very loud tone.

"Sometimes he would walk about the room by the hour together whilst undressed, and then return to bed. Such conduct occurred from time to time during the whole period we lodged together. His conduct was always that of a mild, inoffensive, and humane man. I have frequently seen him, when we have been going out to take a walk, put crumbs of bread into his pocket to feed the birds with. He appeared to be very fond of children, and I have observed him watch the children at play for hours; he said he liked to see their innocence.

"The last time I saw the prisoner was in July 1842, when we walked together for a short distance. I thought he was altered, both in manner and appearance, for when I looked at him he always dropped down his head and looked on the ground. His conversation was not so connected as formerly.

"I have known the prisoner burst out into immoderate fits of laughter without any cause whatever; at other times he would moan. I never knew him to attend any political meetings, or express any extravagant political opinions. When I last saw him he told me, in the course of a conversation, that when he was in London he went one night to the House of Commons, and heard Sir Robert Peel, Lord John Russell, and Mr. O'Connell speak, and he expressed himself highly delighted. He said he thought Sir Robert Peel had arrived at what Lord Byron had said of him, 'that he would be something great in the State'; he said he thought Lord John Russell was very inferior as a speaker to Sir Robert Peel, and that Mr. O'Connell was inferior to both."

"Did you ever hear him, either on that or any other occasion, speak at all disrespectfully of Sir Robert Peel?"

"Certainly not."

Cross-examined by the lawyer Waddington for the Crown about these "ejaculations" and "laughter" of M'Naughten's, Gilchrist suggested that "the ejaculations which I have spoken of, and also the laughter, might have been caused by the recollection of something he had previously heard, and of which I was not aware."

"Did you ever hear him speak about Sir R. Peel's political character?"

"Never."

"Or utter any threat towards him?"

"No."

A Glasgow tailor, John Hughes, was examined by Monteith and confirmed the evidence of the previous witness, going on to explain that "the prisoner lodged at my house during the year 1835."

"A person of the name of M'Cordigan, who slept in the same bed with the prisoner, made several complaints to me about the prisoner disturbing him during the night, and left me in consequence.

"The prisoner did not appear to be fond of society, and scarcely ever spoke unless first spoken to, and then his replies were quick and hurried, as if he wished to avoid conversation. I also noticed that when any person spoke to him, if their eye caught his he immediately looked down to the ground, as if ashamed; whenever he asked for anything he appeared confused.

"In consequence of his very strange manner I gave him notice to leave, but he was very unwilling to go away. Another reason I had for wishing him to leave was in consequence of the infidel doctrines he maintained, and the books of such a character which he was in the habit of reading. I always have family worship in my house every Sunday, and generally in the week days. The prisoner mostly attended on Sundays."

The solicitor general asked whether he had given these reasons as part of his notice to M'Naughten.

"I did not tell him the true reason why I wished him to leave my house. I assigned as a reason that my wife could not wait upon him any longer."

"Did you observe any particular difference in his behaviour whilst he was at your house?"

"Yes, I thought his appearance just before he left was more strange than when I first saw him."

Justice Coleridge asked whether Hughes had any children living in his house.

"I have, my Lord."

"Did the prisoner seem fond or take any notice of them?"

"He never used to take any notice of them."

William Carlo, a wood-turner in Stockwell Street, Glasgow, explained to defence counsel Clarkson, that he had known the prisoner for seven years, and was in his employ as journeyman for nearly three years, up until 1838.

"By 1840 he had a very good business. I purchased it in 1841. Whilst I was in his employ he frequently complained of a pain in his head, and would often keep his hand to his head, as if in pain, the greater part of the evening. When in this state I have known him on several occasions to go and bathe in the Clyde, which is near the premises, in order to get rid of it.

"I have very frequently seen him since 1841, but never observed anything particularly the matter with him till about six months ago. I had frequently heard it stated during the last eighteen months that there was something wrong about him, but I did not believe it. In consequence of those rumours, however, I went to see him whilst lodging at Mrs. Patterson's.

"We then walked out together, and he gave me a description of his visit to France; the only motive he assigned to me for going there was curiosity. He told me he was very much persecuted by certain parties, who always followed him about wherever he went, and that he could get no rest for them night or day. He said they were using all their influences against him, in order to prevent his getting a situation; whether he went to France, England, or Scotland, the spies were always about him. He told me it was immaterial in what country he was, for they were sure to send their emissaries before him, and he was known wherever he went.

"I asked him who the parties were, and he told me they were Scotchmen, and natives of Glasgow. I told him it was all imagination, and endeavoured to persuade him to think nothing more about it. I also told him that if any person ill-used him or slandered him I would have them punished, as I considered his character was very good. He said he would do so, and added that if he could once set his eyes upon them they should not be long in the land of the living.

"After the conversation had continued for some time he became very much excited; and, seeing that he was labouring under some extraordinary excitement, I considered it prudent to drop the subject. In consequence of that conversation I immediately came to the conclusion that he was not in his right mind."

Waddington followed up with a question regarding this conversation.

"I never noticed anything extraordinary in his behaviour till the period I have just mentioned," Carlo allowed, "although his habits were rather eccentric."

"What do you mean by eccentric?"

"Why, that he was very hard-working and penurious; he was also eccentric in his dress. The last few times that I saw him, I noticed that he was not quite so cheerful as usual, though he was generally sullen and reserved, and always evinced a disposition to evade conversation."

"What did you pay him for his business?" Justice Coleridge inquired.

"18£."

"Did that sum include the tools?"

"Yes; but there were very few, and most of them were worn out."

Bodkin, for the defence, called Jane Drummond Patterson to take the stand.

"I know the prisoner. He lodged in my house two years ago. I observed something very peculiar in his manner. His eyes presented a very strange appearance; he looked wild, and very different from what he used to do. He was also very restless in his sleep. I frequently heard him moan and groan in his sleep, and sometimes he spoke as if disturbed.

"He went away twice, and told me he had been to France. I told him he had better stop away altogether; to which he replied that he could not stop either in London or in France, as he was constantly haunted by a parcel of devils following him, and they said they were persons from Glasgow. He appeared then rather angry. I at length began to be afraid of him, and expressed a wish for him to leave my house. He said he would leave as soon as possible; he could get situations anywhere, but it was of no use, as they were all haunted with devils.

"A few days before he left in September, I found some pistols in his room. I said, 'What in the name of God are you doing with pistols there?' He said he was going to shoot birds with them. On one occasion, when I was speaking to him about getting a situation, he laid hold of me, made use of an oath, and looked very wild.

"When he went away he took nothing with him but the clothes on his back. I noticed when he went away that he looked very wild and frightsome-like."

The solicitor general asked her when she first came to notice this aspect of his manner: "I noticed the peculiarity when he first came to lodge with me, but he did not mention anything about being haunted by devils till three or four months afterwards."

Monteith of the defence had Henry C. Bell, one of the deputy sheriffs and a resident of Glasgow, called to the stand:

"I believe the prisoner to be the person who called upon me about nine or ten months ago and complained that he was harassed to death by a system of persecution which had for some time been adopted towards him, and for which he could obtain no redress whatever.

"I told him I would render him any assistance in my power, and asked him the nature of the persecution he complained of. He made a long, rambling, unintelligible statement in reply, from which I gathered, as far as I can recollect, that he was constantly beset by spies, and that he considered his life and property in danger. I told him that I thought he must be labouring under some very erroneous impression, and advised him, if he had any criminal charge to make against any person, to go to the Procurator-Fiscal, or if his complaint was of a civil nature, to apply to some man of business.

"He said it would be perfectly useless to make any such application, and appearing dissatisfied with my answer, he went away. He called upon me again about a fortnight or three weeks afterwards. I asked him whether he had seen the Procurator-Fiscal or a man of business, and he said he had not. He then made another statement of a precisely similar character, but I told him that I could not render him any assistance, and he then went away. I certainly concluded that he was not right in his intellects, that he was labouring under some very extraordinary delusion and I made a remark to that effect to my clerk."

To describe a visit he'd had from M'Naughten about twelve months previously, Alexander Johnston, the M.P. for Glasgow, was examined by Clarkson for the defence:

"He complained of being subjected to an extraordinary system of persecution, and wished for my advice as to the best method of getting rid of it. On subjects of general business he talked very rationally, but with respect to this particular business he said that he had for a considerable time been persecuted by the emissaries of a political party, whom he had offended by interfering in politics.

"He also complained of being attacked through the newspapers, and said the persons of whom he complained followed him night and day; that he could get no rest for them; that they had destroyed his peace of mind, and what to do he really did not know. I reasoned with him, and told him that I thought he must be mistaken; assured him that nobody followed him about, and advised him, if he received any annoyances, to apply to the captain of police. He then said that he thought his persecutors would be satisfied with nothing less than his life. When I told him that I thought he was mistaken, he said that he was quite certain that he was not. He assured me that he was perfectly sound in his mind, and in good bodily health. He then left me."

"What was the impression left upon your mind by that interview?" Clarkson wanted to know.

"I certainly thought that what he stated was his firm conviction. In about a week or ten days the prisoner again called upon me, and he then told me that his persecutors were still pursuing him, and wished me to take some steps in order to deter them from so doing. I again recommended him to go to the sheriff, and assured him that if he was in reality annoyed as he had described, he would be protected. I merely told him that in order to get rid of him, feeling assured that he was labouring under a delusion. About a month after the last interview, I came to London, and in a few days I received a letter from the prisoner, reiterating the same complaints, and begging of me to interfere in his behalf; to that communication I wrote the letter produced."

"Have you the letter you received from the prisoner?"

"No, I have not."

Clarkson requested the letter Johnston had written to M'Naughten be entered into evidence. This was done and the clerk of the court read it out:

Reform Club, May 5, 1842. Sir, I received your letter of the 3rd of May, and am sorry I can do nothing for you. I fear you are labouring under an aberration of mind, and I think you have no reason to entertain such fears. I am, &c., Alexander Johnston. – Mr. D. M'Naughten

The solicitor general followed up and cross-examined Mr. Johnston about what he knew of the prisoner.

"I had no knowledge of him previous to his calling upon me; neither had I any other conversations with him but those I have stated."

Cockburn himself rose and asked for Sir James Campbell, lord provost of Glasgow to be sworn in, following which he told the court of an encounter he had had with M'Naughten:

"I am Lord Provost of Glasgow, and was so in the year 1842. In the month of May in that year, the prisoner called upon me; he said he wanted my advice and protection. He said that he was the victim of an extraordinary persecution; that he was followed and beset by spies night and day, and that he could not get rid of them; they dogged him wherever he went, and he could not in consequence get any rest night or day; that he was afraid to go home, and had therefore been compelled to sleep in the fields in the suburbs of the town.

"I asked him who his persecutors were, and he told me they were persons who had an ill-feeling towards him, and that he considered his life in danger in consequence. I at once saw that he was labouring under a strange delusion, and told him that he was labouring under some hypochondriac affection, for which he ought to have advice, and asked him whether he had ever been treated as an insane person? He said he had not, and endeavoured to persuade me that he was in the enjoyment of sound mind and health.

"After some further conversation, I advised him to consult with his friends upon the subject, and suggested the propriety of seeing some medical gentleman. He did not appear to be satisfied with what I stated to him, and he then went away. I immediately sent for the prisoner's father, in order to let him know what had taken place, but he did not wait upon me, and I took no further steps in the affair. I felt no doubt at the time that the prisoner was labouring under some species of insanity."

Waddington asked the witness his observations on the prisoner's appearance.

"I did not notice anything particular in his appearance, and I should not have observed there was anything wrong about him had it not been for what he stated. He was a total stranger to me, and I should think the conversation did not last more than five minutes."

The Rev. Alexander Turner spoke to a similar interview with the prisoner:

"I am the minister of the parish of Gorbals. About seven or eight months ago I recollect the prisoner calling upon me at my residence. He told me that he was the son of Mr. M'Naughten, the turner, who was a member of my congregation. He told me, that for some time past he had been very much persecuted by a number of persons, who constantly followed him about, and who annoyed him in various ways; that, in order to escape their persecutions, he had gone to France, but had not been able to free himself from them. I think he said they had found him out in France; and that, as he could not get rid of them, his life was rendered perfectly miserable, and he talked about being haunted by them.

"He also told me that he had called on the Sheriff and Sir James Campbell, and likewise upon the Procurator-Fiscal, but they refused to do anything for him. I observed that he appeared to be labouring under a very great degree of excitement, which was evident from large drops of perspiration on his brow. I certainly thought that he was insane. In consequence of that interview, I called upon his father a day or two afterwards, and told him that I thought he ought to be put under restraint."

Clarkson asked Campbell to mention again when this had been: "To the best of my belief, that conversation took place about seven or eight months ago. I never saw the prisoner afterwards."

Commissioner of police for Glasgow, Hugh Wilson, recalled for Bodkin his experiences with M'Naughten:

"I have known the prisoner for about ten or twelve years. I recollect his calling upon me, about eighteen months ago, to make a complaint. He said that he had come to consult me on a very delicate matter; and, after some hesitation, said that he was the object of some persecution, and added, that he thought it proceeded from the priests at the Catholic chapel in Clyde Street, who were assisted by a parcel of Jesuits.

"I asked him what they did to him, and his reply was, that they followed him where ever he went, and were never out of his sight, and when he went into his bedroom he still found them with him. He was perfectly calm and collected when he first came in, but when he began to talk about the persecution, he became very much excited; and I then thought he was daft. I saw that he was extremely anxious upon the subject, and therefore told him to call again on the following Tuesday, and I would see what could be done for him.

"A few days afterwards I again saw him, when I promised to speak to Miller, the superintendent, about it. When I again saw him, I told him that I had seen Miller, who said it was all nonsense and there was nothing in it; to which the prisoner replied that Miller was a bad one, that he saw it in his face, and he wanted to deceive both him and me. Having again run on about the Catholics and the Jesuits, he went away.

"In two or three days he again called, and on alluding to the subject, said, the Tories had joined with the Catholics, that he could get no rest either night or day, through their persecuting conduct, and he felt quite sure they would throw him into a consumption.

"At that interview I told him he had spoilt the scheme which I had planned for the purpose of finding out his persecutors, at which he appeared to be very much disappointed. I desired him not to look either to the right or to the left, and, if possible, let them see that he did not observe them. He said he would do so. After that interview, I did not see him for three or four months, when he again came to me and said he was worse than ever. I told him he should get out of their way. He said he had been to Boulogne, and asked me if I knew the watch-box on the Custom House Quay there? I told him I did.

"He then said that as soon as he landed, he saw one of his spies peep from behind it, and added, that it was no use going further into France, and spending his money, when he could get no relief. He appeared then worse than ever, and I advised him to go into the country and amuse himself by working, and not to think anything more about it; but he said it was no use going there, as they would be sure to follow him. I had several other interviews with him, and the last time I saw him was about the month of August last, when he made the same sort of complaint, and the delusion then appeared to be stronger in his mind than ever."

To this the solicitor general put a question about the manner of his appointment as police commissioner, whether he felt M'Naughten might have had occasion to be involved with him in some political connection.

"The office I hold is not one of a political character," he informed Follett. "I have not canvassed the prisoner for his vote within the last twelve months. I have solicited his vote, but that was three or four years ago. When I saw him in August last, he was very much excited. He said the police, the Jesuits, the Catholic priests, and Tories were all leagued against him." What Cockburn had established was a fairly compelling body of observation and lay opinion as to M'Naughten's condition at or around the time of shooting. It was now the turn of the experts to convert these observations into medical opinion which might bear upon his culpability.

Chapter Eighteen

ORIGINALLY FOUNDED IN 1247 as a priory for the sisters and brothers of the Order of the Star of Bethlehem, by the time of M'Naughten's trial in 1843 Bethlehem Hospital in London (known as "Bethlem") was recognized as the world's first and oldest psychiatric hospital providing care to the mentally ill. By virtue of his thirty years as a practising physician at Bethlem, with insanity the subject of his work, Dr. Edward T. Monro was called as the first expert witness for the defence, Cockburn himself doing the questioning.

"How did you come to examine the prisoner Daniel M'Naughten?"

"I was requested by the friends of the prisoner to visit him in Newgate prison. I was accompanied by Sir A. Morrison, Mr. M'Clure, and other professional gentlemen."

"You met on that occasion some medical gentlemen, who were deputed on the part of the Crown to visit the prisoner, did you not?"

"I met Dr. Sutherland, Jr. and Dr. Bright."

"I believe you all saw the prisoner together?"

"Yes, we saw and examined the prisoner together."

"How was the examination conducted?"

"We all asked the prisoner questions in turn."

"Did you make at the time any note of the examination?"

"No; but I made some notes afterwards."

"When did that examination take place?"

"On the 18th of February."

"What did the prisoner say in answer to the questions put to him?"

"With the permission of the Court, I will state the substance of what he stated. In reply to the questions put to him, the prisoner said he was persecuted by a system or crew at Glasgow, Edinburgh,

Liverpool, London, and Boulogne. That this crew preceded or followed him wherever he went; that he had no peace of mind, and he was sure it would kill him; that it was grinding of the mind. I asked him if he had availed himself of medical advice. He replied that physicians could be of no service to him, for if he took a ton of drugs it would be of no service to him; that in Glasgow he observed people in the streets pointing at him, and speaking of him. They said, 'that is the man,' 'he is a murderer,' 'the worst of characters.' That everything was done to associate his name with the direst of crimes. He was tossed like a cork on the sea, and wherever he went, in town or country, on sea or shore, he was perpetually watched and followed.

"At Edinburgh he saw a man on horseback watching him. Another person there nodded to him and exclaimed, 'That's he.' He said he had applied to the authorities of Glasgow for protection and relief. His complaints had been sneered and scowled at by Sheriff Bell, who had it in his power to put a stop to the persecution, if he had liked. If he had had a pistol in his possession, he said he would have shot Sheriff Bell dead as he sat in the court-house; he also said that Mr. Salmond, the procurator-fiscal, Mr. Sheriff Bell, Sheriff Alison, and Sir R. Peel might have put a stop to this system of persecution if they would; that on coming out of the court-house he had seen a man frowning at him, with a bundle of straw under his arm; that he knew well enough what was meant; that everything was done by signs; that he was represented to be under a delusion; that the straw denoted that he should lie upon straw in an asylum.

"He believed that whilst on board the steamboat on his way from Glasgow to Liverpool he was watched, eyed, and examined closely by persons coming near him; that they had followed him to Boulogne on two occasions; that they would never allow him to learn French, and wanted to murder him. He stated he was afraid of going out after dark, for fear of assassination, that individuals were made to appear before him, like those he had seen at Glasgow.

"He mentioned having applied to Mr. A. Johnston, M.P. for Kilmarnock, for protection; Mr. Johnston had told him that he (the prisoner) was labouring under a delusion, but that he was sure he was not. That he had seen paragraphs in *The Times* newspaper containing allusions which be was satisfied were directed at him; he had seen articles also in the *Glasgow Herald*, beastly and atrocious, insinuating things untrue and insufferable of him; that on one or two occasions something pernicious had been put into his food; that he had studied anatomy to obtain peace of mind, but be had not found it. He said that he imagined the person at whom he fired at Charing Cross to be one of the crew, a part of the system that was destroying his health."

"When you referred to the person whom he had fired at Charing Cross, how did you put your question?"

"I cannot recollect the exact question. I have no doubt I asked him who be thought the person was."

"State, Dr. Monro, as correctly as you can, what the prisoner said on this point?"

"He observed that when he saw the person at Charing Cross at whom he fired, every feeling of suffering which he had endured for months and years rose up at once in his mind, and that he conceived that he should obtain peace by killing him."

"I believe all the medical men heard the questions put to him and the answers?"

"Yes. Drs. Bright and Sutherland were present. I do not know if they saw the prisoner yesterday."

"Do you think that your knowledge of insanity enables you to judge between the conduct of a man who feigns a delusion and one who feels it?"

"I do, certainly."

"Do you consider, Dr. Monro, that the delusions were real or assumed?"

"I am quite satisfied that they were real. I have not a shadow of a doubt on the point. Supposing you had heard nothing of the examination which took place in Newgate, but only the evidence which has been adduced in court for the last two days, would you then say that the prisoner was labouring under a delusion?"

"Most certainly."

"The act with which he is charged, coupled with the history of his past life, leaves not the remotest doubt on my mind of the presence of insanity sufficient to deprive the prisoner of all self-control. I consider the act of the prisoner in killing Mr. Drummond to have been committed whilst under a delusion; the act itself I look upon as the crowning act of the whole matter, as the climax – as a carrying out of the pre-existing idea which had haunted him for years."

"It is consistent with the pathology of insanity, is it not, that a partial delusion may exist, depriving the person of all self-control, whilst the other faculties may be sound?"

"Certainly; monomania may exist with general sanity. I have frequently known a person insane upon one point, exhibit great cleverness upon all others not immediately associated with his delusions. I have seen clever artists, arithmeticians, and architects, whose mind was disordered on one point. An insane person may commit an act similar to the one with which the prisoner is charged, and yet be aware of the consequences of such an act. The evidence which I have heard in Court has not induced me to alter my opinion of the case. Lunatics often manifest a high degree of cleverness and ingenuity, and exhibit occasionally great cunning in escaping from the consequences of such acts. I see a number of such cases every day."

Dr. Monro's formulation was that "monomania" had caused a "partial delusion" (or later a "morbid delusion") in M'Naughten. At the time monomania was seen as a disorder that permitted the accused to, in general respects, carry on as if normal. The famous physician Henry Maudsley described the condition of monomania in his *Responsibility in Mental Disease*:[1] "When [the patient] exhibits insane delusions on one subject or in regard to certain trains of thought, and talks sensibly in other respects, he is said to have 'monomania.'" It was thus described as a "partial insanity." This description is most consistent with what would presently be referred to as "Delusional Disorder":[2]

Nonbizarre delusions (i.e., involving situations that occur in real life, such as being followed, poisoned, infected, loved at a distance, or deceived by spouse or lover, or having a disease) of at least one month's duration.

. . .

Apart from the impact of the delusion(s) or its ramifications, functioning is not markedly impaired and behaviour is not obviously odd or bizarre.

Perhaps the leading authority on insanity at the time of the trial was the American Isaac Ray, the author of an often cited text, *A Treatise on the Medical Jurisprudence of Insanity*.[3] (Ray was quoted by Cockburn in his opening speech to the jury.) Mania was seen in M'Naughten's day

SKETCH PORTRAIT OF DANIEL M'NAUGHTEN AT THE TIME OF HIS TRIAL
SOURCE: ILLUSTRATED LONDON NEWS, MARCH 1843.

as due to structural aberrations in the brain, either acquired or congenital. These structural changes could come in the form of "lesions" or other anomalies. Where not observable during an autopsy, the inference was that the techniques of the day were incapable of detecting the lesion or other structural flaw. The structural flaw was presumed to create an "irritation," which was the initial stage of the mental disease. From this irritation the disease progressed (in an unstated manner) to the point where "disorganization" occurred as the final stage.

The deranged function of the brain manifested itself in qualitatively different ways depending upon where this irritation occurred. The irritation could set off a chain of events that would cause the brain to function abnormally without leaving any observable evidence at an autopsy. As well, the irritation was thought to be able to operate within a small enough area of the brain such that a full-blown inflammation of the brain did not occur. Therefore, the mania or insanity may not have been pervasive but limited to certain functions of the brain, and may often have been undetectable unless the individual was operating in a particular environment or amongst certain individuals.

Further, the view as far as Ray was concerned was that mental illness was a disease with precisely the same features as other diseases of the body, with periods of incubation, development, and termination in cure or death. His authoritative text indicates that what are symptoms of mania in one person may be indications of normalcy in another. Ray advises that it is really change in disposition, rather than the nature of the change, that is diagnostic.

Solicitor-General Follett put several questions to Dr. Monro in cross-examination.

> "You have stated that Drs. Bright and Sutherland were present at the examination. Did they hear your examination of the prisoner?"
>
> "Yes, they were present and heard the examination. They were there on the part of the Crown. I asked all the questions."
>
> "Is it not the practice of the Crown to have medical gentlemen present at the examination of a person charged with such serious crimes as the prisoner is now accused of?"
>
> "I believe it is."
>
> "I believe you attended in the case of Oxford [acquitted by reason of insanity in 1840] on the part of the Crown?"

"I saw Oxford by myself; no other medical man was present."

"Who were present when you examined M'Naughten?"

"Sir A. Morrison, Mr. M'Clure, doctors Bright and Sutherland. On the two last occasions on which I saw the prisoner, Mr. Hutcheson and Dr. Crawford were present at the request of the friends of the prisoner. They examined the prisoner almost exclusively on that occasion, and, in accordance with the usual practice, gentlemen in behalf of the Crown also attended."

"I should like you to acquaint the Court with the exact form of the question you put to him which had a reference to his firing the pistol at Mr. Drummond, at Charing Cross."

"I did not take any notes at the time."

"Did you ask him if he knew whom he fired at?"

"I am not quite certain. I think I asked the prisoner whom he fired at."

"Did anyone present ask the prisoner if he knew that it was Sir Robert Peel he shot at?"

"I think he was asked the question more than once. He hesitated and paused, and at length said he was not sure whether it was Sir Robert Peel or not. This was asked in my presence."

"Please do refer to your notes, and tell me whether he did not say that if he thought it was not Sir Robert Peel, he would not have fired at all?"

"I have no notes to that effect. The notes that I have with me were made at home, and not at the time of the examination."

"Did he not say he would not have fired if he had known that it was not Sir Robert Peel?"

"No, I think he did not. On this point he observed that the person at whom he fired gave him as he passed a scowling look. At that moment all the feelings of months and years rushed into his mind, and he thought that he could only obtain peace by shooting him. He stated this in answer to my questions. I avoided all leading questions. There was much repetition in the questions put to him. The gentlemen from Scotland also examined him."

"What was the form of the question which related to his firing at Sir Robert Peel?"

"I think the question was, 'Did you know whom you were firing at?' In reply he observed, 'He was one of the crew that had been following me.'"

"Do you mean to say, Dr. Monro that you could satisfy yourself as to a person's state of mind by merely going into a cell and putting questions to him?"

"In many instances I can; I will mention a case in point. A short time back I was called in to examine a man who was confined in Newgate under sentence of death. It was thought that he had feigned insanity. After an attentive examination, in conjunction with Mr. M'Murdo, I at once detected that his insanity was assumed, and such turned out to be the fact. I had the satisfaction afterwards of hearing that the man himself confessed prior to the execution that he had feigned insanity."

"I wish to know whether your skill would enable you to ascertain the nature of the delusion under which the prisoner was labouring without seeing the depositions taken in his case?"

"Certainly. I have formed my opinion from an examination of the prisoner personally, in conjunction with the depositions."

"Is it not necessary to examine the bodily symptoms in these cases; for instance, the pulse?"

"Yes, sometimes. I did not feel his pulse, neither did I lay much stress upon the appearance of his eye." [In Dr. Ray's text an accelerated pulse and a "wild and glassy look to the eye" were described as possible indications of mania.]

"Do you always assume that the party tells you what is passing in his mind?"

"Not always."

"What do you mean by insanity? Do you consider a person labouring under a morbid delusion of unsound mind to be insane?"

"I do."

"Do you think insanity may exist without any morbid delusion?"

"Yes; a person may be imbecile; but there is generally some morbid delusion; there are various shades of insanity. A person may be of unsound mind, and yet be able to manage the usual affairs of life."

"May insanity exist with a moral perception of right and wrong?"

"Yes; it is very common."

"A person may have a delusion and know murder to be a crime?"

"If there had existed antecedent symptoms I should consider the murder to be an overt act, the crowning piece of his insanity. But if he had stolen a 10£ note it would not have tallied with his delusion."

"But suppose he had stolen the note from one of his persecutors?"

The first part of Monro's answer was not heard, owing to the laughter which followed the Solicitor-General's observation. "A delusion like M'Naughten's," he continued, "would carry him quite away. I think a person may be of unsound mind, labour under a morbid delusion, and yet know right from wrong."

"Have you heard of what is called moral insanity?"

"I have."

"Have you read the works of M. Marc?"

"I understand what monomania means. It is attended by an irresistible propensity to thieve or burn, without being the result of particular motives."

In re-examining Dr. Monro, Cockburn clarified with him the issue of the prisoner's moral perceptions.

"You said, Dr. Monro that a person might labour under a particular form of insanity without having his moral perceptions deranged. For illustration, a man may fancy his legs made of glass. There is nothing in that which could affect his moral feelings?"

"Certainly not."

"You have not the slightest doubt that M'Naughten's moral perceptions were impaired?"

"No."

Further to Dr. Monro's testimony, Clarkson on behalf of the defence then questioned Dr. A. Morison, a physician at St. Luke's Hospital and also affiliated with Bethlem Hospital and the Surrey Asylum:

"I believe, Dr. Morison, that you were one of the gentlemen who saw the prisoner in conjunction with Drs. Monro, Sutherland, and Bright?"

"I was."

"You have been in Court during the whole of the day?"

"I have."

"Were you not present during the whole of the examination of the prisoner in Newgate?"

"I was."

"Did you arrive at any conclusion as to the prisoner's state of mind?"

"I did."

"Please do state to the Court what your impression was?"

"That M'Naughten was insane."

"After having heard the evidence adduced today in Court, has your opinion undergone any alteration?"

"I am still of the same opinion, that the prisoner was insane at the time he committed the act with which he is charged."

"The prisoner's morbid delusions consisted in his fancying himself subject to a system of persecutions?"

"Yes; that was the peculiar cause of his insanity."

"What effect had this delusion upon his mind?"

"It deprived the prisoner of all restraint over his actions."

"Do you speak with any doubt upon the point?"

"Not the slightest."

To this, Solicitor-General Follett put a question in cross-examination:

"Dr. Morison, had you formed your opinion in consequence of reading the depositions?"

"It is the result both of reading the depositions and examining the prisoner. I had, however, arrived at a conclusion of his insanity before I read the depositions."

Dr. William M'Clure, a London surgeon who had accompanied Monro and Morison in the prison examination of M'Naughten, confirmed the previous evidence of the witnesses for the defence: "I consider when he fired at Mr. Drummond, at Charing Cross, he (the prisoner) was suffering from an hallucination which deprived him of all ordinary restraint."

Dr. W. Hutcheson, physician to the Royal Lunatic Asylum at Glasgow, gave evidence to the same effect: "The prisoner had lost all self-control at the moment he fired at Mr. Drummond. The act flowed immediately from the delusion."

The solicitor general, in cross-examination, sought to clarify Hutcheson's conclusion: "Do you mean to say that the delusion prevented the prisoner from exercising any control over his actions?"

"I said that the act was the consequence of the delusion, which was irresistible. The delusion was so strong that nothing but a physical impediment could have prevented him from committing the act. He might have done the same thing in Glasgow if the disease of the mind had reached the same point."

"From what period do you date his insanity?"

"From the time when M'Naughten called upon the commissioner of police, Mr. Wilson, for protection."

"Was he insane at that time?"

"Yes."

"When was that?"

"Eighteen months back."

Cockburn took this point a step further: "Supposing at that time the same morbid notion had seized him, do you think he would have committed a similar act?"

"I do not think he could have resisted any impulse springing from the morbid delusions under which he suffered."

"When patients exhibit symptoms similar to those which the prisoner manifested they are generally, I believe, placed under restraint?"

"Yes. Such symptoms often gradually develop themselves, whereas many have these delusions for some time and are harmless, and then they may suddenly impel them to the commission of crime. I have known cases of that kind."

Dr. P.J. Crawford, a professor of medical jurisprudence at Anderson's University in Glasgow, as well as Mr. Aston Key, of Guy's Hospital in London, both confirmed the testimony of the previous defence witnesses.

Final evidence confirming M'Naughten's insanity was then given, in response to questions from Clarkson, by the surgeon Forbes Winslow who had authored a book on insanity in criminal cases:

"Mr. Winslow, you are a surgeon residing in Guildford Street?"

"I am."

"You are the author of *The Plea of Insanity in Criminal Cases*, and other works on the subject of insanity?"

"Yes."

"I think Mr. Winslow that you have been in Court during the whole of the trial and have not been summoned on either side, and have heard all the evidence on the part of the Crown and for the defense?"

"I have."

"Judging from the evidence which you have heard, what is your opinion as to the prisoner's state of mind?"

"I have not the slightest hesitation in saying that he is insane, and that he committed the offence in question whilst afflicted with a delusion, under which he appears to have been labouring for a considerable length of time."

At this moment Chief Justice Tindal intervened: "Mr. Winslow, will you repeat what you have just stated?" Winslow again expressed his unqualified opinion of M'Naughten's insanity.

A Dr. Philips from the Westminster Hospital was also called, though neither he nor Winslow had personally examined M'Naughten. The findings of both gentlemen were given very serious consideration by the court, however, as they were merely observers, effectively corroborating the evidence of other witnesses based on independent assessment of its "scientific" nature.

Indeed, it was at this point that Chief Justice Tindal interrupted the proceedings and addressed Follett: "Solicitor General, are you prepared, on the part of the Crown, with any evidence to combat this testimony of the medical witnesses who now have been examined, because we think if you have not, we must be under the necessity of stopping the case. Is there any medical evidence on the other side?"

"No, my Lord," Follett replied.

Chief Justice Tindal continued: "We feel the evidence, especially that of the last two medical gentlemen who have been examined, and who are strangers to both sides and only observers of the case, to be very strong, and sufficient to induce my learned brothers and myself to stop the case."

Follett then addressed the jury:

"Gentlemen, after the intimation I have received from the Bench, I feel that I should not be properly discharging my duty to the Crown and to the public if I asked you to give your verdict in this case against the prisoner. The Lord Chief Justice has intimated to me the very strong opinion entertained by himself and the other learned judges who have presided here today, that the evidence on the part of the defendant, and more particularly the evidence of the medical witnesses, is sufficient to show that this unfortunate man at the time he committed the act was labouring under insanity; and, of course, if he were so, he would be entitled to his acquittal.

"I was anxious, however, to say, on the part of the Crown, that they have had no object whatever but the attainment of public justice, and I believe I am right in saying that, on the part of the prosecution, every facility has been given to the defense. There is no wish, there can be no wish on the part of the public prosecutor, but that the ends of public justice shall be attained; and, certainly, when in the streets of this metropolis a crime of this sort was committed, it was incumbent on those who have the care of the public peace and safety to have the case properly investigated. The safety of the lives and persons of all of us requires that there should be such an investigation.

"On the part of the Crown I felt it my duty to lay before you the evidence we possessed of the conduct of this young man. I cannot agree with the observations my learned friend has made on the doctrines and authorities that have been laid down in this case, because I think those doctrines and authorities are correct law; our object being to ascertain whether at the time the prisoner committed the crime he was at that time to be regarded as a responsible agent, or whether all control of himself was taken away. The Lord Chief Justice, I understand, means to submit that question to you. I cannot press for a verdict against the prisoner. The learned judge will submit the case to you, and then it will be for you to come to your decision."

Chief Justice Tindal duly addressed the jury:

"In this important case which has excited very great anxiety during the two preceding days, the point I shall have to submit to you is whether on the whole of the evidence you have heard, you are satisfied that at the time the act was committed, for the commission of which the prisoner now stands charged, he had that competent use of his understanding as that he knew that he was doing, by the very act itself, a wicked and a wrong thing.

"If he was not sensible at the time he committed that act, that it was a violation of the law of God or of man, undoubtedly he was not responsible for that act, or liable to any punishment whatever flowing from that act. Gentlemen, that is the precise point which I shall feel it my duty to leave to you.

"I have undoubtedly been very much struck, and so have my learned brethren, by the evidence we have heard during the evening from
the medical persons who have been examined as to the state of the
mind of the unhappy prisoner, for unhappy I must call him in reference to his state of mind.

"Now, gentlemen, I can go through the whole of the evidence, and
particularly call back your attention to that part of it to which I at first
adverted, but I cannot help remarking, in common with my learned
brethren, that the whole of the medical evidence is on one side, and
that there is no part of it which leaves any doubt on the mind. It seems
almost unnecessary that I should go through the evidence.

"I am, however, in your hands; but if on balancing the evidence in
your minds you think the prisoner capable of distinguishing between
right and wrong, then he was a responsible agent and liable to all
the penalties the law imposes. If not so, and if in your judgment the
subject should appear involved in very great difficulty, then you will
probably not take upon yourselves to find the prisoner guilty. If that is
your opinion then you will acquit the prisoner. If you think you ought
to hear the evidence more fully, in that case I will state it to you, and
leave the case in your hands. Probably, however, sufficient has now
been laid before you, and you will say whether you want any further
information."

Here the court came very close to what is known as a "directed
verdict." That is, the Chief Justice telling the trier of fact, which in
this case was the jury, that the only possible verdict available on the
evidence is a verdict of "not guilty by reason of insanity." This is rarely
done but is appropriate in overwhelming circumstances where, in a
justice's mind, it would be unwise to leave any discretion to the jury
who, if left to their own devices, might return a perverse verdict. The
Chief Justice did not go quite that far but, at the same time, strongly
intimated that the verdict was obvious and inevitable. Three members
of the House of Lords – Chief Justice Tindal, and Lords Williams and
Coleridge – presided at M'Naughten's trial. It is clear that the members of the bench, lords Tindal, Williams, and Coleridge, had been
discussing the case as it progressed and decided that the nature of the
evidence was such that it compelled them to intervene:

"We require no more, my Lord," said the foreman of the jury.

"If you find the prisoner not guilty," the Chief Justice instructed, "say on the ground of insanity, in which case proper care will be taken of him."

"We find the prisoner not guilty, on the ground of insanity."

By order of the court, the clerk then directed the jailer to keep the prisoner in safe custody till Her Majesty's pleasure be known. M'Naughten was then removed and the jury members were discharged. Eleven days later, on Wednesday, 15 March, he was moved by order of the Right Honorable Sir James Graham, secretary of state, from Newgate Prison to Bethlehem Hospital.

PART III

The M'Naughten Rules

Chapter Nineteen

REACTION TO THE M'Naughten verdict was swift in coming. His acquittal outraged many and was criticized by most for it didn't seem to make sense. Queen Victoria, who was far from amused, was known to have said: "How could he have been found not guilty? He *did* it, didn't he?"

A March 6th letter to the editor of *The Times* gave pointed expression to the public mood:

> Sir, if the result of M'Naughten's trial satisfies the end of justice, by proving the moral irresponsibility of the murderer, it undoubtedly leaves the security of Her Majesty's subjects from similar murderous attacks in a very unsatisfactory state. M'Naughten is not the only dangerous lunatic at large – nay, his case is so common, that a term has been invented to designate it, and was employed by his counsel, viz., "homicidal monomania"; in plain English, an irresistible impulse on the part of the maniac for blood – to put some one to death.
>
> The question then is, is the law sufficient for the protection of the public? Is there no responsibility on the part of the relatives in leaving such dangerous lunatics at large? It appears in evidence that the father was twice warned as to the state of his son's mind – once by the Provost of Glasgow, whose station ought to have given weight to his opinion; but to neither was any attention paid, and it is to be regretted that such culpable neglect and recklessness of consequences cannot be visited by the law.
>
> We read in Dr. Monro's evidence that the assassin said, that at one time he would have shot Mr. Sheriff Bell dead in his seat in the court of justice, if he had a pistol, and no one can doubt that Mr. Bell might have been the victim. Again, it appears that one of his illusions

What did the jury mean by saying he was not guilty! I will never believe that anyone could be "not guilty" who wanted to murder a conservative Prime Minister!

Victoria R

Queen Victoria's comment on the attempted assassination of Sir Robert Peel on January 20, 1843, reflected the attitude of the people of England. When Daniel McNaughton shot Peel's secretary, in the mistaken belief that he had killed the Prime Minister, and was absolved of the crime on the grounds of insanity, the public was outraged. As a consequence of the storm of controversy and publicity occasioned by the trial, the first set of rational and consistent rules for determining criminal insanity was formulated.

QUEEN VICTORIA'S REACTION TO THE M'NAUGHTEN VERDICT

was, that he had been attacked by paragraphs in *The Times* and the *Glasgow Herald*; it is quite as probable that M'Naughten should have carried out his revenge on his fancied persecutors, and exercised his "homicidal monomania" by waiting at the office of your journal, Sir, and shooting the first man who came out of the door as that he should have taken away the life of Mr. Drummond.

One word on the affected sentimentality of the day: a perusal of the last two days' proceeding in the Central Criminal Court would almost persuade us to give our sympathy to the murderer, and not to the murdered. No words applicable to such a deed of horror are used, though our forcible Anglo-Saxon idiom supplies them in abundance. The prisoner is "unfortunate," "is in an unhappy situation," and "all must regret the fate of this victim." Such is the dainty language in vogue, which tends to foster the false morality of the morbid humanitarians of the day.

Another letter to the editor addressed, with biting sarcasm, the diagnosis of monomania that the defence obtained from Dr. Monro:

Sir, I have in contemplation the accomplishment of a certain pet project, which unfortunately involves some degree of violence in its attainment; I mean, however, to retain beforehand some of the most eminent medical men of the day as witnesses in proof of my monomaniacal possession, and in the meantime I hope, through the assistance of your journal, to ascertain when the public (who I understand considers itself rather outraged by the acquittal of my friend Mr. M'Naughten) are sufficiently tranquillized to render it safe and expedient for a British court of Justice and a British jury to reward my perseverance with a comfortable and permanent abode in Bethlehem Hospital at the expense of the nation. I confess this latter consideration has much weight with me, as I am at present out of work, and have the much more disagreeable alternative of a union workhouse staring me in the face.

Still another from the *Standard*, which came in verse, was reprinted in *The Times*:

Ye people of England! Exult and be glad,
For ye're now at the will of the merciless mad.
Why say ye that but three authorities reign –

Crown, Commons, and Lords? – You omit the insane?
They're a privileg'd class, whom no statute controls,
And their murderous charter exists in their souls.
Do they wish to spill blood – they have only to play
A few pranks – get asylum'd a month and a day –
Then heigh! To escape from the mad doctor's keys,
And to pistol or stab whomsoever they please.

Now, the dog has a human-like wit – in creation
He resembles most nearly our own generation:
Then if madmen for murder escape with impunity,
Why deny a poor dog the same noble immunity?
So, if dog or man bite you, beware being nettled,
For crime is no crime – when the mind is unsettled.

The humour magazine *Punch* produced a satirical ad announcing the opening of a new school in London, the "Monomaniac Academy: Bethlem Hospital," which would be run by James Hadfield and Daniel M'Naughten:

An Academy for the instruction of youth in the art of insanity that will enable young criminals to escape punishment, pickpockets to become monomaniacs *pro tempore*, and enable others to remove all impediments to legacies.

While it is not known whether newspapers of the day received any letters applauding the M'Naughten verdict, there were those who suggested the public shouldn't have been surprised or dismayed, one person writing to *The Times*:

Sir, many of my respectable friends are alarmed at a late verdict, but in my opinion very unnecessarily, since all that the Government has to do is to perform their duty to the country, as pointed out by the act of 39 and 40 George III, cap. 94, (*Criminal Lunatics Act*, 1800) by which it is provided that "whenever any person charged with murder shall be acquitted on the ground of being insane at the time of committing such offence, it shall be lawful for the Crown to give such order for the safe custody of such person during pleasure, in such place, and in such manner, as to the Crown shall seem fit.

MONOMANIACS

An unfortunate creature was brought up charged with having a mania for splitting open policemen's skulls, without any cause whatever. The unhappy individual, for whom every one present felt the deepest commiseration, had broken the heads of two policemen, and threatened to do the same thing for the whole of the division to which they belonged. The policemen whom the poor fellow had attacked, came into court to give their evidence, and the state of their heads made every one feel sincerely for the unhappy man, whose state of monomania must be pitiable indeed, to have hurried him into the infliction of such extensive injuries as the policemen's heads presented.

The following examination of the prisoner, whose unfortunate condition was the object of general commiseration, was then gone into.

Magistrate.—What induced you to perpetrate this unaccountable piece of violence ?

The prisoner returned no answer.

Magistrate.—What books do you read ?

Prisoner (sullenly).—Boxiana!

Magistrate (shaking his head).—Poor fellow, he must be taken care of. *(To the defendant).* Where did you pass your time previous to this unhappy circumstance ?

Prisoner.—At the Duke's-head public-house.

Magistrate.—Why did you break the policemen's heads?

Prisoner.—Because they interfered with me !

Magistrate (in a tone of great feeling).—Poor creature ! What an awful condition of monomania he seems reduced to.

A medical witness was then called.

Magistrate.—Be good enough to state to me the result of a professional examination of the unfortunate person at the bar.

Medical Witness.—When I examined him at the station-house, I found his eyes fixed but his head rolling about, and, pathologically speaking, I think the action of the cerebellum was increased to a high state of irritation.

Magistrate (somewhat wonder-struck).—Go on, sir, if you please.

Medical Witness.—The perceptive organs were no doubt a good deal obscured ; and this, acting on the moral propensities, added to a degree of excitement which was probably local—considering that he came from a public-house—would in my opinion account for what has happened.

Counsel for the Prisoner.—May not a coagulation of moral agencies existing coequally with a highly inflammatory condition of the muscular fibres, produce such a result as that which is now the subject of inquiry ?

Medical Witness (after a few minutes' consideration, during which the whole Court was in a state of breathless suspense).—I think it may !

Magistrate.—Then there is an end of the case. The unhappy man at the bar is a subject of pity, not of punishment. *(To the prisoner).* You will be taken where every comfort will be provided for you. Have you any objection to go ?

The victim of monomania answered mechanically, that he had not, and has since been placed in the infirmary, where every indulgence will be granted him, until he is in a fit state to be restored to liberty.

The decision seemed to give perfect satisfaction to every one, except to the two policemen ; but, as they are since dead, their dissent can be of little consequence.

The friends of the monomaniac have applied to have him restored to them ; and, if they give proper assurance that they will take care of him, their request will of course be readily acceded to.

SOURCE: PUNCH MAGAZINE, 1837

INSANITY MADE EASY.

EELING, as we must, that it is very desirable that those "unfortunate persons" who are subject to monomania, should be protected from the penal consequences of their calamity—particularly when their affliction is liable to reach the climax of murder—it is due to those very much-to-be-pitied persons, that the proof of their mental aberration should be made as easy as possible. We, therefore, beg leave to subjoin a few facts, upon proof of which acquittals may be at once obtained in cases of the very gravest nature.

1. To have habitually declared one's self the victim of persecution.

2. When in Newgate on a charge of murder, to amuse the medical men by fantastic assertions on the subject of certain imaginary plots, crews, and conspiracies.

It would be idle to go through a long catalogue of these defences, which will admit of endless variety ; but, as insanity will henceforth become an essential part of the science of crime, we should not be surprised at thieves and assassins taking lessons from professors of the " art of going mad, with a view to the establishment of irresponsible agency."

SOURCE: PUNCH MAGAZINE, 1837

For its part, reminding readers of the balanced coverage it had given the story all along, *The Times* ran an editorial that it hoped would placate the hostile public and, at the same time, ask "the learned and philosophic gentlemen" responsible for the verdict (i.e., the judges) to help ordinary people better understand what is meant by "sanity" and "insanity":

> When we expressed our determination to abstain from offering any observations upon the moral guilt or innocence of M'Naughten until all the circumstances of the dreadful deed for which he was to be arraigned had been judicially investigated, we merely paid that tribute of deference and respect which is due to the dignity, the impartiality, and the justice of our tribunals.
>
> The same feeling of respect which then induced us to withhold such comments on the prisoner's state of mind as the publication of many facts connected with his former life might have suggested, now prevents us from questioning the justice of his acquittal, or the propriety of the motives which dictated that acquittal.

A jury of Englishmen has pronounced the murderer of Mr. Drummond NOT GUILTY, on the score of insanity. To that verdict we, in common with the rest of the community, are bound to defer. They have, in consequence of the professional, as well as the general testimony produced, and in accordance with the direction of the learned Chief Justice who tried the case, averred their perfect and sincere belief, that the wretched prisoner at the moment that he perpetrated the assassination was in such a state of mind as disabled him from calculating the consequences or recognizing the nature of his crime.

While we bow with due humility to a decision so solemn as that of a British jury, given too upon the high authority of a most eminent and learned judge – whilst we frankly admit that the concurrent and consentient testimony of the medical witnesses did not leave it open for his Lordship to adopt any other course than that which he did adopt – and whilst we do not presume to cavil at or dispute the great scientific qualifications, the eminent professional lore, and the pathological attainments of the physicians subpoenaed on the occasion, still we would, not captiously nor querulously, but in a spirit of humble and honest earnestness, of hesitating and admiring uncertainty, and of almost painful dubitation, ask those learned and philosophic gentlemen *to define, for the edification of common-place people like ourselves, where sanity ends and madness begins*; and what are the outward and palpable signs of the one or the other?

Mr. Cockburn laid it down that a man might be mad on one point, and sane on all others; that M'Naughten, although he wrote very excellent businesslike letters, in which he evinced no slight shrewdness and providence, and although he expressed himself on general topics in a clear, intelligent, and intelligible manner, yet unfortunately laboured under a species of monomania, which the learned counsel called "homicidal monomania." In this proposition he was borne out by the evidence of Sir A. Morrison and Dr. Munro, who declared their conviction that the prisoner had laboured under a morbid delusion, of which this murder was the climax.

Now, we do not presume to question the correctness of this theory. In fact, we have heard it stated before, though not in quite such learned phraseology. It is usual enough to hear it advanced that all men are less sane upon some points than others; that all men have some oddity, some queer habit, some peculiar fancy, by fostering or humouring which exclusively they would become decidedly mad on one particular point. This is common enough. But we never before heard this self-engendered insanity pleaded in defense of crimes to the perpetration of which it might have contributed.

However, it is neither our duty nor our wish to cavil at the verdict of the jury. They, doubtless, performed their part conscientiously enough. We only want to know, for the benefit of simple folks, what in future is to be considered sanity? It appears that it is not enough that a man should talk and write correctly on matters of business, give a good account of what is passing around him, or pronounce a correct opinion of men and measures, in order to be considered sane; but, if he indulge in the humours of a morbid melancholy, and cherish the fancies of a diseased imagination, this is sufficient to obtain for him the character of a monomaniac; and if he only proceeds to commit murder, that is the climax of his monomania.

Now, we fear that there are many monomaniacs in the world: and we suppose that they have as various tastes and whims as their saner neighbours. We are not philosophers enough to know whether they are superior to the impulses of vanity, avarice, or revenge. From all that we know, or have read, of human propensities, we rather believe that these are the predominant passions of most monomaniacs. In that case it certainly is desirable that they should be known by some accurate and general description in time to guard their intended victims from a monomaniacal pistol or a climacteric stiletto. It may be a pleasing fancy for such men to contemplate the prospective *otium cum copia* of Bedlam and the grandeur of lionized insanity; but it would be more agreeable to the interests of society if they could be introduced to these pleasures without the preparatory noviciate of unprovoked and unexplained assassination; for, highly curious as the phenomenon may be in a medical point of view, it is but poor consolation to reflect that a fellow man has been prematurely cut off from the duties and enjoyments of a well-spent life by the unsuspected blow of an assassin who: "laboured under a morbid delusion, of which murder was the climax."

Naturally, the medical profession was quick in responding to the verdict. The following is the lead article from *The Lancet*, 18 March 1843:

The circumstances connected with the death of Mr. Drummond, painful as the review of them must be to all right-thinking men, suggest several considerations of such importance that we regard it as a duty to comment upon them at some length.

Leaving the medical details of the case, we would advert to one of the most momentous, and what has been made one of the most difficult questions in jurisprudence or in morals. The intricacy of the subject resides, first, in the difficulty of determining the precise line of demarcation between the extremes of bad temper, fanaticism, or moral depravity, and the commencement of actual insanity; and, secondly, where the insanity of the party is indisputable, – in the difficulty of holding, with a just hand, the balance between the compassion that is due to the miserably afflicted being, and the value of an indefinite number of human lives, which may be sacrificed, immediately, to his hallucination, or, more remotely, to the contagious example of his misguided acts.

The first of these difficulties, however, applies to the subject when regarded in a moral, or pathological, rather than in a legal light, because the law never has made, and never can make, subtle distinctions between sanity and insanity; while, at the same time, extenuating circumstances, arising out of the various conditions of body and mind in which an individual may have been placed at the time of the commission of a given act, – have always been allowed some influence in modifying the rigid course of criminal law.

It is with the second difficulty, then, that we have principally to deal, namely, that involved in the case of a lunatic who commits murder. In such a case the murder may have been committed during a paroxysm of furious insanity, or during a lucid interval, or, what is much more frequent than either, under the influence of a permanent monomania. If the crime have been perpetrated during a lucid interval, the law cannot deal with the lunatic otherwise than as with a sane person, in the event of his execution, a moral view of the case must leave a painful impression on the mind arising from the doubt how far a lunatic is, at any time responsible for his actions.

But, if the fatal deed has been committed under circumstances which show that the perpetrator is unequivocally mad at the time of its commission, the law in its present state acquits him of all guilt. The question, then, becomes whether the law ought to remain as it is in such cases, or to be altered. It has been contended that a lunatic can incur no moral guilt under any circumstances, and that the argument must, therefore, be taken up on an entirely different ground. The execution of a lunatic for murder could answer no end of justice; but the points for consideration are, whether his execution would act as an example to deter other madmen from similar desperate deeds, and, admitting that it would do so, whether we should be justified in sacrificing the life of one madman in order to promote the safety of an indefinite number of other lives.

Now, on the one hand, it may be argued, first, that we have no right, on the ground of simple expediency, or to prevent a contingent evil, to sacrifice the life of any human being, for, on the same principle, we might be justified, at the first outbreak of an highly malignant and contagious disease, in putting to death the first persons who were seized with it, and burying their bodies with quick-lime.

Secondly, that madness being the most dreadful calamity which can afflict a human being, it would be the height of cruelty for man to raise his arm against one already so awfully stricken by the hand of GOD. Thirdly, that lunatics, although readily influenced by the contagion of crime, are much less apt to be impressed by the example of punishment. On the other hand, to the first and second of these arguments it may be answered, that there is no true parallel between the case of a lunatic and that of a man seized with a malignant and contagious disease, because the life of the latter is of value to himself and others, while that of a mischievous lunatic is but a fitful and dismal dream, the termination of which, by natural causes, should be hailed as a blessing.

In answer to the third argument it may be urged, that the effect of example in deterring lunatics from committing murder, has been found to be considerable, if we may judge from the few instances in which the lives of madman have been sacrificed by the law; while the influence of example in promoting the propensity to murder and suicide has been most strikingly exemplified in this metropolis, within the last two or three years. In 1810, BELLINGHAM, unquestionably a lunatic, was hanged for the murder of Mr. PERCIVAL, and from that time until 1841, not a single political assassination was perpetrated in this country, throughout the most exciting and troubled times that have been known to England. OXFORD was acquitted for his late attempt on the life of the QUEEN, on the ground of insanity, though in our opinion, with very doubtful propriety; and other similar attempts almost immediately followed. Not a week had elapsed from the trial of M'Naughten for the murder of MR. DRUMMOND, and his acquittal on the ground of insanity, ere another madman openly threatened the lives of her MAJESTY and Sir ROBERT PEEL, and that of Mr. GOULBURN was measured by a person for whom, had he put his threats in execution, the plea of insanity would probably have been set up.

Such, we conceive, is a fair and simple statement of the question. It is one in which the most important interests of society, and that political justice which bind the state to protect the lives of citizens, appear to be at variance with our feelings of humanity towards a dangerous and offending yet guiltless individual.

Since the foregoing remarks were written the subject of the plea of insanity in cases of imputed murder has been introduced in the House of Lords, in a very elaborate speech by the LORD CHANCELLOR, who suggested that the judges should be called, questioned and required to explain what they deem to be the existing state of the law in relation to that great branch of criminal judicature.

When we have heard the exposition of these learned and influential persons we shall return to the subject, in the meantime embracing this opportunity of stating it to be our firmly-established conviction that at the late trial of M'NAUGHTEN evidence was received which was not strictly admissible – that in the opening speech of the counsel for the prosecution no reference to the *insanity* of the accused ought to have been received, that the opinions of medical men who had only heard *the trial* ought not to have been received, that the counsel for *the prosecution* should have replied to the arguments and pernicious statements of the counsel for *the prisoner*, that the judge should have summed up on the *whole* case, leaving it fairly to *the jury* to found their verdict upon the belief which they conscientiously entertained, after hearing the evidence, whether M'NAUGHTEN did or did not know that he was doing was *wrong* when he leveled the pistol at the back of his unfortunate victim.

Chapter Twenty

ACCORDINGLY, WHEN THE House of Lords was presented with the question of "where sanity ends and madness begins," as well as what the nature and extent of the unsoundness of mind was "which would excuse the commission of a felony of this sort," they determined to seek the opinion of the judges on the law governing such cases, and on the 19th of June all the judges attended their lordships and the following questions of law were put to them for consideration:[1]

"First, what is the law respecting alleged crimes committed by persons afflicted with insane delusion, in respect of one or more particular subjects or persons: as, for instance, where at the time of the commission of the alleged crime, the accused knew he was acting contrary to law, but did the act complained of with a view, under the influence of insane delusion, of redressing or revenging some supposed grievance or injury, or of producing some supposed public benefit?

"Second, what are the proper questions to be submitted to the jury, when a person alleged to be afflicted with insane delusion respecting one or more particular subjects or persons, is charged with the commission of a crime (murder, for example), and insanity is set up as a defense?

"Third, in what terms ought the question to be left to the jury, as to the prisoner's state of mind at the time when the act was committed?

"Fourth, if a person under an insane delusion as to existing facts, commits an offence in consequence thereof, is he thereby excused?

"Fifth, can a medical man conversant with the disease of insanity, who never saw the prisoner previously to the trial, but who was present during the whole trial and the examination of all the witnesses, be asked his opinion as to the state of the prisoner's mind at the time of the commission of the alleged crime, or his opinion whether the prisoner was conscious at the time of doing the act, that he was acting contrary to law, or whether he was labouring under any and what delusion at the time?"

Mr. Justice Maule registered misgivings about what was being expected of him and his fellow justices:

"I feel great difficulty in answering the questions put by your Lordships on this occasion, first, because they do not appear to arise out of, and are not put with reference to, a particular case, or for a particular purpose, which might explain or limit the generality of their terms, so that full answers to them ought to be applicable to every possible state of facts, not inconsistent with those assumed in the questions: this difficulty is the greater, from the practical experience both of the bar and the Court being confined to questions arising out of the facts of particular cases. Secondly, because I have heard no argument at your Lordships' bar or elsewhere, on the subject of these questions; the want of which I feel the more, the greater are the number and extent of questions which might be raised in argument. And thirdly, from a fear of which I cannot divest myself, that as these questions relate to matters of criminal law of great importance and frequent occurrence, the answers to them by the Judges may embarrass the administration of justice, when they are cited in criminal trials.

"For these reasons I should have been glad if my learned brethren would have joined me in praying your Lordships to excuse us from answering these questions; but as I do not think they ought to induce me to ask that indulgence for myself individually, I shall proceed to give such answers as I can, after the very short time which I have had to consider the questions, and under the difficulties I have mentioned; fearing that my answers may be as little satisfactory to others as they are to myself.

"The first question, as I understand it, is, in effect, 'What is the law respecting the alleged crime, when at the time of the commission of it, the accused knew he was acting contrary to the law, but did the act with a view, under the influence of insane delusion, of redressing or revenging some supposed grievance or injury, or of producing some supposed public benefit?'

"If I were to understand this question according to the strict meaning of its terms, it would require, in order to answer it, a solution of all questions of law which could arise on the circumstances stated in the question, either by explicitly stating and answering such questions, or by stating some principles or rules which would suffice for their solution. I am quite unable to do so, and, indeed, doubt whether it be possible to be done; and therefore request to be permitted to answer the question only so far as it comprehends the question, whether a person, circumstanced as stated in the question, is, for that reason only, to be found not guilty of a crime respecting which the question of his guilt has been duly raised in a criminal proceeding, and I am of opinion that he is not.

"There is no law, that I am aware of, that makes persons in the state described in the question not responsible for their criminal acts. To render a person irresponsible for crime on account of unsoundness of mind, the unsoundness should, according to the law as it has long been understood and held, be such as rendered him incapable of knowing right from wrong. The terms used in the question cannot be said (with reference only to the usage of language) to be equivalent to a description of this kind and degree of unsoundness of mind. If the state described in the question be one which involves or is necessarily connected with such an unsoundness this is not a matter of law, but of physiology, and not of that obvious and familiar kind as to be inferred without proof.

"Second, the questions necessarily to be submitted to the jury are those questions of fact which are raised on the record. In a criminal trial, the question commonly is, whether the accused be guilty or not guilty: but, in order to assist the jury in coming to a right conclusion on this necessary and ultimate question, it is usual and proper to submit such subordinate or intermediate questions, as the course which the trial has taken may have made it convenient to direct their attention to. What those questions are, and the manner of submitting them, is a matter of discretion for the Judge – discretion to be guided by a consideration of all the circumstances attending the inquiry. In performing this duty, it is sometimes necessary or convenient to inform the jury as to the law; and if, on a trial such as is suggested in the question, he should have occasion to state what kind and degree of insanity would amount to a defense, it should be stated conformably to what I have mentioned in my answer to the first question, as being, in my opinion, the law on this subject.

"Third, there are no terms which the Judge is by law required to use. They should not be inconsistent with the law as above stated, but should be such as, in the discretion of the Judge, are proper to assist the jury in coming to a right conclusion as to the guilt of the accused.

"Fourth, the answer which I have given to the first question is applicable to this.

"Fifth, whether a question can be asked, depends, not merely on the questions of *fact* raised on the record, but on the course of the *cause* at the time it is proposed to ask it; and the state of an inquiry as to the guilt of a person charged with a crime, and defended on the ground of insanity, may be such, that such a question as either of those suggested, is proper to be asked and answered, though the witness has never seen the person before the trial, and though he has merely been present and heard the witnesses: these circumstances, of his never having seen the person before, and of his having merely been present at the trial, not being necessarily sufficient, as it seems to me, to exclude the lawfulness of a question which is otherwise lawful; though I will not say that an inquiry might not be in such a state, as that these circumstances should have such an effect.

"Supposing there is nothing else in the state of the trial to make the questions suggested proper to be asked and answered, except that the witness had been present and heard the evidence; it is to be con- sidered whether that is enough to sustain the question. In principle it is open to this objection, that as the opinion of the witness is founded on those conclusions of fact which he forms from the evidence, and as it does not appear what those conclusions are, it may be that the evi- dence he gives is on such an assumption of facts, as makes it irrelevant to the inquiry. But such questions have been very frequently asked, and the evidence to which they are directed has been given, and has never, that I am aware of, been successfully objected to.

"Evidence, most clearly open to this objection, and on the admis- sion of which the event of a most important trial probably turned, was received in the case of *The Queen v. M'Naughten*, tried at the Central Criminal Court in March last, before the Lord Chief Justice, Mr. Justice Williams, and Mr. Justice Coleridge, in which counsel of the highest eminence were engaged on both sides; and I think the course and practice of receiving such evidence, confirmed by the very high authority of these Judges, who not only received it, but left it, as I understand, to the jury, without any remark derogating from its weight, ought to be held to warrant its reception, notwithstanding the objection in principle to which it may be open. In cases even where the course of practice in criminal law has been unfavourable to parties accused, and entirely contrary to the most obvious principle of justice and humanity, as well as those of law, it has been held that such practice constituted the law, and could not be altered without the authority of Parliament."

Lord Chief Justice Tindal then spoke:

"My Lords, Her Majesty's Judges (with the exception of Mr. Justice Maule, who has stated his opinion to your Lordships), in answering the questions proposed to them by your Lordships' House, think it right, in the first place, to state that they have forborne entering into any particular discussion upon these questions, from the extreme and almost insuperable difficulty of applying those answers to cases in which the facts are not brought judicially before them. The facts of each particular case must of necessity present themselves with endless variety, and with every shade of difference in each case; and as it is their duty to declare the law upon each particular case, on facts proved before them, and after hearing argument of counsel thereon, they deem it at once impracticable, and at the same time dangerous to the administration of justice, if it were practicable, to attempt to make minute applications of the principles involved in the answers given by them to your Lordships' questions.

"They have therefore confined their answers to the statement of that which they hold to be the law upon the abstract questions proposed by your Lordships; and as they deem it unnecessary, in this peculiar case, to deliver their opinions seriatim, and as all concur in the same opinion, they desire me to express such their unanimous opinion to your Lordships.

"The first question proposed by your Lordships is this: 'What is the law respecting alleged crimes committed by persons afflicted with insane delusion in respect of one or more particular subjects or persons: as, for instance, where at the time of the commission of the alleged crime the accused knew he was acting contrary to law, but did the act complained of with a view, under the influence of insane delusion, of redressing or revenging some supposed grievance or injury, or of producing some supposed public benefit ?'

"In answer to which question, assuming that your Lordships' inquiries are confined to those persons who labour under such partial delusions only, and are not in other respects insane, we are of opinion that, notwithstanding the party accused did the act complained of with a view under the influence of insane delusion, of redressing or revenging some supposed grievance or injury, or of producing some public benefit, he is nevertheless punishable according to the nature of the crime committed, if he knew at the time of committing such crime that he was acting contrary to law; by which expression we understand your Lordships to mean the law of the land.

"Your Lordships are pleaded to inquire of us, secondly, 'What are the proper questions to be submitted to the jury, where a person alleged to be afflicted with insane delusion respecting one or more particular subjects or persons, is charged with the commission of a crime (murder, for example), and insanity is set up as a defense?' And, thirdly, 'In what terms ought the question to be left to the jury as to the prisoner's state of mind at the time when the act was committed?'

"And as these two questions appear to us to be more conveniently answered together, we have to submit our opinion to be, that the jurors ought to be told in all cases that every man is to be presumed to be sane, and to possess a sufficient degree of reason to be responsible for his crimes, until the contrary be proved to their satisfaction; and that to establish a defense on the ground of insanity, it must be clearly proved that, at the time of the committing of the act, the party accused as labouring under such a defect of reason, from disease of the mind, as not to know the nature and quality of the act he was doing; or, if he did know it, that he did not know he was doing what was wrong.

"The mode of putting the latter part of the question to the jury on these occasions has generally been, whether the accused at the time of doing the act knew the difference between right and wrong: which mode, though rarely, if ever, leading to any mistake with the jury, is not, as we conceive, so accurate when put generally and in the abstract, as when put with reference to the party's knowledge of right and wrong in respect to the very act with which he is charged.

"If the question were to be put as to the knowledge of the accused solely and exclusively with reference to the law of the land, it might tend to confound the jury, by inducing them to believe that an actual knowledge of the law of the land was essential in order to lead to a conviction; whereas the law is administered upon the principle that every one must be taken conclusively to know it, without proof that he does know it.

"If the accused was conscious that the act was one which he ought not to do, and if that act was at the same time contrary to the law of the land, he is punishable; and the usual course therefore has been to leave the question to the jury, whether the party accused had a sufficient degree of reason to know that he was doing an act that was wrong: and this course we think is correct, accompanied with such observations and explanations as the circumstances of each particular case may require.

"The fourth question which your Lordships have proposed to us is this: 'If a person under an insane delusion as to existing facts, commits an offence in consequence thereof, is he thereby excused?' To which question the answer must of course depend on *the nature of the delusion*: but, making the same assumption as we did before, namely, that he labours under such partial delusion only, and is not in other respects insane, we think he must be considered in the same situation as to responsibility *as if the facts with respect to which the delusion exists were real*. For example, if under the influence of his delusion he supposes another man to be in the act of attempting to take away his life, and he kills that man, as he supposes, in self-defense, he would be exempt from punishment. If his delusion was that the deceased had inflicted a serious injury to his character and fortune, and he killed him in revenge for such supposed injury, he would be liable to punishment.

"The question lastly proposed by your Lordships is: 'Can a medical man conversant with the disease of insanity, who never saw the prisoner previously to the trial, but who was present during the whole trial and the examination of all the witnesses, be asked his opinion as to the state of the prisoner's mind at the time of the commission of the alleged crime, or his opinion whether the prisoner was conscious at the time of doing the act that he was acting contrary to law, or whether he was labouring under any and what delusion at the time?' In answer thereto, we state to your Lordships, that we think the medical man, under the circumstances supposed, cannot in strictness be asked his opinion in the terms above stated, because each of those questions involves the determination of the truth of the facts deposed to, which it is for the jury to decide, and the questions are not mere questions upon a matter of science, in which case such evidence is admissible. But where the facts are admitted or not disputed, and the question becomes substantially one of science only, it may be convenient to allow the question to be put in that general form, though the same cannot be insisted on as a matter of right."

Lord Brougham responded on behalf of the House:

"My Lords, the opinions of the learned Judges, and the very able manner in which they have been presented to the House, deserve our best thanks. One of the learned Judges has expressed his regret that these questions were not argued by counsel. Generally speaking, it is most important that in questions put for the consideration of the Judges, they should have all that assistance which is afforded to them by an argument by counsel: but at the same time, there can be no doubt of your Lordships' right to put, in this way, abstract questions of law to the Judges, the answer to which might be necessary to your Lordships in your legislative capacity. There is a precedent for this course, in the memorable instance of Mr. Fox's bill on the law of libel; where, before passing the bill, this House called on the Judges to give their opinions on what was the law as it then existed."

Lord Campbell:

"My Lords, I cannot avoid expressing my satisfaction, that the noble and learned Lord on the woolsack carried into effect his desire to put these questions to the Judges. It was most fit that the opinions of the Judges should be asked on these matters, the settling of which is not a mere matter of speculation; for your Lordships may be called on, in your legislative capacity, to change the law; and before doing so, it is proper that you should be satisfied beyond doubt what the law really is. It is desirable to have such questions argued at the bar, but such a course is not always practicable. Your Lordships have been reminded of one precedent for this proceeding, but there is a still more recent instance; the Judges having been summoned in the case of the Canada Reserves, to express their opinions on what was then the law on that subject. The answers given by the Judges are most highly satisfactory, and will be of the greatest use in the administration of justice."

Lord Cottenham:

"My Lords, I fully concur with the opinion now expressed, as to the obligations we owe to the Judges. It is true that they cannot be required to say what would be the construction of a Bill, not in existence as a law at the moment at which the question is put to them; but they may be called on to assist your Lordships, in declaring their opinions upon abstract questions of existing law."

Lord Wynford:

"My Lords, I never doubted that your Lordships possess the power to call on the Judges to give their opinions upon questions of existing law, proposed to them as these questions have been. I myself recollect, that when I had the honour to hold the office of Lord Chief Justice of the Court of Common Pleas, I communicated to the House the opinions of the Judges on questions of this sort, framed with reference to the usury laws. Upon the opinion of the Judges thus delivered to the House by me, a Bill was founded, and afterwards passed into a law."

The Lord Chancellor:

"My Lords, I entirely concur in the opinion given by my noble and learned friends, as to our right to have the opinions of the Judges on abstract questions of existing law; and I agree that we owe our thanks to the Judges, for the attention and learning with which they have answered the questions now put to them."

And so ended the opinion of the House of Lords.

WHILE *Hadfield's Case* of 1800 is said to mark the beginning of modern jurisprudence with respect to the defence of insanity, *M'Naughten's Case*[2] is certainly of equal if not greater importance in so far as it precipitated the establishment of specific rules governing the defence of insanity. Interestingly, while it is often said that the so-called M'Naughten Rules were distilled from the M'Naughten case *per se*, that is inaccurate. The "not guilty" verdict in *M'Naughten's Case* was based not on M'Naughten's Rules at all, but upon a rather equivocal test not entirely consistent with the tests used in *Hadfield's Case*.

In fact the M'Naughten Rules came about as a result of the *responses to questions* put to the judges before the House of Lords *subsequent* to M'Naughten's "not guilty on the ground of insanity" verdict, a verdict that, as we have seen, prompted such controversy that the lords were called upon to act. The responses given by the judges then – arising from the case of Daniel M'Naughten – would serve, it was hoped, as rules by which judges and juries could be guided when considering cases where an accused pleads not guilty by reason of insanity. The rules are categorized thus:

1) Presumption of sanity and burden of proof
2) Disease of the mind
3) Nature and quality of the act
4) Knowledge that the act was wrong
5) Crimes without specific intent
6) The function of the jury
7) Sentencing

It should also be recognized that the "Rules" are somewhat of an anomaly in that they are neither the *ratio* of a decided case nor are they the substance of a British *statute*. They are the opinions of the judges solicited after M'Naughten's acquittal. Nevertheless, the M'Naughten Rules, as interpreted by the common law over the past 160 years and more, remain the law regarding insanity in England today.[3] Indeed, the M'Naughten Rules have been exported to a number of common law jurisdictions including Canada and most American jurisdictions.[4] That is not to say that the Rules have not been the subject of much controversy and critique.

While it is not the purpose of the present discussion to exhaustively present the intricacies of the debate, a summary of the more important concerns is as follows:

1) The advisory opinion is not a judgment based upon definite facts that can be compared to other similar situations.
2) The questions put to the judges were directed only to the issue of delusional thinking in which paranoid symptoms were the most striking feature. As well, the judges knew quite well that it was the

case of M'Naughten that was the final precipitant. It has therefore been said that the very nature of the questions left the opinions applicable to a very narrow fact situation.

3) The opinions, if they were to be taken as a comprehensive view of the law of insanity, appear to disregard the statement of the law as set out in *Hadfield's Case* where the court clearly found the accused to be insane in a situation where he knew the nature and quality of the act with which he was charged, and knew that it was wrong. Nevertheless, the accused person's unshakeable delusions were held by the court to be a sufficient foundation for a verdict that "the prisoner is not guilty, he being under the influence of insanity at the time the act was committed." Presumably, if the M'Naughten Rules were applied to the facts of *Hadfield's Case* such a finding would not have been made.

4) The questions put to the judges and the answers received were very confusing and somewhat inconsistent. "It is difficult to determine just what the judges meant to say, because of the number of times they said it. By rewording their rules in several different ways, they left the test no more uniform than it had been before."[5]

5) "Right and wrong" tests in general belong to the realm of ethics. The standard of what is right and wrong varies over time and across ethnic populations so much so that it may be very short-lived and/or unworkable in a culturally diverse jurisdiction.

6) The emphasis on intellectual factors leaves other aspects of mental disorder not considered and, in particular, ignores the importance of emotional dimensions.

7) As well, and as importantly, the test does not consider the volitional component of behaviour. It "takes no account of the fact that while mental deterioration may not have progressed sufficiently to satisfy the cognitive knowledge tests of responsibility, it might yet exist to a degree which has destroyed the subject's control over his instinctive urgings."[6]

Although the pronouncement of the lords was less than satisfactory, it marked the beginning of a "codification" of the rules. This simple fact was an improvement in itself. It provided a framework within which rules could be articulated so that everyone would be applying more or less the same test.

In M'Naughten's case we heard in the arguments of learned counsel and the summing up of the trial judge himself, a hopeless confusion of tests – arguments and summary that came from the brightest legal minds of the day. We heard that lack of criminal responsibility was produced by fierce delusions, diseased intellect, inability to know what is morally wrong, no self-control, ungovernable impulses, behaviour that was not "willful," inability to know good from evil, frenzied impulses, and involuntary impulses.

Even in these considerations one can see a potential for confusion as to what we would recognize today as psychotic thought process, cognitive deficit, intellectual disability, and non-volitional acts. Although each is relevant in its own way, in a general sense these deficits are not all specifically relevant to the modern test for insanity.

In Canada, a version of the M'Naughten Rules was part of our first *Criminal Code* in 1892;[7] the applicable section at the time was S.11, as set out as follows:

11. (1) No person shall be convicted of an offence by reason of an act done or omitted by him when labouring under natural imbecility, or disease of the mind, to such an extent as to render him incapable of appreciating the nature and quality of the act or omission, and of knowing that such act or omission was wrong.

(2) A person labouring under specific delusions, but in other respects sane, shall not be acquitted on the ground of insanity, under the provisions hereinafter contained, unless the delusions caused him to believe in the existence of some state of things which, if it existed, would justify or excuse his act or omission.

(3) Every one shall be presumed to be sane at the time of doing or omitting to do any act until the contrary is proved.

The preceding provisions have survived to date with periodic modernizing of language, but no significant substantive changes have been made, other than that the first part of the test has been made explicitly "disjunctive" rather than "conjunctive." That is, an accused may now rely upon either arm of the test – he may show that he was "incapable of appreciating the nature and quality of the act or omission," *or* show that he was incapable of "knowing that such act or omission was wrong."

While the so-called Rules may have their problems and may not be as comprehensive as one might wish, they have provided us with a relatively clear articulation of the law as it was understood by the House of Lords. Consistency was certainly lacking with respect to how "insanity," in the legal context, was understood. One can readily see that at the conclusion of M'Naughten's trial there was a lack of differentiation between the concepts of knowledge, intent, self-control, control of impulses, volition, and consciousness. These faculties, all potentially affected by mental disorder, tended to be lumped together in a rather confusing manner. Now, we more carefully parse these concepts and group them as relevant to either the *mens rea* (guilty mind) or *actus reus* (guilty act) of the particular offence – the two components of every criminal offence.

Daniel M'Naughten would very likely obtain the same verdict of "not criminally responsible" today. There is little doubt that he would have been diagnosed as suffering from a paranoid disorder of one description or another. It is unclear but unlikely that M'Naughten would today obtain a diagnosis of schizophrenia. It is likely that he would obtain the more circumscribed diagnosis of paranoid psychosis. According to the criteria of the *Diagnostic and Statistical Manual of Mental Disorders* (fourth edition), the characteristic symptoms of schizophrenia, of which at least two must be present, are as follows:

1) delusions
2) hallucinations
3) disorganized speech (e.g., frequent derailment or inchoherence)
4) grossly disorganized or catatonic behaviour
5) negative symptoms (e.g., affective flattening, alogia, or avolition)

As well, for a significant period of time after the onset of the symptoms, one or more major areas of functioning such as work, interpersonal relations, or self-care are markedly below the level achieved prior to onset. The symptoms must have been present for at least six months. To obtain the particularization of "paranoid type" the individual must experience preoccupation with one or more delusion or frequent auditory hallucinations. The most conspicuous symptom observed in M'Naughten was his fixed and long-standing delusion regarding the Tories, although careful scrutiny of the evidence supports the episodic presence of virtually all symptoms. As his counsel summarized:

"He appears to have been from the commencement a man of gloomy, reserved, and unsocial habits. He was, moreover, as you will hear, though gloomy and reserved in himself, a man of singularly sensitive mind – one who spent his days in incessant labour and toil, and at night gave himself up to the study of difficult and abstruse matters; but whose mind, notwithstanding, was tinctured with refinement . . . I mention these things to show that, from the earliest period, the prisoner had a pre-disposition to insanity."[8]

All observers testify to the fact that M'Naughten's delusional thinking regarding the Tories antedated the killing of Drummond by several years. His deterioration was evident from the testimony of his father: "He seemed more distant than formerly, but I knew no reason for his being so. He would frequently pass me in the street and did not speak to or notice me." M'Naughten, Sr., refers to his son's "extraordinary delusions" as problematic two years before the shooting. The delusions were of such an intensity that the Tories were with him day and night spying on him . . . they were there every time he turned around . . . they laughed at him and shook their fists in his face. They chased him from Glasgow to England to France . . . there was no escape, he was a desperate man hoping only to free himself from his tormentors: "He [Sir Robert Peel] shall break my peace no longer."

He attempted to have the police intervene on his behalf, but to no avail. He then took matters into his own hands and deliberately struck back in what for him was a last resort. The fact that he was able to plan and execute a complicated course of action in no way detracts from the diagnosis, despite what the Crown counsel would have had the jury believe. Today it is recognized that individuals suffering from paranoid psychoses are often singularly affected and appear normal in most other respects. Even in everyday conversation the delusional thought may not be detectable. It is only when the conversation moves into the afflicted zone that the depth of the disorder becomes apparent. While M'Naughten's symptoms would be described in different terminology today, a jury would in all likelihood view his culpability in much the same way.

Chapter Twenty-one

TEN DAYS AFTER his trial, Daniel M'Naughten – "this wretched criminal," as *The Times* described him[1] – was removed from Newgate Prison. He received the information that he was to be taken to Bethlehem Hospital "with evident satisfaction, and walked with a quick firm step to the outer prison gate where a hackney cabriolet was waiting for him." The governor of the prison, a Mr. Cope, accompanied the prisoner and upon arriving at the hospital handed him over to the custody of the hospital governor, who conveyed him to the section of the building reserved for "criminal lunatics" where an apartment had been prepared for him, a cell previously occupied "by several of the more notorious criminals of late years," but a commodious space nonetheless on the ground floor of the hospital.

Following his committal, *The Times* gave its readers a glimpse of M'Naughten's first few days at Bethlehem:

> He was constantly watched by two turnkeys who were relieved every 12 hours, and with these individuals the wretched man at all times entered into conversation with considerable alacrity. He frequently made inquiries as to the political movements which were going on, and manifested great anxiety when in the performance of their duty the officers attempted to evade answering his questions. His excitement when conversing on this subject appears to have impressed all those who were brought into contact with him, with a belief that his mind was affected.
>
> His conversation is generally stated to have been extremely interesting, frequently turning on mechanical subjects; but it is a curious circumstance, that on one occasion only did he allude to the fearful crime committed by himself, and then only in the most unconcerned

33 & 34 VICT. c. 75.

Reg: 75.

Schedule A.

STATEMENT RESPECTING CRIMINAL LUNATICS,

To be filled up and transmitted to the Medical Superintendent with every Criminal Lunatic.

Name - - - - - -	Daniel McNaughton.
Age - - - - - -	29 on admission.
Date of Admission - - -	March 13th 1843
Former Occupation - - -	Turner.
From whence brought - -	Newgate.
Married, Single, or Widowed - -	Single
How many Children - - -	———
Age of Youngest - - -	———
Whether First Attack - - -	———
When previous Attacks occurred -	———
Duration of existing Attack - -	
State of Bodily Health - - -	Moderate.
Whether Suicidal or Dangerous to others -	No. No.
Supposed Cause - - -	———
Chief delusions or Indications of Insanity -	Imagines the Tories are his enemies they'd retiring in his manner —
Whether subject to Epilepsy - -	No.
Whether of temperate habits - -	Yes.
Degree of Education - - -	Fair.
Religious Persuasion - - -	Episcopalian.
Crime - - - - -	Murder —
When and where tried - - -	Central Crim.l Court. 1843.
Verdict of Jury - - - -	Found to be Insane
Sentence - - - -	Her Majestÿs Pleasure —

London : SHAW & SONS, Fetter Lane.

BETHLEHEM HOSPITAL: M'NAUGHTEN'S ADMISSION STATEMENT

manner. He appeared to have no anxiety as to his defense, and saw his solicitor only two or three times.

He was impatient of confinement, and would sometimes pace his cell backwards and forwards for half an hour at a time. He slept remarkably well, generally retiring about 10 o'clock, and seldom waking during the night. Since his acquittal he has been visited by his father, but no other relative has seen him. He attended service in the prison chapel twice on Sunday last, and took part in the prayers with great apparent feeling and propriety.[2]

A week later, when the predominant public feeling seemed to be that "the villain" M'Naughten had escaped with impunity, and that anyone with a desire to be "comfortably provided for" need only commit a murder "to attain that blessing," *The Spectator*[3] ran an article in an attempt to correct "misrepresentations" about what M'Naughten's life in prison would be like:

> The insane man is doomed to undergo "the next thing to capital punishment," said Lord Brougham, on the very evening when the Press was ignorantly suggesting an incentive to assassination by trumpeting forth an assurance that a repetition of the act would meet not only with a similar immunity but with the reward of a well found home and every reasonable indulgence.
>
> Many depraved creatures may know little of madhouses beyond what is contained in such paragraphs as the Press issues; and upon their authors, in case it should by their falsehood tempt some destitute wretch to crime, must rest an unenviable accountability. Since the law is not altered – since insanity is still regarded as a pitiable disease to be treated by restraint rather than killing, and since the power of deciding upon its [i.e. sanity's] existence is still left to a jury, it should be at the present moment the object of all who sincerely deplore M'Naughten's deed, to paint as vividly as possible all the terrors to which, under the most merciful sentence, he is doomed.
>
> A heartfelt desire to deter others from this crime might indeed be expected to show itself by an exaggeration of those terrors; but even, if this desire be wanting, those who set forth a madhouse as a temptation should, in fairness to the beings upon whose minds their influence may tell, describe its unfavourable features as well as its delights. Amid their most glowing terms they should still confess that

drawbacks are to be found; that in these happy homes the inmates, Rasselas-like, pine night and day for escape; that here the violent seem to loathe an existence subject to perpetual coercion, and that the most vigilant watch is scarcely effectual to guard against their unceasing desire to die.

That the timid mope in corners scared by the fierceness of those by whom they are surrounded, and that the more rational only endure an increased bitterness from a dreadful consciousness of their true position; that in prisons there may be hope of companionship – perhaps also eventual release – but that in the madhouse all is discordant, that there is not even companionship in vice, that there is no escape but the grave; and that all delights which the depraved most cherish – the frequent dram and every brutal gratification, are here forbidden.

Perhaps, also, as men – especially those who seek for "notoriety" are much guided in their ideas of what is desirable by the estimation which it receives from others, it might be as well to mention, that sane people visiting those receptacles are apt to experience emotions which no after-impressions can erase; that some of sound mind, confined but for a short time, have become hopelessly deranged; that even the very neighbourhood of the building is intuitively shunned; and that, such is the inconsistency of human nature, it is even probable that the writers by whom it is described as offering more than ordinary temptations would rather wander penniless through the world – lie sore and bedridden in an hospital, or submit to a violent death – than be compelled to taste during the remainder of their lives the enjoyment of such "comfortable provision."

It is difficult to describe with any degree of certainty the sort of care M'Naughten would have received while in Bethlehem. There is no clear evidence of particular treatments of choice in mid-Victorian England, although compared with methods in practice earlier in the century and before, it is thought to have been an era of relatively benign, non-invasive treatment that focused more on management and diet. An inquiry into the conditions at asylums three years after M'Naughten's trial touted the virtues of the latter:

It appears to be now generally allowed that the insane, as a class, require a liberal and nutritious though simple diet. The mere change indeed, on admission into a pauper asylum, from a scanty to a liberal diet, has in many cases appeared to effect a recovery without the employment of any more special means. I believe there can be no question that in institutions where the diet is liberal, the general health will be promoted; and that consequently in such institutions, other things being equal, the recoveries will be more numerous and the mortality lower than when the reverse obtains. Water broths and soups, containing large quantities of peas or other flatulent vegetables, are seldom adapted to the wants of the insane; and their too liberal use in asylums, in connection with an otherwise scanty diet, has been found to be connected with the prevalence of dysentery and diarrhea.[4]

Indeed, what is clear from such texts as Roy Porter's *Madness: A Brief History*,[5] is that the nineteenth century marked the beginning of an asylum industry. The numbers of people housed in asylums exploded relative to population growth. Along with the growth in the number of institutions and the number of people housed in these institutions, came innovations in their treatment. During the eighteenth and early-nineteenth century, lunatics were being treated in a variety of ways that included the use of electricity, sedation, physical restraint, cold water bathing, purging, and bleeding. To achieve "humoral" fluid balance, lunatics were put on "cooling" or "diluting" diets which consisted of salads, barley water, and milk, with red meat and wine to be avoided. Early forms of treatment appear to be quite bizarre from today's vantage point, although they were theoretically sound in their time. For example, in his *Primitive Physick*, John Wesley prescribes the following:[6]

For Raving Madness:

1. It is a sure rule that all madmen are cowards, and may be conquered by binding only, without beating (Dr. Mead). He also observes that blistering of the head does more harm than good. Keep the head close shaved, and frequently wash it with vinegar.

2. Apply to the head clothes dipped in cold water.

3. Or, set the patient with his head under a great waterfall, as long as his strength will bear; or pour water on his head out of a tea-kettle.

4. Or, let him eat nothing but apples for a month.

5. Or, nothing but bread and milk. Tried.

However, by the 1830s invasive treatments and "restraint" were, for the most part, no longer in vogue. Leading medical scientists at the time of M'Naughten's hospitalization believed that insanity was triggered by irritation and inflammation of the brain. From here, the disorder progressed to the point where the patient became disorganized due to a derangement of the brain's functioning, which may or may not have been evidenced by observable structural changes at the time of an autopsy.[7] While leading lights such as the American, Dr. Isaac Ray, believed that insanity observed the same pathological laws as other diseases, his treatise is conspicuously vague with respect to treatment.

Though Ray acknowledged treatments such as the judicious administration of medicines, he doubted the efficacy of bathing, bleeding, and digitalis. Indeed, all forms of mechanical intervention were to be replaced and free rein given ... but with supervision. The "new technique" consisted largely of treating patients with "respect and dignity" and ensuring that they were well fed and looked after. It was also thought that a key to the restoration of mental health was keeping busy. Reading, writing, cleaning, sewing, painting, gardening – anything that kept one busy was a step towards recovery. Activity precluded troubling ruminations. As a result, it was common to see massive asylums essentially run by the lunatic residents, tending to the gardens and livestock, tending to the kitchens, performing cleaning and housekeeping duties. These institutions were virtually self-sustaining enterprises that often included fully operational farms and woodshops.

In this respect, the architecture of these buildings and the layout of their grounds were of great importance. All were designed to optimize patient rehabilitation. And classification of patients was greatly valued as well. Men had to be separated from women and all lunatics were classified by the amount and type of their debilitation, although it was held as therapeutic in many places to allow men and women the occasional opportunity to mix. The asylums were built to exacting standards, ensuring that details such as drainage, lighting, and security were to the highest specifications. In 1837, Dr. W.A. F. Browne, head of the Montrose Royal Lunatic Asylum in Scotland produced a work entitled *What Asylums Were, Are, and Ought to Be*:[8]

> Conceive a spacious building resembling the palace of a peer, airy, and elevated, and elegant, surrounded by extensive and swelling grounds and gardens. The interior is fitted with galleries, and workshops, and

music rooms. The sun and the air are allowed to enter at every window, the view of the shrubberies and fields, and groups of labourers, is unobstructed by shutters or bars; all is clean, quiet and attractive. The inmates all seem to be actuated by the common impulse of enjoyment, all are busy and delighted by being so. The house and all around appears to be a hive of industry.

. . .

There is in this community no compulsion, no chains, no whips, no corporal chastisement, simply because these are proved to be less effectual means of carrying any point than persuasion, emulation, and the desire of obtaining gratification.

. . .

Such is a faithful picture of what may be seen in many institutions, and of what might be seen in all, were asylums conducted as they ought to be.

One must resist the urge to chuckle at this picture of such happy well-adjusted people living in blissful harmony, and perhaps find oneself perplexed, in a way, that such seemingly harmless people should be labelled as lunatics and have had their liberty stripped away. Nevertheless, this image of asylum life was transported to North America and fairly depicts, at least, the typical quality of many institutions dating from the mid-nineteenth to early-twentieth centuries. Some of these grand hospitals set on large, country-estate properties remain in existence today, vestiges of a bygone age; however, many are gone.

As has been said, it is likely that M'Naughten would have been cared for in a simple, non-invasive manner and left to recover spontaneously. It is likely that what we refer to today as "spontaneous remission"[9] was at the time all that one could hope for, and such restoration not necessarily due to the "treatment" being provided.

But the asylums turned out not to be the panaceas they were originally hoped to be. Stays tended to be interminable. Abuse was not uncommon, both with respect to the treatment and care one received upon admission to the asylum, as well as with respect to the sorts of individuals who were being admitted. Most often, there was no automatic review mechanism and individuals often found themselves tucked away in an asylum for many years on the basis of a dubious diagnosis, with little recourse. This was typically, and remains, a very "under-lawyered"

PHOTOGRAPH OF DANIEL M'NAUGHTEN TAKEN CIRCA 1856
SOURCE: BETHLEHEM HOSPITAL ARCHIVES

population and one would have had exceeding difficulty extricating oneself from the clutches of the asylum, even if a patient had the wherewithal as well as the means to pursue litigation. "Inconvenient" relatives were not infrequently dumped into these "bins" that as a rule offered little more than the most basic custodial care.

With the advent of psychotropic medications in the 1950s, the great deinstitutionalization movement swept across Western Europe and North America. For the first time drugs offered a "cure" for mental illness. Their promise was so compelling that governments almost gleefully began shutting down the enormous and very costly asylums. Thousands of mentally disordered individuals were released into communities, governments universally promising that the money saved from the shutting down of the institutions would be reinvested in community treatment.

As we have witnessed over the past forty to fifty years, both promises have been broken. The drugs, while dampening the so-called positive symptoms of major mental illness, have done nothing to lift the so-called negative symptoms. Positive symptoms refer to those things that mentally ill people do that we do not do: for example, hallucinate and harbour fixed false beliefs (delusions). Negative symptoms refer to things that we can do that mentally ill people have difficulty doing: for example, concentrating, focusing, and thinking in an abstract manner. It is clear that there have been no cures. It is also clear that many mentally ill individuals have great difficulty surviving in the communities they re-entered.

As well, as indicated, the reinvestment in community mental health care, even assuming its efficacy, has generally not been as extensive as promised. In most Western European and North American cities the numbers of mentally disordered individuals living on the streets has grown exponentially as a result of deinstitutionalization.

The deinstitutionalization movement was also fuelled by new mental health legislation driven by civil libertarians and advocates that ensured patient review. Whereas institutionalization was previously, for the most part, predicated upon a "need to treat," with the new legislation, institutionalization was based upon "danger to self or others." The determination of who is and who is not dangerous, remains an elusive pursuit; suffice it to say, we might have replaced one imperfect system with a different but no less perfect one.

Today the process of psychiatric care and security for the individual obtaining a verdict of "not criminally responsible due to mental disorder" would look considerably different than it must have to Daniel M'Naughten. An individual who is found to be not criminally responsible on the basis of mental disorder, first of all, is only confined by the state so long as he or she remains a "significant threat to the safety of the public." Being mentally unwell, by itself, is not a basis for confining anyone. If the state is not able to convince a court or review panel that an individual found to be not criminally responsible is a significant threat to the safety of the public, they are discharged, regardless of whether or not they suffer from a mental illness, and regardless of the seriousness of the offence. This approach is consistent with legislation found in most Western European and North American jurisdictions.

As well, even where an individual obtaining a verdict of "not criminally responsible on the basis of mental disorder" is found to be a significant threat to the safety of the public, his liberty is only curtailed to the extent necessary to contain the risk they pose. Not all of these individuals are locked up in psychiatric hospitals the way Hollywood would have us believe. In Ontario, for example, approximately two-thirds of the accused who have obtained such a verdict are actually living in the community, subject to certain conditions that are prescribed to meet the needs of the particular individual and the risks they pose. This approach is consistent with the "least onerous and least restrictive intervention" philosophy that runs through most modern mental health legislation.

At present, once an individual obtains a verdict of not criminally responsible due to mental disorder, most jurisdictions have built provisions for systematic review by either the court or a specially designed tribunal into their legislation. In Canada, individuals must be reviewed by a board at least once a year. It is up to the state to demonstrate at each review that the accused remains a significant threat to the safety of the public. If that is not demonstrated the accused is discharged absolutely, regardless of the seriousness of the index offence.

An accused found not criminally responsible due to mental disorder in respect to a homicide may be quickly stabilized and discharged quite soon after the verdict. Conversely, an individual found not criminally responsible due to mental disorder in respect to a relatively minor offence may be kept in a hospital for a long period of time if he or she remains a significant threat to the safety of the public. The point to be made is that there is no correlation between the seriousness of the offence committed and the duration of hospitalization.

In most jurisdictions, individuals who have been found not criminally responsible as a result of mental disorder cannot be treated with psychotropic medications unless they consent to that treatment. Where the individual, by virtue of his or her mental illness, lacks the capacity to consent to or refuse treatment, statutory provisions enable substitute decision-makers to consent or refuse medications on the patient's behalf. While psychopharmacology does not yet provide cures, it does provide prognoses that are generally positive in the sense that the medications will generally improve the patient's condition. Medications can typically be expected to both calm the patient and dampen positive symptoms. Most mentally disordered accused will end up living in the community or will have significant community access.

If Daniel M'Naughten had received a verdict of "not criminally responsible" on grounds of mental disorder (insanity) today, it is likely, given what we know about him, that he would not have spent a great deal of time in hospital. It is reasonably clear that he suffered from some type of paranoid psychosis. It is further clear that he was a fairly subdued and compliant individual even though he was unmedicated. It is therefore likely that he would have been receptive to taking prescribed medications.

Paranoid disorders have a reasonably good prognosis. Relative to major mental disorders such as schizophrenia, the range of symptomatology is typically more limited. Assuming compliance with current anti-psychotic medications, the positive symptoms of his disorder would likely have been diminished, if not erased. One could reasonably expect that Daniel M'Naughten might have been back living in the community within a few years of his offence, and might have been, depending upon his compliance with treatment, absolutely discharged from Her Majesty's grasp, were the state not able to demonstrate that he continued to represent a significant threat to the safety of the public.

After twenty years in Bethlehem Hospital, Daniel M'Naughten was moved to Broadmoor, a new psychiatric institution that opened its doors in 1863. It was the first custom-built criminal lunatic asylum in the world, with a fine library (as had been the case at Bethlehem) and music in the evenings upon occasion, when male and female inmates were permitted to intermingle and some even to dance. Although it is hard to picture him gliding across the floor in three-quarter time with a woman in his arms, it is quite probable that M'Naughten did spend a great deal of his time in the library, reading quietly, free from the persecutions of Tories and other imagined enemies intent on doing him harm. Yet, who can say?

He died in the Broadmoor asylum two years later, of natural causes. He was fifty-two years old.

Acknowledgments

THIS BOOK HAS been "under construction" for well over a decade. Original *Times of London* coverage from 1843 was, at the time of the book's writing, only available on microfiche obtained from Bell & Howell. This was "copy typed" over several months as the quality was too poor to be scanned. In her spare time my secretary Sarah Takhsha generously assisted me with this arduous task. I am indebted to Sarah for her valuable assistance. I would also like to thank Jeff Miller at Irwin Law for his ideas as to how the original text could be improved upon ... there were many. Paul Illidge, our writer friend, was of invaluable assistance in converting what was originally a rather documentary manuscript into one which was much more of a story. Finally, I would like to thank Pam Erlichman for her expert editorial skills and Heather Raven at Irwin Law for her beautiful organization of the text.

Endnotes

INTRODUCTION

1   Richard Moran, in his thoroughly researched text *Knowing Right from Wrong* (New York: Free Press, 1981), attempts to explain the outcome of the trial in terms of the political conspiracy and socioeconomic forces of the times, an interpretation that has not received a lot of support. See, for example, J. Thomas Dalby, "The Case of Daniel McNaughton: Let's Get the Story Straight" (2006) 27:4 American Journal of Forensic Psychiatry at 17–32.

2   *Diagnostic and Statistical Manual of Mental Disorders* (fourth edition), known as the DSM-IV (Washington, DC: American Psychiatric Association, 1994) at xxi.

3   For example, see the *Mental Health Act* of Ontario, R.S.O. 1990, s. 1.

4   See s. 1.

5   *R. v. Cooper*, [1980] 1 S.C.R. 1149.

6   [1996] O.J. No. 4688.

7   *R. v. Malcolm* (1989), 50 C.C.C. (3d) 351 (Ont. C.A.).

8   "Proof" of any defence in a criminal context is "on a balance of probabilities."

9   R.D. Schneider, *Statistical Survey of the Provincial and Territorial Review Boards* (Ottawa: Department of Justice, 7 April 2000).

10 *Burke's Peerage, Baronetage & Knightage* (London: Burke's Peerage, 1970) at 2098.

CHAPTER ONE

1   See, for example, Roy Porter, *Madness: A Brief History* (Oxford: Oxford University Press, 2002).

2   See, for example, Gregory Zilboorg, *A History of Medical Psychology* (New York: W.W. Norton & Co., 1941); C.E. Goshen, ed., *Documentary History of Psychiatry* (New York: Philosophical Library, 1967).

3 H. Kramer & J. Sprenger, *The Malleus Malificarum* [1484], trans. Rev. Montague Summers (New York: Dover Publications, 1971).

4 In England, because these persons were less frequently seen as possessed "demoniacs," they remained a nuisance and were herded, along with rogues, vagabonds, sturdy beggars, and vagrants, into some "secure place" – a lock-up, bridewell, or house of correction – pursuant to the provisions of the English *1714 Vagrancy Act*. The "disturbed of mind" were thus lumped together with the "disturbers of the peace." See, for example, Roy Porter, *Madmen: A Social History of Madhouses, Mad-Doctors & Lunatics* (Stroud, UK: Tempus Publishing, 2004) at 19.

5 As reported in "Exorcism Goes Horribly Wrong" (2007) 18:7 *Law Times* at 24.

6 27 How. St. Tr. 1282.

7 Nigel Walker, *Crime and Insanity in England,* vol. 1, *The Historical Perspective* (Edinburgh: Edinburgh University Press, 1968) at 15–16.

8 *Ibid.* at 15.

9 Royal pardons were also required to excuse serious offences committed by accident, self-defence, or if the accused was an infant.

10 Walker, above note 7.

11 *Ibid.*

12 *Ibid.* at 25.

13 *Ibid.* at 19–23.

14 *Ibid.* at 26.

15 *Ibid.*

16 *Ibid.*

17 *Ibid.*

18 (1603), 2 Coke's Rep. 568 at 571.

19 Sir Matthew Hale, *Historia Placitorum Coronae* [1736], vol. 1 (London: Professional Books, 1971).

20 *Ibid.* at 14; see Chapter II, *Concerning the Several incapacities of persons, and their exemptions from penalties by reason thereof.*

21 *Ibid.* at 17.

22 In Chapter IV, Hale indicates as follows (at 29–30):

> Now concerning another sort of defect or incapacity, namely *ideocy, madness* and *lunacy*: For tho by the law of England no man shall avoid his own act by reason of these defects (a), tho his heir or executor may, yet as to capital offenses these have in some cases the advantage of this defect or incapacity (b); and this defect comes under the general name of *Dementia*, which is thus distinguished.

I. *Ideocy*, or *fatuity a nativitate vel dementia naturalis*; such a one is
    described by *Fitzherbert*, who knows not to tell 20s. nor knows who
    his father or mother, nor knows his own age; but if he knows let-
    ters, or can read by the instruction of another, then he is no ideot.
    F.N.B.233.b. These, tho they may be evidences, yet they are too nar-
    row and conclude not always; for ideocy or not is a question of fact
    triable by jury, and sometimes by inspection.

II. *Dementia, accidentalis, vel adventitia*, which proceeds from several
    causes; sometimes from distemper of the humours of the body, as deep
    melancholy or adult choler; sometimes from the violence of a disease,
    as a fever or palsy; sometimes from a concussion or hurt of the brain, or
    its membranes or organs; and as it comes from several causes, so it is of
    several kinds or degrees; which as to the purpose in hand maybe thus
    distributed: 1. There is a partial insanity of mind; and 2.a total insanity.

... and this partial insanity seems not to excuse them in the committing of any offense for its a matter capital; for doubtless most persons,
that are felons of themselves, and others are under a degree of partial
insanity, when they commit these offenses: it is very difficult to define
the individual line that divides perfect and partial insanity, but it must
rest upon circumstances duly to be weighed and considered both by the
judge and jury. [emphases added]

23 *Ibid.*
24 Henry Weihofen, *Mental Disorder as a Criminal Defense* (Buffalo, NY:
    Dennis & Co., 1954) at 55.
25 W. Hawkins, *A Treatise of the Pleas of the Crown* (London: E. Sayer, 1724).
26 *Ibid.* at 1–2:

> The Guilt of offending against any Law whatsoever, necessarily suppos-
> ing a wilful Disobedience, can never be imputed to those, who are either
> uncapable of understanding it, or of conforming themselves to it: There-
> fore, before I come to the several Kinds of Offences, I shall shew what
> Degrees of Discretion and Freedom are required in the Commission of
> them; for the better Understanding whereof, I shall consider what Of-
> fenders are excusable,
>
> 1. In respect of their Want of Reason;
> 2. In respect of their Subjection to the Power of others.
>
> *Sect.* 1. As to the first Point it is to be observ'd, (a) That those who are
> under a natural Disability of distinguishing between Good and Evil,
> as Infants under the Age of Discretion, Ideots and Lunaticks, are not
> punishable by any criminal Prosecution whatsoever. [emphasis added]

Sect. 2. Indeed it was (b) anciently holden, in Respect of that high Regard which the Law has for the Safety of the King's Person, That a Madman might be punish'd as Traitor, for killing or offering to kill the King; but this is (c) contradicted by the later Opinions.

Sect. 3. And it seems agreed at this (d) Day, That if one, who has committed a capital Offence, become *Non Compos* before the Conviction, he shall not be arraigned; and if after Conviction, he shall not be executed.

Sect. 4. But by 12 *Anne*, 23, which seems to be agreeable to the (e) ancient Common Law, a dangerous Madman may be kept in Prison till he recover his Senses; and by the Common Law, if it be doubtful whether a Criminal, who at his Trial is in (f) appearance a Lunatick, be such in Truth or not, it shall be tried by an Inquest of Office, to be returned by the Sheriff of the County wherein the Court sits; and if it be found by them that the Party only feigns himself mad, (g) and he still refuse to answer, he shall be dealt with as one who stands mute.

27 (1843), 10 Clark & Fin. 200.
28 16 How. St. Tr. 695.
29 See, for example, Weihofen, above note 24.
30 *Ibid.*
31 (1760), 19 How. St. Tr. 886.

CHAPTER TWO

1 *The Times* pointed out that M'Naughten's case was a "headliner" not only because of the notoriety of the victim, his circumstances, and the intended victim but also because of the legal "dream team" who acted as counsel. As well, a medical dream team was assembled to attend to the victim, Edward Drummond – the most prominent surgeons in all of England. Drummond's chief surgeon, G.J. Guthrie, was born in London on May 1st in 1775 and died May 1st in 1856 at the age of seventy-one. Remarkably, he was qualified by the College of Surgeons on the 5th day of February 1801 while not quite sixteen years of age! His early medical career was with the military where he gained expertise in the treatment of gunshot wounds and other battle injuries. Mr. G.J. Guthrie was a most prominent surgeon in London at the time of M'Naughten's trial, with an international reputation resulting from his many scholarly works. He was a very highly regarded surgeon who is credited with the first amputation through the hip joint in which the patient survived. His impact, however, was varied. In 1823 he recognized a condition that caused a hardening of the eye for which he coined the term "glaucoma."

He was also the president of the Royal College of Surgeons and Professor of Anatomy and Surgery and was regularly called upon to give evidence before commissions and inquests. Mr. Guthrie was married twice and was survived by a son who was a surgeon, an unmarried daughter, a widow, and an infant son.

Bransby B. Cooper was also one of the most prominent medical men in London in 1843. Again, Cooper's reputation was international and he had produced many scholarly works. He was born 2 September 1792 in Great Yarmouth, the fourth son of Reverend Samuel Cooper, the elder brother of the much more famous Sir Astley Cooper. Bransby later published a biography of Sir Astley. His early career was in the Navy; however, he returned to school and studied medicine at the Norwich Hospital. After two years of medical study he came to London upon the advice of his uncle. In 1812 he entered the Royal Artillery as an assistant surgeon. He returned to the University of Edinburgh in 1815 and became a member of the Royal Medical Society in the same year. He later became president of that society. In 1843, the year of M'Naughten's trial, he was elected an honorary fellow of the Royal College of Surgeons of England. He taught in the Anatomy Department at the Surgical School of Guy's Hospital in London. As well, he lectured and published extensively on the topic of anatomy. He died very suddenly on 18 August 1853.

Little is known of Richard Jackson. However, it seems relatively clear that he was in fact not a "surgeon and apothecary," as described in this account of the *Times*, but rather an apothecary.

2 (1840), 9 Car. & P. 525 at pp. 550–52.

3 39 & 40 Geo. III c. 94.

4 *Hadfield's Case* (1800), 27 How. St. Tr. 1282 at 1312–314.

5 Furthermore, *complete* insanity would render the accused unfit to stand trial such that the matter of culpability would not have been put before the court.

6 *Hadfield's Case*, above note 4 at 1321.

7 Up until the proclamation of Bill C-30, in 1992, "specific delusions" were included in s. 16(3) of the *Criminal Code of Canada* as a particular basis for a finding of insanity. Although reference to specific delusions has since been deleted, this was as a result of the provision being viewed as unnecessary rather than as an intended change in the law.

8 The same provisions were imported into Canada, because the *Criminal Lunatics Act* was incorporated into the provisions of the draft English *Criminal Code*, which was never proclaimed in England but was adopted by Canada in 1892.

9   Thomas Dalby, "The Case of Daniel McNaughton: Let's Get the Story
    Straight," American Journal of Forensic Psychiatry, 2006, 27(4): 17–32.

CHAPTER THREE

1   B.R. Davies, *A Street Map of London, 1843* (Moretonhampstead, Devon,
    UK: Old House Books, 1992).
2   The following table sets out the remarkable number of watershed events
    that take place at the time of our present story:

Events in 1843

February 11:	Giuseppe Verdi's opera *I Lombardi* premieres in Milan.
March 15:	Victoria, British Columbia, was founded by the Hudson's Bay Company as a trading post and fort.
May 4:	Natal is proclaimed a British colony.
May 22:	The first major wagon train headed for the northwest sets out with one thousand pioneers from Elm Grove, Missouri, on the Oregon Trail.
May 23:	Chile takes possession of the Strait of Magellan.
July 19:	The SS Great Britain is launched from Bristol.
August 15:	Tivoli Gardens, one of the oldest still intact amusement parks in the world, opened in Copenhagen, Denmark.
October 13:	In New York City, Henry Jones and 11 others found B'nai B'rith (the oldest Jewish service organization in the world).
November 28:	Ka La Ku'oko'a: Hawaiian Independence Day. The Kingdom of Hawai`i was officially recognized by the United Kingdom and France as an independent nation.
December 19:	First publication of Charles Dickens' *A Christmas Carol.* The world's first commercial Christmas Cards are printed by Sir Henry Cole in London. James Joule quantifies the conversion of work into heat. In Barbados, the first black man, Samuel Jackson Prescod, is elected to the House of Assembly. First tunnel under the Thames is finished. Argentina supports Rosas of Uruguay and begins a siege of Montivideo. The *Economist* is first published. Bishops University is founded. Abbeville is founded by descendants of Acadians from Nova Scotia.

First publication of Edgar Allan Poe's short story *The Tell-Tale Heart*.

Births in 1843

January 10:	Frank James, American Outlaw (d. 1915)
January 29:	William McKinley, 25th President of the United States (d. 1901)
April 4:	William Jackson, photographer (d. 1942)
April 15:	Henry James, American writer (d. 1916)
May 21:	Charles Albert Gobat, Swiss politician, recipient of the Nobel Peace Prize (1914)
June 3:	King Frederick VIII of Denmark (d. 1912)
June 9:	Bertha von Suttner, Austrian writer and pacifist, recipient of the Nobel Peace Prize (d. 1914)
June 15:	Edvard Grieg, Norwegian composer (d. 1907)
June 30:	Sir Ernest Satow, British diplomat and scholar (d. 1928)
July 7:	Camillo Golgi, Italian physician, recipient of the Nobel Peace Prize in Physiology or Medicine (d. 1926)
July 29:	Johannes Schmidt, German linguist (d. 1901)
August 1:	Robert Todd Lincoln, American statesman and businessman (d. 1926)
August 20:	Christina Nilsson, Swedish operatic soprano (d. 1921)
August 31:	Georg von Hertling, Chancellor of Germany (d. 1919)
November 25:	Henry Ware Eliot, American industrialist, philanthropist and the father of T.S. Eliot (d. 1919)
November 27:	Cornelius Vanderbilt II, American railway magnate (d. 1899)
December 11:	Heinrich Hermann Robert Koch, German physicist, recipient of the Nobel Peace Prize in Physiology or Medicine (d. 1896)
	Jang Seung-eop, Korean painter (d. 1897)
	Alexander Herrmann, German magician (d. 1896)
	Pierre Lallemont, French inventor of the bicycle (d. 1891)

Deaths in 1843

January 11:	Francis Scott Key, American lawyer and lyricist (b. 1779)
March 21:	Robert Southey, English poet (b. 1774)
March 25:	Robert Murray M'Cheyne, Scottish clergyman (b. 1813)
March 27:	Karl Salamo Zachariae Von Lingenthal, German jurist (b. 1769)
April 15:	Noah Webster, American lexicographer (b. 1758)
April 17:	Samuel Morey, American inventor (b. 1762)

June 6:   Friedrich Hölderlin, German writer (b. 1770)

July 7:   John Holmes, American politician (b. 1773)

July or August: Sequoyah, creator of the Cherokee syllabary (b. circa 1767)

December 18:   Thomas Graham, Lord Lynedoch, British Governor-
                 General of India (b. 1748)
                 William Abbot, English actor (b. 1798)

3   Charles Dickens, *A Christmas Carol* (London: Chapman and Hall, 1843) at 125.

4   William Drummond, 4th Viscount Strathallan (d. 1746). Killed at Culloden, his name and that of his eldest son, James, were included in the *Bill of Attainder* passed in 1746. Robert Burns, Scotland's national bard, wrote "Strathallan's Lament" for William Drummond. It appears in the second volume of Johnson's *Museum*.

> **Strathallan's Lament**
> Thickest night, o'erhang my dwelling!
> Howling tempests, o'er me rave!
> Turbid torrents, wintry swelling,
> Roaring by my lonely cave!
>
> Crystal streamlets gently flowing,
> Busy haunts of base mankind,
> Western breezes softly blowing,
> Suit not my distracted mind.
>
> In the cause of Right engaged,
> Wrongs injurious to redress,
> Honour's war we strongly waged,
> But the Heavens denied success.
>
> Ruin's wheel has driven o'er us,
> Not a hope that dare attend,
> The wide world is all before us –
> But a world without a friend.

CHAPTER FOUR

1   *The Times,* January 23, 1843.

CHAPTER FIVE

1   *Diagnostic and Statistical Manual of Mental Disorders* (fourth edition), known as the DSM-IV (Washington, DC: American Psychiatric

Association, 1994) at 629. The DSM-IV is the most commonly used diagnostic manual. It is a massive volume that catalogues various diagnoses by presenting symptoms rather than by aetiology. A personality disorder is defined in the DSM-IV as "an enduring pattern of inner experience and behaviour that deviates markedly from the expectations of the individual's culture, is pervasive and inflexible, has an onset in adolescence or early adulthood, is stable over time, and leads to distress or impairment."

CHAPTER SIX

1   *The Times of London*, January 24, 1843.
2   *Ibid.*
3   *The Times*, January 25, 1843.

CHAPTER SEVEN

1   Also in the news:

> A DELICATE AFFAIR – An exceedingly distressing affair has recently come to light, in which a fascinating young lady moving in the highest circles of fashion in Dublin occupies a very prominent position. The facts are these: – Miss L., daughter of Captain L., who resides in Jone's-road, in the neighbourhood of Mountjoy-square, became enamoured of her father's servant, James Kane, and for some weeks past meditated an elopement; but some difficulty or other frustrated their plans. However, on Thursday evening they determined on giving friends and family the slip, and, accordingly, Kane bundled up her clothes and such habiliments as he had of his own, and, having secreted them in the shrubbery facing the house, he returned to Miss L., who fixed 10 o'clock that evening as the "witching hour of flight." In matters of this kind, especially where "love is the theme," some evil genius appears to blight every hope, and prevent the fulfillment of our wishes; so it was in this case, for the captain and his two sons became acquainted with the intended elopement, and, each having loaded pistols, they concealed themselves in the shrubbery, resolved upon shooting the gay Lothario and rescuing the girl. Miss L. overheard a conversation between her brothers, in which they vowed every kind of revenge against Kane, and she contrived to convey a slip of paper to him, cautioning him not to move that night. He took the hint; but, little dreaming that there was danger in even going to the shrubbery, he ventured there to remove the clothes till a more favourable opportunity. Captain L. and his sons immediately pounced upon him,

and charged him with having stolen the clothes. The unfortunate fellow was brought before the magistrates of Henry-street yesterday, and committed for trial. – *Globe*.

CHAPTER EIGHT

1   Allyson Nancy May, *The Bar & the Old Bailey, 1750–1850* (Chapel Hill and London: University of North Carolina Press, 2003) at 20.
2   Dr. Monroe (also spelled "Monro") was one of a dynasty of medical Monroes who ran Bethlem Hospital for a total of 128 years.
3   Except as part of the name of nearly every faux English pub in North America!

CHAPTER TWELVE

1   It should be noted that indictments of the time were exhaustive in their detail. Today, charges are articulated much more economically. The problem with the elaborate detail of the time was that the Crown could stand to lose a prosecution due to its failure to prove a particular averred in the indictment.
2   Peter Ackroyd, *London: The Biography* (London: Chatto & Windus, 2000) at 250.

CHAPTER THIRTEEN

1   State Trials Report.
2   Fieschi attempted the life of Louis Philippe in this way on 28 July 1835.
3   27 St. Tr. 1314.
4   In *Oxford's Case*, State Trials Report at 508.
5   Collinson, at 636–74.
6   5 C. & P. 168.

CHAPTER FOURTEEN

1   The impropriety of this witness's behaviour was not lost upon observers of the trial as demonstrated in the following: "This certainly was a specimen of 'entangling a man in his talk,' for which Mr. John Tierney deserves, and we hope will receive, a severe reprimand." From *Fraser's Magazine for Town and Country*, vol. 22 (January–June 1843) (London: G.W. Nickisson) at 446.

2 *Ibid.* at 448. Observers noted that Cockburn, when he spoke, appeared to be suffering from a severe cold and hoarseness but within a few hours after commencing the next day seemed to have overcome this difficulty.

CHAPTER FIFTEEN

1 Isaac Ray, *A Treatise on the Medical Jurisprudence of Insanity* (Boston: Charles C. Little and James Brown, 1838).
2 27 St. Tr. 1314.
3 Ray, above note 1, s. 10 at 18.
4 673*n.*
5 5 C. & P.168 at 508.
6 Ray, above note 1, s. 15 at 29.
7 Mr. Roscoe died March 25, 1836 in his thirty-seventh year.
8 Roscoe's *Criminal Evidence* at 876.

> M. Marc, in his treatise [at p. 25] "De la Folie," says: –
>
> "Homicidal monomania is a partial delusion characterised by an impulse, more or less violent, to murder; just as suicidal monomania is a partial delusion characterised by a disposition, more or less voluntary, to destroy oneself. This monomania presents two very distinct forms. In some cases the murder is provoked by an internal but raving conviction, by the excitement of a wandering imagination, by a false reasoning, or by the passions in delirium. The monomaniac is impelled by some motive obvious but irrational; he always exhibits sufficient signs of partial delirium, of the intelligence or of the affections. Sometimes his conscience makes him turn with horror from the act which he is about to commit; but his will is overcome by the violence of his impulse; the man is deprived of his moral liberty; he is a prey to a partial delirium; he is a monomaniac; he is mad. In the other cases the homicidal monomaniac does not present any alteration of the intelligence or affections; he is carried away by a blind instinct, by something indefinable, which impels him to kill."

9 5 C. & P.168; and see above, at 547.
10 *Hume's Commentaries on the Law or Scotland*, vol. 1, at 37.
11 The prisoner.

CHAPTER SIXTEEN

1 Isaac Ray, *A Treatise on the Medical Jurisprudence of Insanity* (Boston: Charles C. Little and James Brown, 1838), s. 17 at 32.

280 RICHARD D. SCHNEIDER

2   M. Marc, *De la Folie*, at 25.
3   The right of summing up the evidence in cases of felony and misdemeanour was conferred on prisoners and their counsel in 1865 by 28
& 29 Vict. c. 18. s. 2 (*Denman's Act*). Similar provisions had already been
enacted as regards civil trials by the *Common Law Procedure Act*, 1854, 17
& 18 Vict. c. 125. s. 18.

CHAPTER EIGHTEEN

1   Henry Maudsley, *Responsibility in Mental Disease* (New York: D. Apple-
ton and Company, 1896) at 73.
2   *Diagnostic and Statistical Manual of Mental Disorders* (fourth edition)
(Washington, DC: American Psychiatric Association, 1994) at 301
(known as the DSM-IV).
3   Isaac Ray, *A Treatise on the Medical Jurisprudence of Insanity* (Boston:
Charles C. Little and James Brown, 1838).

CHAPTER TWENTY

1   House of Lords, Mews' Dig. i. 349; iv 1112, S.C. 8 Scott N.R. 595; 1 C. and
K. 130; 4 St. Tr. N.S. 847 May 26, June 19, 1843.
2   (1843), 10 Clark & Fin. 200.
3   See, for example, E. Baker, "The Law of Insanity in England and Wales"
(1996) 6 Intl. Bull. L. & Ment. Health at 19. Curiously, the insanity defence is rarely used in England as a combined result of "hospital
orders" that are possible upon a conviction and the fact that the defence
of diminished responsibility is possible in England. A successful plea of
diminished responsibility does not have attached to it the presumption
of indefinite restriction of liberty. As a result of the recent *The Criminal
Procedure (Insanity and Unfitness to Plead) Act*, 1991, c. 25, the defence may
be enjoying somewhat of a renaissance due to a softening of the dispos-
itional options available upon the verdict.
4   For example, see Henry Weihofen, *Mental Disorder as a Criminal Defense*
(Buffalo, NY: Dennis & Co., 1954) at 63.
5   *Ibid.*
6   *Ibid.*
7   The *Criminal Code, 1892*, 55–56 Vict., c. 29.
8   State Trial Rep.

CHAPTER TWENTY-ONE

1   14 March 1843.
2   *Ibid.*
3   21 March 1843.
4   *Hansard*, 26.8, 1846, col. 1040–41.
5   Roy Porter, *Madness: A Brief History* (Oxford: Oxford University Press, 2002).
6   From the middle of the eighteenth century and cited in Roy Porter, *Madmen: A Social History of Madhouses, Mad-Doctors & Lunatics* (Stroud, UK: Tempus Publishing, 2004).
7   Isaac Ray, *A Treatise on the Medical Jurisprudence of Insanity* (Boston: Charles C. Little and James Brown, 1838) at 88.
8   As quoted by Porter in *Madness: A Brief History*, above note 5 at 117–18.
9   Spontaneous remission refers to a situation where observable symptoms of the mental disorder vanish spontaneously. At one time it was thought that shocking a patient could precipitate a spontaneous remission. Shock could take the form of a frightening event, a startle, or implosion in cold water. Again, the apparent efficacy of these approaches was based upon spurious correlation rather than any real connection with the biology of the disorder.

Index

About the Author

Hon. **Richard D. Schneider**, Ph.D. LL.M., C.Psych., is a justice of the Ontario Court of Justice, where he presides at Toronto's Mental Health Court, and Alternate Chair of the Ontario and Nunavut Review Boards. He is also an Assistant Professor in the Department of Psychiatry, Faculty of Medicine, at the University of Toronto, and an Adjunct Lecturer in the Faculty of Law, University of Toronto. Prior to his appointment to the bench, Justice Schneider was a criminal defence lawyer, a clinical psychologist, and counsel to the Ontario Review Board. He was recently appointed Honorary President of the Canadian Psychological Association. He has published extensively in the area of mental disorder and the law.